'Rosy' Wemyss, Admiral of the Fleet

ADMIRAL OF THE FLEET LORD WESTER-WEMYSS
G.C.B. ,C.M.G. ,M.V.O., D.C.L. (Oxon.) LL.D. (Cam.)

To Pete, with best wishes

'Rosy' Wemyss
Admiral of the Fleet
THE MAN WHO CREATED ARMISTICE DAY

JOHN JOHNSON-ALLEN

[signature: John Johnson-Allen]

Whittles Publishing

Published by

Whittles Publishing Ltd,
Dunbeath,
Caithness, KW6 6EG,
Scotland, UK

www.whittlespublishing.com

© 2021 John Johnson-Allen

ISBN 978-184995-485-3

CONTENTS

PART 3: POST BELLUM

ACKNOWLEDGEMENTS

I would like to thank the following for their assistance:

The Master and Fellows of Churchill College, Cambridge for their permission to reproduce extracts from the archives of The Papers of Admiral of the Fleet Lord Wester-Wemyss and The Papers of Sir Brian Godfrey-Faussett.

The Archivists and staff of the Churchill Archive Centre at Churchill College Cambridge for their great help, freely given, for the many times that I was there.

Commodore Angus Menzies RN For his careful reading of the drafts to ensure that there were no errors in Royal Naval terminology.

Beth Ellis of P&O Heritage Collection for her help in finding illustrations relating to the *Ophir*.

Glyn Evans for permission to use the image of the Kenneth Shoesmith painting in his private collection.

The staff of the National archive for their assistance.

Mr and Mrs Michael Wemyss for their considerable assistance and warm hospitality.

The team, Keith, Sue and Kerrie at Whittles Publishing for their enthusiastic assistance.

Caroline Petherick, editor without equal, for her assistance in polishing my work to its final state.

As always, and most importantly, my wife Clare for her forbearance, support and patience as she suffered a husband whose mind was more or less completely obsessed by Rosy Wemyss for over a year.

Any mistakes that appear in these pages are all mine and I take full responsibility for them.

Author's note: for those of my readers who are not familiar with Scottish names, Wemyss is pronounced Weemz.

ENCOMIUM

Admiral Mark Kerr CB CVO (1864–1944)

Of the 48 cadets who joined the *Britannia* in July 1877, Rosy Wemyss passed in as number 18. I was two places below him. He had many friends, as he was the most cheerful fellow of his term. In particular were Fitzherbert, Benson, Robinson, Cust, Dormer, Heathcote Grant and myself.

Wemyss did not indulge in games very much but liked walking and talking, and his unbounded cheerfulness and good temper made him the best of pleasant companions. On passing out he did very well, as he gained ten months' promotion out of a possible twelve, by which he became a midshipman two months after leaving the *Britannia*.

During the voyage of the 'Flying Squadron', in 1881 and 1882 he was a midshipman on board *Bacchante* with several of his old teammates, including Their Royal Highnesses Prince Edward and Prince George of Wales. I was a midshipman on board the flagship of the squadron, the *Inconstant*, and Rosy and I used to meet sometimes onshore and occasionally on board; but as the times at sea were so long there was not much ship-visiting when we got into harbour. I think the longest time between ports was 50–60 days, as we were nearly always cruising under sail.

On the way to Australia from the Cape of Good Hope, the *Bacchante* gave us a great deal of anxiety as she had her rudder smashed by a following sea, and nothing was heard of her until we arrived at Melbourne when, to our great joy, we heard that she had arrived in safety at Albany, in West Australia, and was lying at anchor in St George's Sound.

Rosy was the first lieutenant of the *Astraea* in the Mediterranean in 1895 – when I was first lieutenant of the *Cambrian*. I was thus senior to Rosy, having been to the royal yacht as a sub-lieutenant and promoted early on account of having served in the naval brigade in the Egyptian War.

We were fortunate in the *Cambrian* as being at the top of the fleet in drills, shooting and games, and in the cupboard on the half-deck we had 21 cups for these various events. Rosy came on board to see me one day and the following is very typical of his generosity. He said: 'I have applied to go to the royal yacht, but I have heard that you were applying, and as the *Cambrian* is the top ship here you certainly ought to go before me.' I told him that I had had one royal yacht promotion, and I would certainly not have my name put forward again. I'm glad to say he got the job and was promoted before I was. During the war, Rosy, on coming home from the eastern Mediterranean in the summer of 1917, stopped at Taranto on board my flagship, the *Queen*. He told me that he was going to be made Commander-in-Chief of the Mediterranean, and he asked me if I would mind coming out and serving under him, to run the whole of the anti-submarine warfare and convoying of merchant ships, as he said he had had no experience of these matters, or of air escort, and he approved of my ideas and of what I had been doing. He was very shy about asking me to serve under him, as I had formerly been his senior, and he was very happy when I told him that nothing would give me greater pleasure. I cannot tell you how I looked forward to the prospect – and how disappointed I was when Geddes kept him at the Admiralty. When I came home from the Adriatic in August 1917, Rosy, who was then Deputy First Sea Lord of the Admiralty, asked me if I would go over to the Air Board to assist in forming the Royal Air Force, as I was the only senior officer in the Navy who was an air pilot, and also because I had been doing my best to push the Air Service for some years. I at once consented.

Before I joined the Air Board, when I was saying goodbye to him he told me that he had sent in my name on the Naval Honours List for the KCB for my work in the Adriatic. ...

He was a great and loyal friend, a modest and exceptionally intelligent officer with great tact and honesty, and with a great quantity of friends and very few enemies.[1]

---

1 Churchill Archive WYMS 1/2

FOREWORD

Admiral Sir Nigel Essenhigh GCB, former First Sea Lord

At first glance the subject of this biography, Admiral of the Fleet Baron Rosslyn Wester Wemyss, might appear to be the typical product of the late Victorian Navy, a man who, along with so many other of its officers, found himself in a very different world in the 20th century. Yet here, the author shines a light on the career of one man in a way that not only tells what it was like to be in the Senior Service in those days, but much about his character and that of those around him, and the nature of the turbulent period of change through which the Navy was going.

Wemyss joined the Navy at the age of 13 in 1877, and the first years of his service were spent at sea in ships which although fitted with steam reciprocating engines were severely limited in range by coal supplies, and thus spent much of their time under sail. It was a navy that had not been seriously tested in battle since Trafalgar, and one in which performance was often judged as much by ships' appearance and their crews' sail-changing prowess and sporting achievements as by genuine operational efficiency. These factors moulded the characters of many officers and left them ill at ease with the technological advances that produced dreadnoughts and submarines and aircraft, and which forced the Royal Navy of the First World War to adopt a very different approach to the one that had prevailed throughout much of the 19th century.

Yet three snapshots from Wemyss' career illustrate that, unlike some of his brother officers, he had grasped the need for change, and to work to match the world in which the Navy was operating. The first was the enlightened appointment he was given to set up the Royal Naval College at Osborne on the Isle of Wight where, for the first time ever seaman officers and engineers were given their initial training alongside each other. He saw to it that their basic naval education became focused on the realities of the day rather than on what were fast becoming the increasingly outmoded skills that had been needed in a navy of sails and muzzle-loading cannons. The second was his pivotal role in organising the evacuation of Allied forces from the Dardanelles under the noses of Turkish troops, thereby averting an even worse end to what had been a disastrous campaign. The third was his outstanding service in the Middle East as Commander-in-Chief of the East Indies station during the period 1916–17, when he played a pivotal part in organising the Navy to support the land campaigns in the Middle East. The words of T E Lawrence sum this perfectly:

> Admiral Wemyss was in glorious contrast to the soldiers – no jealousy, no stupidity, no laziness … His support in the mixed councils and conferences was hearteningly useful … In practical affairs he did all the Navy can do on land.

Praise indeed from one of the most critical of critical observers.

His eventual transition to the post of First Sea Lord at the Admiralty in Whitehall in December 1917 was not a move that he relished, and was an appointment that he appears to have accepted with some reluctance. Yet the moment was right for this officer to lead the Navy through a very difficult period, when his conciliatory and diplomatic skills served him and the service well. His important roles in the conduct of the armistice negotiations in 1918 and at the 1919 Paris Peace Conference marked the pinnacles of an exceptionally varied 40-year career. This book shows clearly that in many ways Wemyss was more a naval officer of the 21st century than of the 19th into which he had been born.

INTRODUCTION

Rosslyn Erskine Wemyss was universally known throughout the Navy as Rosy, and therefore it is as Rosy that I refer to him throughout this book. As I have come to know him through his own letters and from those from others I found the man behind the naval officer. He was, certainly in his younger years, an energetic sportsman with a great sense of fun – he would dress up as a ballerina for a ship's entertainment evening to carry out a dance, with his monocle firmly fixed, on the heaving deck. He loved his wife and daughter very deeply. He also had a temper, which he learned to keep in check. He was a man of his time: as a naval officer he fitted the mould of not being too clever, but he was also, somewhat unusually, very considerate of his junior officers and men.

He entered the Royal Naval College Dartmouth as a cadet at the age of 13, in July 1877 and retired, after over 40 years' service, as an Admiral of the Fleet.

His first ship, *HMS Bacchante,* nearly new in 1879, was a ship which, although it had an engine, was still a sailing ship and sailed most of the time. He was in her for two years; this cemented his lifelong friendship, which had started at Dartmouth and continued when they joined their first ship together, with his distant cousin Prince George, son of the Prince of Wales and who later became King George V. Their time in *Bacchante* was still in the years of the Pax Britannica, the period of peace which had started in 1815 and came to an abrupt end in 1914. The Navy had not seen any significant action since Trafalgar, and was set in its ways, which were mainly unchanged until the coming of war. In his early career, Rosy advanced quickly, helped by his friendship with Prince George. Referred to by some other officers as a 'Court officer', he had had appointments on two of the royal yachts, was appointed second-in-command of HMS *Ophir* for the royal tour of Prince George and Princess Mary 1901, and was in command of HMS *Balmoral Castle* for the royal visit to South Africa nine years later.

In 1915, as a rear admiral, after a boring spell patrolling the Western Approaches in command of a squadron of elderly cruisers, he was sent by Churchill to Mudros, off the coast of Gallipoli, to create the naval base for that invasion, controlling the harbour and creating a base for the troops that bivouacked there before the attack. He was in command of all the landings of troops and materiel, then at the end of that disastrous campaign it fell to him to evacuate all the troops and their equipment. This he did so successfully that of all the tens of thousands of troops taken off the beaches only one man was lost.

He was then posted to command the East Indies and Red Sea Station, based in Egypt, for 18 months. His station stretched as far east as Colombo, in Ceylon (now Sri Lanka), but as the eastern shore of the Red Sea was occupied by Turkey, which had joined the war on the Axis side on 31 October 1914, his efforts were mainly concentrated there. He supported the Arab Revolt through the ships of the Red Sea Patrol, and came to know both T E Lawrence and Emir Feisal, with whom he remained friends after the war.

Back in London in 1917 he was appointed Deputy First Sea Lord, becoming First Sea Lord after Jellicoe departed at the end of December. As First Sea Lord, Rosy represented the Allied navies in the Armistice negotiations in November 1918 at Compiègne and, with Marshal Foch, was the creator of Armistice Day, by agreeing on the cessation of hostilities at 11:00 a.m. on 11 November. The next year, as the British naval representative at the Versailles peace conference, he defended the British position to the extent that he became embroiled in a furious argument with the American Admiral Benson, which nearly ended in fisticuffs.

He left the Navy on 1 November 1920, having been promoted to an Admiral of the Fleet and raised to the peerage as Baron Wester Wemyss. He retired to the home he loved in Cannes where, except for the war years, he had lived since his marriage to Victoria. After dabbling in business, which was not a success – sailors ashore are not always good businessmen – his health eventually failed him and he died one month after his 69th birthday.

He was a very admirable man; in all my works of research I found only two comments that criticised him in any way. Having spent 12 months immersed in the man and his life, I am left wishing that I had known him.

John Johnson-Allen

PART ONE: PAX

1: FROM BIRTH TO *BRITANNIA*

On 29 March 1864 James Hay Erskine-Wemyss died at his home at Buckingham Gate, London, within a few hundred yards of Buckingham Palace and Wellington Barracks. He was only 35. In early spring at Wemyss Castle, he had been standing with his sister, looking out of the windows overlooking the Firth of Forth, when a lump of masonry fell from a newly reconstructed terrace. Wemyss Castle, like so many ancient buildings, is said to be haunted. He turned to her and said, 'I am a dead man, for as a warning to the owner of Wemyss Castle of his early approaching death a piece of masonry always falls.'[2] Within a few weeks he had died.

Two weeks after that, on 12 April, his fifth child, Rosslyn Erskine-Wemyss, was born, so his arrival cannot have been greeted with anything other than a muted welcome. The new baby joined two sisters and two brothers; his eldest brother, Randolph, inherited the castle and the family estates.

The Wemyss family were Scottish through and through, with a lineage traced directly to Michael of Methil and Wemyss, of the late 12th century. The family boasted that not a drop of English blood flowed in their veins; so Scottish were they that when they had to venture south to England they tried to associate only with fellow Scots. They also had a strong naval heritage, stretching back into the 18th century: Rosslyn's grandfather, James, had joined the Navy as a first class volunteer at the age of 12, on HMS *Unicorn*, commanded by his uncle, Charles Wemyss. James was promoted to lieutenant in 1808, serving on HMS *Victor*. As a result of his conduct in action he was chosen as flag lieutenant to Sir Edward Pellew, who rose to become Lord Exmouth. Pellew described himself as 'pockmarked, ugly, uninteresting and uneducated'. He was also 'tough, brave,

2 Lady Wester Wemyss The Life and Letters of Lord Wester Wemyss (London, 1935) 13

skilful, lucky and unscrupulous'.[3] When James Wemyss was appointed to be his flag lieutenant, Pellew was Commander-in-Chief East Indies. This appointment coincided with the mutiny on HMS *Nereide,* which became a *cause célèbre* because of the excessively harsh behaviour of her captain, Ronald Corbet.

James Wemyss was promoted to commander four years later and achieved post rank as captain in 1814. But on his return to England in the same year he was placed on half-pay. So, retaining his commission he entered Parliament, where he became an active member. Rising through the list of captains, he eventually was promoted rear admiral in 1850, but as a rear admiral 'without distinction of squadron' he was, in the naval term of the period, a 'yellow admiral'. He lived into old age and died only ten years before the death of his son, who had also joined the Navy but had had only a brief career because of his fragile health. Rosslyn was therefore more or less destined, provided he could meet the necessary entry requirements, to enter the Navy.

His mother, Millicent, was also from an illustrious family. Her mother, the Lady Augusta, was one of the children of the liaison between the Duke of Clarence and the actress Mrs Jordan. When the Duke of Clarence succeeded to the throne as William IV the children of this liaison were not cast aside; the boys were found careers in the Army, the Navy and the Church; the five daughters all were married into good families. His fourth daughter, Augusta, married the Hon. John Kennedy, heir to the Erskines of Dun, whose family seat was Dun in Angus. They had three children: William Henry, Wilhelmina and Millicent. It was a relatively short marriage, however, as John Kennedy Erskine died of consumption at the age of 28. After four years of widowhood Augusta married Admiral Lord Frederick Gordon.

Both Wilhelmina and Millicent married on the same day in 1855, Wilhelmina marrying her cousin, Lord Munster, and Millicent marrying James Hay Wemyss of Wemyss Castle.

After his sudden death, she found herself, with five young children, managing an estate deep in debt, to which she applied herself with great energy and considerable success. Her efforts, over a period of 15 years, enabled her to pass the estate to her eldest son free of debt and with a rental income of over £30,000 per annum.[4]

*James Hay Wemyss
(Author's collection)*

3 N A M Rodger Command of the Ocean (New York 2004) 386
4 Lady Wester Wemyss Life and Letters, 20

The family lived mainly in Princes Gate, London, and it was from there that Rosslyn went to preparatory school in Farnborough. There are few details about his time there, but a comment from a contemporary, Esmé Howard (who became Lord Howard of Penrith and was a long-time friend), gives a perhaps subjective description of him at that time: 'I don't think I ever knew any man who changed so little from his schooldays. He was from the first keen about work and play but what I remember best was his keen enjoyment of anything humorous and his great love of fun. He also had a keenly critical side to his nature even in those days.'[5]

After his school days, Rosy, as he became universally known, sat for the examination to enter the Royal Navy at the Britannia Royal Naval College. The examinations in those days were not as searching or rigorous as they later became, so Rosy's main hurdle was the eyesight test. The sight in his right eye was defective – he wore a monocle in later life – but happily the doctor carrying out the examination had sailed with his father, so he succeeded in passing an 'easy test'.[6]

The Navy that he was to join had not been engaged in a major conflict since the end of the Napoleonic Wars; instead it had successfully policed the world in the era of the Pax Britannica. This lack of action had had an enervating effect on the service, even though improvements had been made, for example in the 1850s when Sir James Graham had reformed the administration, replacing the antiquated system with one of five departments, each led by a principal officer, each of those reporting to one of five lords – the four sea lords and the First Lord of the Admiralty, who was a politician.

The enervating effect on the Navy was noticed by the younger officers in particular. Lieutenant Reginald Bacon commented

> the fleet possessed the lowest level of efficiency of material since the middle of the 18th century. The officers and men were just as zealous, the love of their profession just as great, but they were imbued with ideas that had not altered with the times. Sail drill still occupied a place in the scale by which efficiency was measured. Gun range was too short to evoke any real interest in gunnery as an art and coupled with slow ships it was clear that tactics had not advanced beyond ideas of a close range melee. Fleet manoeuvres – the practice of altering the formation of ships – were exercised but no one appreciated whether these gyrations would be of use in fighting or not![7]

---

5 Lady Wester Wemyss Life and Letters, 25

6 Lady Wester Wemyss Life and Letters, 26

7 Captain John Wells The Royal Navy, an Illustrated Social History 1870-1982 (Stroud 1994) 38

By 1903 Reginald Bacon was described by Admiral Sir John Fisher as 'the cleverest man in the Navy'. He retired six years later, having spent much of his later career in shore posts, ending his career as Director of Naval Ordnance in 1909. He was recalled to service in 1914, and in 1915 was made Commander-in-Chief Dover, with part of his remit being to develop new gunnery methods with the monitors (small, shallow-draught inshore ships fitted with large naval guns for shore bombardment). He was removed as Commander-in-Chief Dover in January 1918, a week after Rosy had succeeded Sir John Jellicoe as First Sea Lord.[8]

The rigid and hidebound ways of the Navy were exemplified by the disaster during fleet manoeuvres in the Mediterranean in 1893, when Admiral Sir George Tryon, a forbidding and autocratic officer who had a reputation for his enthusiasm for such manoeuvres and for ordering unexpected changes in the formation of the fleet, made a signal for the two columns of the fleet to alter course by 180 degrees, turning towards each other. On his flagship, HMS *Victoria*, as the lines turned inwards it became apparent on her bridge and on the bridge of the rapidly approaching HMS *Camperdown* that collision was inevitable. *Camperdown* went to collision stations and closed watertight doors accordingly. She collided with *Victoria*'s starboard bow, causing damage that resulted in the flagship sinking 12 minutes later, taking 700 of her crew, including Admiral Tryon, with her.

In addition to sail drills and out-of-date ideas, the appearance of the ships was a matter of the greatest importance and of considerable rivalry. Promotion depended more on the appearance of the ship both externally and internally, than on her performance. Wealthy officers who could afford such extravagances as gold leaf, brass finials for the ship's boats and enamel paint had an advantage over less well-off officers. The result of this split and polish was that 'there is no doubt that on Sunday morning the whole ship presented a blaze of splendour to the captain as he went on his round of inspection'.[9]

This, then, was what awaited Rosy, when on 15 July 1877 he joined HMS *Britannia* at Dartmouth. She had been a three-deck ship of the line which had been turned into a training ship for officers in 1858, and had been joined in 1864 by the two-deck ship HMS *Hindustan*, which was moored close to *Britannia* to provide extra accommodation. The education was similar to that taught in public schools, although there had been unfavourable press comments about the standards of the education. Only five years after Rosy arrived, an article in *The Times* had claimed 'that subjects taught were inappropriate, age entry was too

---

8 Eamonn Welch 'The Operational Impact of the Loss of HMS Paragon in the Straits of Dover, 17 March 1917' in The Mariner's Mirror Vol.105, 1 February 2019

9 Peter Padfield Rule Britannia: The Victorian and Edwardian Navy (London 2002) 197

low and the entrance examination all wrong'.[10] The response from the Admiralty was a 'hands off' attitude, to the extent of regarding criticism as impertinence. Further criticism on the standards at *Britannia* came from a Captain Bowden Smith, who was in command there at the time, who firmly believed that the 13-year-old entry excluded boys who developed later or who had not at 12 years old decided on the Navy as a career, because, he stated, 'we want the best men we can get to officer the Navy and by cutting off the supply at such an early age we may be losing valuable services'.[11]

The theoretical subjects that Rosy was taught were mathematics (arithmetic, algebra, geometry, and plain and spherical trigonometry), physics, practical and theoretical navigation, charts, instruments, French, essay-writing and drawing. In addition – and most importantly – seamanship, which attracted as many marks in the final exam as the first three branches of mathematics. The seamanship studies included the rules of the road to assist in the prevention of collision at sea. These rules had been developed over the previous 30 years, and while Rosy was at Dartmouth whistle signals were introduced. This improvement did not, however, prevent the disastrous collision in 1878 off Erith in the River Thames when the paddle-steamer *Princess Alice* was hit by the collier *Bywell Castle*. The *Princess Alice* broke into three and sank more or less immediately. Despite gallant efforts by boatmen to rescue the men, women and children who had been on board her for a pleasure cruise, very few of the nearly 700 were saved.

Although drawing may not seem an obvious subject, it was important because it was naval officers who provided the Hydrographic Department with sketches of coast and port entrances for inclusion in Admiralty pilot books and charts. In the years before photography these were an important addition to safe navigation.

Every afternoon, cadets went ashore for sport – cricket, rugby, soccer or lacrosse – and they would go rowing and sailing in a variety of craft. In addition, in the year after Rosy arrived, the Britannia Beagles were founded, and twice a week cadets could follow the hounds on foot, getting good exercise over the Devon hills. Rosy's love of hunting, which was remarked upon in the coming years, would, if not started then, have developed during his time at Dartmouth. The Britannia Beagles are still in existence to this day.

Among the cadets who joined with Rosy were two brothers whose arrival had caused some controversy within their family as to the suitability of the Navy as a career. Prince George and his elder brother Prince Albert Victor, known as Eddy,

---

10 Captain John Wells The Royal Navy 40

11 Captain John Wells Ibid, 40

both joined the same term. Prince George, as the second son of the Prince of Wales, was thought unlikely to succeed to the throne; it was considered therefore that his entry to the Navy was important, as it would instil in him, it was felt, the qualities of punctuality, obedience and attention to duty. Eddy's future also had to be considered, as heir to the throne; however, he was listless and backward, and showed no interest in learning. Here there was clearly a problem, as their tutor Canon Dalton noted:

> Prince Albert Victor requires the stimulus of Prince George's company to induce him to work at all … Difficult as the education of Prince Albert Victor is now, it would be doubly or trebly so if Prince George were to leave him. Prince George's lively presence is his mainstay and chief incentive to exertion, and [turning] to Prince George again, the presence of his elder brother is most wholesome as a check against that tendency to self conceit which is apt at times to show itself to him. [If he went with his brother he would not develop] those habits of promptitude and method, of manliness and self reliance in which he is somewhat deficient[12]

The principal opposition came from their grandmother: Queen Victoria did not approve of the two princes joining the Navy together. She commented

> their positions (if they live) will be totally different and it is not intended that they should both enter the Navy … the very rough sort of life to which boys are exposed on board ship is the very thing not calculated to make a refined and amicable Prince who, in after years (if God spares him) is to ascend the throne.[13]

As it was allegedly said many years later of Prince George that he could swear for longer and worse than any other man in the Navy, she may have had a point! However, her advice was not taken, so the two princes, accompanied by Canon Dalton, entered the Navy in July 1877.

As George's grandmother had said, the Navy was rough even at *Britannia*, as Prince George noted:

> It never did me any good to be a prince … and many was the time I wished I hadn't been. It was a pretty tough place and so far from making any allowances for our disadvantages the other boys made the point of taking it out of us on the grounds that they'd never be able to do it later on. There

---

12 Denis Judd The Life and Times of George V (London 1973) 24

13 Captain John Wells Ibid 24

was a lot of fighting among the cadets and rule was if challenged you had to accept. So they used to make me go up and challenge the big boys – I was awfully small then – and I'd get a hiding time and again.[14]

Prince George and Rosy became friends and remained close friends for the remainder of their lives. Rosy was also friendly with Eddy, but was a particular friend of George. They passed out of Dartmouth in 1879; Rosy's results show a solid but not exciting performance, which resulted in him achieving 13th place in his class. The cadets now joined their first ships. Rosy found himself on the same ship as Princes George and Eddy. It had been agreed to further broaden George's life experience that he should be embarked on a training ship. Eddy was embarked as well, as it was felt that he would be supported by George and by Canon Dalton, although the latter was somewhat reluctant. Although the Queen had initially not been in favour of the princes joining the Navy, she was now wholeheartedly in favour of this idea – but the Cabinet and the prime minister, Disraeli, were not. Disraeli was, however, eventually persuaded, and the royal view prevailed.

---

14 Denis Judd Ibid 25

2: *BACCHANTE*: COWES TO THE CAPE

All midshipmen, as part of their training, were required to keep a journal, which took the general form of a ship's log. It was illustrated by sketches and chartlets, and formed a continuous record during their time as a midshipman. Rosy's has not survived, but that of his contemporary at Dartmouth, Bryan Godfrey-Faussett, does survive and is a particularly well written and illustrated example.[15] His habit of writing carried on into his career, as will be seen in a later chapter. The logs of Prince George and Prince Eddy were published as a book, edited by Canon Dalton.

Rosy's first ship was HMS *Bacchante*,[16] to which he was appointed on 25 July 1879; he joined her on 6 August, at anchor off Cowes. Although he joined her as a cadet, he was promoted midshipman on 23 September.

Bacchante was a nearly new ship. Built in 1876 she was classified as a corvette, but carried initially 14 muzzle-loading rifled guns (although four of these were removed and replaced by four 6-inch breech-loading rifled guns). The guns were mounted in the old way, for firing as broadsides, the guns equally distributed to either side of the gun deck. As well as her three fully rigged masts, she was fitted with Rennie compound steam engines, which gave her a top speed of 15 knots under power, whilst under sail her top speed was 11½ knots. With her armament all on the gun deck, as Conrad Dixon comments 'she had, as a contemporary observed, all her teeth in the lower jaw'.[17]

She became part of the Detached Squadron, 'showing the flag' around the world. Showing the flag, in the days before telegraph and wireless was a support

---

15 Churchill archive (CA) BGGF 1/13

16 Unless otherwise noted, all references and quotations in this and the next chapter are from The Full Cruise of HMS Bacchante, compiled from the Private Journals of Prince Albert Victor and Prince George (London, 1886)

17 Conrad Dixon Ships of the Victorian Navy (Southampton 1987) 20

to the Foreign Office, who valued the naval presence in far-flung parts of the world – and, as Arthur Marder comments somewhat cynically, it also 'pleased … the consuls' daughters who needed tennis and dancing partners'.[18]

She was under the command of the Right Hon. Lord Charles Scott. The officers included a naval instructor, as she carried ten midshipmen. Two of those were Princes Albert Victor (Eddy) and George, who also joined her on 6 August. They had been brought down by their parents, the Prince and Princess of Wales. Canon Dalton, somewhat unwillingly, was accompanying them and became the ship's acting chaplain. Amongst the remaining midshipmen were the Hon. John Scott, the Hon. George Hardinge and the Right Hon. Lord Francis Osborne.

Bacchante stayed at anchor off Cowes for Cowes Week, then sailed to Plymouth on 11 August, undergoing various trials on her passage, to ascertain her manoeuvrability under steam and sail, arriving on 16 August. She was joined the next day by the royal yacht *Victoria and Albert,* in which Rosy was later to serve. She was carrying the Prince of Wales who was to be present at the laying of the foundation stone of the new Eddystone lighthouse which was to be carried out by the Duke of Edinburgh who arrived on board the Trinity House Vessel *Galatea.*

Bacchante sailed from Plymouth later that day for more exercises, and then turned back to arrive at Spithead on 26 August. As a result of the trials she went alongside Gun Wharf Quay to have three of her guns removed in order to improve her trim and therefore her sailing ability.

When she sailed for Portland two days later she had been joined by the Prince of Wales, Prince and Princess Edward, and Prince Herman of Saxe-Weimar. The short passage of 4½ hours was, from the Needles onwards, entirely in fog, at an average speed of over 10 knots. The Collision Regulations state that in fog vessels should go at a moderate speed; this speed seems to suggest either that the fog was not thick or that the royal presence on board meant that a specific time of arrival had to be met.

After a week at Portland, she sailed, initially under sail until out of sight of Portland when, as the south-west wind was, given their course, directly ahead, the sails were furled and they proceeded under steam.

Once they had left Portland, the ship settled down to its normal daily routine. For the midshipmen, their daily routine for drills was laid down by the first lieutenant, the Hon. A G Curzon Howe. Every morning of the week the day started at 7:30 a.m., with 30 minutes of cutlass or rifle drill. From 9:00 a.m. to 11:30 a.m. the morning was spent at school studies, followed by the procedure leading up to noon sights of the sun, from 11:30 a.m. to 12:00 noon. The afternoons were taken

18 Arthur Marder From the Dardanelles to Scapa Flow Vol.1 (Barnsley 1961) 39

up with further drills; on Monday, gun drill and seamanship; Tuesday, company drill and more seamanship; Wednesday, gunnery and torpedo drill; Thursday, for steam (engineering studies) and Friday, the preparation of watch bills (the making of lists of the particular allocations of men for specific manoeuvres or drills, such as the setting or furling of sails or harbour manoeuvres) and logbooks. All midshipmen were also busy keeping the log of their daily activities, including illustrations and charts of their progress.

By 27 September, they had left the Channel behind; all sail was made and the propeller shaft was raised to lessen drag. Removal of the guns in Portsmouth had had a beneficial effect on her sailing ability; the wind had gone round to the north-east, and despite it only being a gentle breeze, she averaged just under 5 knots over the following 24 hours. There was a heavy swell from the west and the removal of the guns made her livelier. The wind increased over the following days, so that by the last day of the month they were sailing at around 7 knots, heeling over to about 14 degrees. On 2 October two more cadets were promoted to midshipman. Rosy's promotion to that rank ten days before had reflected his position in the final rankings at *Britannia*, as he was ranked 13th in his term of over 30.

Two days later, on Saturday, the midshipmen had choir practice; whether this was due to the influence of Canon Dalton is not known but the addition in their log by one of the princes of an extract from Psalm 103 in Latin – here quoted from the King James Bible 'In wisdom had thou made them all: the earth is full of thy riches. So is this great and wide sea where in are things creeping innumerable, both small and great beasts. There go the ships, there is that leviathan, whom thou hast made to play in' suggests that the Canon may have had some say in the matter.

They passed Cape Trafalgar early in the morning of 6 October and arrived at Gibraltar, to anchor at 11:30 a.m.

The next day they sailed for Port Mahon in Menorca, on the way exercising the main guns including a broadside controlled by electricity for the first time; the Gatling gun fired one drum of 240 and the troops fired 300 rounds from their Martini rifles. After three days they arrived at their destination, where they remained for a week. The weather was very pleasant with only a light breeze and daily temperatures of about 70°F (21°C). A party of officers and midshipmen were taken on an all-day tour of the island by the British vice-consul to various points of interest. The group had brought their luncheon baskets provided by the ship, and they ate overlooking the sea. Another shore trip was with the captain and four midshipmen to shoot partridge on a farm ashore, overlooking the ship. The result of the day's shooting was disappointing, however, with only three partridges shot. Whether this was due to a dearth of birds or poor shooting was not recorded.

Bacchante sailed on 18 October for Palermo, in Sicily and was under sail for all but 12 miles of the 450-mile passage. Many of the midshipmen had bought ' "turron", a white rock made of pressed almonds, sugar and meal ... which had been extensively purchased and eaten at Port Mahon [the effects of which] are manifestly visible in some members of the gun room mess, so that with a wise compunction many cakes of it remaining unconsumed were consigned to the deep'.[19]

As they arrived at Palermo on 22 October, they were met by a violent squall and heavy rain. This caused the *Bacchante* to let go the anchor in 33 fathoms (60 metres), running out 150 fathoms (300 metres) of cable before securing the chain. Sailing from Palermo after a week, they sailed along the Sicilian coast to Messina where, after a day, they sailed for Gibraltar arriving on 6 November. The two princes called on the governor and his lady, Lord and Lady Napier, who had arrived since the *Bacchante*'s first visit. Lord Napier, commenting on Eddy and mistaking his slowness for 'a profoundly contemplative nature', wrote 'the youngest is the most lively and popular, but I think the eldest is best suited to his situation – he is shy and not demonstrative but does the right things as the young gentleman in a quiet way'.[20]

On 8 November, four of the midshipmen took the steam pinnace and sailed along the coast to an agreed spot, where they were met with horses which then rode along the beach for 5 miles to the local bullring. Continuing on their ride, they met Lieutenant Frere, whose brother Bartle Frere became High Commissioner at the Cape in South Africa, and was instrumental in the decision to tame the Zulu tribe by declaring war on them. Although the Zulus were defeated, Frere's decision was not approved of by Disraeli, as the result was that the potential support of the Zulus as allies against the Boers had been lost and therefore was considered a disastrous mistake.[21]

A further event involving horses occurred three days later, when a party of six midshipmen, led by the commander, had a day's hunting with the Calpe Hunt, whose members were mainly members of the military garrison at Gibraltar.

Bacchante sailed on 15 November on passage to Madeira, where they stayed for a week at anchor, although the heavy swell made their stay uncomfortable and made getting ashore difficult. Leaving on 29 November they sailed in a leisurely manner south to Tenerife, anchoring off Santa Cruz for two days, during which

19 If experimentation is sought, it is available in supermarkets in the UK.

20 Denis Judd The Life and Times of King George V, 28

21 A N Wilson The Victorians (London 2003) 401

time some of the midshipmen made a visit to the cathedral to see Nelson's flags which were on display there, following his action at Tenerife on 24 July 1797.

They sailed on 6 December for Barbados. All but two days of the 18-day passage was made under steam, at a leisurely pace of about 6–7 knots for the most part. A long passage under steam would have been a relief for the seamen, as there were no sails to be handled; not so, though, for the firemen and trimmers in the stokehold, as temperatures rose steadily as they crossed the Atlantic, rising to over 80°F (32°C) by the time they arrived at Barbados. During the passage the midshipmen underwent their half-yearly examinations to assess their progress and ongoing aptitude.

They arrived at Barbados on Christmas Day, anchoring at 11:15 a.m. The ship was soon surrounded by Barbadian washerwomen, who had come out in a swarm of boats. They were led by the six-foot-tall Jane Ann Smith, who had washed for Prince Alfred in the past and fully intended to do the washing for the two princes on board. On Boxing Day coaling commenced, the fuel coming offshore in a succession of lighters. The replenishment of the coal bunkers was a filthy and unpleasant job. David Gregory, in *The Lion and the Eagle*, gives an excellent description of the task:

> Coaling ship was the bane of shipboard life in the ironclad era … for the best part of a day, sometimes longer, the entire crew of the ship would manhandle thousands of sacks of coal on board and down to the nether regions of the vessel. There, the sacks would be broached and the contents shovelled into coal bunkers. It was backbreaking work and, at the end of the process, the crew would be utterly exhausted. Coal dust would be everywhere in the air, and the entire ship coated in a layer of black filth … The sheer awfulness of the experience in the tropics can well be imagined.[22]

On *Bacchante*, the 'entire crew' did not involve the midshipmen. It could be conjectured that as the two princes would not have been expected to take part then the remainder of the midshipmen equally escaped the job. Instead, they went ashore in the afternoon to play tennis and billiards. On 27 December the ship was 'still coaling, but finished at 2:30 p.m. and then began to wash down and get the ship a little bit tidy'.

Sailing on 5 January, their next port was Trinidad; they arrived on 7 January and stayed for two weeks. The day after they arrived the two princes, who up to that time had been naval cadets, were rated as midshipmen, the last out of the term to be promoted. In the afternoon officials from the Jamaican government visited the ship to arrange excursions for the officers and midshipmen for the

---

22 Quoted in John Johnson-Allen TE Lawrence and the Red Sea Patrol (Barnsley 2015) 18

period of their stay. Separate arrangements had been made for the princes to stay ashore for various visits including the obligatory trip to see the pitch lakes. They had returned on board by 19 January, when an afternoon dance was held for over 200 guests including the governor and his aide-de-camp. The dancing continued until 6 pm; smoking was allowed at the after end of the poop, behind a screen of flags; ice creams were served in the chart house and light refreshments under the poop. Rosy clearly enjoyed the occasion, as Lady Wemyss noted: 'Canon Dalton never ceased to chaff him about an incident at a West Indian ball where strange beasties attracted by the light were flying about, and Rosy's solicitous offer to take off one from a rather *décolletée* lady was not appreciated by her as the object he sought to remove was a mole.'[23] They eventually sailed from Trinidad on 22 January to arrive at Grenada on 26 January, where they stayed until the end of the month.

The next leg saw the *Bacchante* island-hopping, calling at the small islands of Grenada, St Vincent and St Lucia before returning to Barbados, then to Dominica and St Thomas. Enjoying sailing in the trade winds with all sails set along the southern shore of Jamaica, by the early evening of 12 March they were approaching Port Royal, where six ships of the Navy were lying. The spit-and-polish ethos of the late Victorian Navy was demonstrated by the *Bacchante* at that point as they moored:

> We were to have picked up number one buoy which Northampton had just vacated, but not liking to lower one of the freshly painted boats [author's italics], sent the men down onto the buoy from the bows of the ship; they had some difficulty in making fast. At the same time the chief engineer, coming up from the engine room, reported that the starting gear had gone wrong and that he could not go ahead or astern as required (and it had been a few turns ahead or astern as required for the last 15 minutes) so ultimately we had to give up making fast for this night, let go an anchor at 8 pm, dusk having thrown a kind veil over our surroundings and proceedings.

Bacchante's embarrassment at this débâcle under the eyes of six other ships would have been excruciating. They succeeded the next day in securing to number one buoy, where they stayed for the next week.

Port Royal was a considerable naval base which had been established over 150 years before *Bacchante* arrived, and had been much enlarged in the mid-19th century, with a coal depot, various victualling stores and an engineering shop (called the smithery). The location of Port Royal was noted around the

---

23 Lady Wester Wemyss Life and Times 28

time of *Bacchante*'s visit by the British government as of potential importance if the Panama Canal were to be completed. In 1884 a programme of dockyard improvements ordered by Gladstone's government included Port Royal's coaling station, which was to have modern fortifications.[24]

The day after *Bacchante* arrived, they were customers of the coaling station, which process occupied the ship for the next two days. On completion of coaling the ship was thoroughly cleaned, as on the evening of the second day they were visited by the acting governor and the commodore together with other guests.

On the following morning virtually all the midshipmen went ashore to the King's House, at the invitation of the owner, Mr Newton, a wealthy planter, to enjoy some time away from the ship. The large swimming pool within the grounds was a considerable attraction and was used both morning and evening, as were the tennis courts. In addition there was an afternoon garden party and an evening reception. The stay ashore went on for four days, taken up with visits and parties.

On 22 March *Bacchante* sailed from Port Royal, slipping her mooring and steaming out of the harbour on passage for Bermuda. Because of their north-easterly course they were initially steaming into a headwind. The passage took them through the Windward Passage, between Cuba and Haiti, in flat calm conditions, then out into the Atlantic. Easter fell early that year and on Easter Sunday, 29 March, the wind came round to the south-west, so the top gallant masts were sent up and all plain sail set, giving them a daily run of over 200 miles, averaging nearly 9 knots over a 24-hour period. The wind strengthened through the day, and so sail was shortened as it was 'a dark, thick, blustery night, force of the wind eight'. They arrived in Bermuda the next morning, mooring to a buoy in Grassy Bay. In the afternoon, orders came through to come into the harbour and make fast alongside, astern of the flagship, HMS *Northampton,* a Nelson class cruiser, much larger than the *Bacchante*. It was noted that 'it is very jolly being alongside a stone wall for a change'.

Bermuda's naval dockyard had been started only five years after the Battle of Trafalgar, in 1810. Its site, Grassy Bay on the south side of Ireland Island, one of the islands of the Bermudan archipelago, was largely of limestone, ideal for building material and the construction of the breakwater and the defences, which took over 50 years. The limestone, which was available locally, caused a law to be passed in 1816 prohibiting the building of any wooden buildings in either the capital, Hamilton, or St George. The only drawback of the limestone is the presence of fissures and unexpected voids, which precluded the building of any dry docks. This problem was resolved by the arrival in 1869 of a floating

---

24 Jonathan Coad *Support for the Fleet: Architecture and Engineering of the Royal Navy's Bases 1700-1914,* 256

dock built on the Thames and capable of a 10,000-ton lift. It was at this time the largest floating dock in the world. Named HMS *Bermuda* for the voyage, it had a crew of 80. Initially it was towed as far as Madeira by HMS *Agincourt* and *Northumberland,* the latter a heavy cruiser, which was to be Rosy's next ship. From Madeira the tow was taken over by the ironclad sister ships HMS *Warrior* and HMS *Black Prince,* with the 25-year-old HMS *Terrible,* the last wooden paddle-steamer left in the Navy, made fast astern as a rudder.

Five years before *Bacchante* arrived, heavy lifting capacity for removing or installing heavy machinery or gun turrets at the main wharf had been created by the construction of massive sheerlegs. The repair facilities were required at the naval dockyard, as Bermuda was the principal Royal Naval base in the western Atlantic and had all the facilities necessary to maintain both the ships and the men of the squadron.[25]

On Sunday 4 April, the men of the *Northampton,* the flagship, led by the ship's band, paraded to church, whilst on *Bacchante* the service, led by Canon Dalton, was held on the main deck. Two days later, the midshipmen were taken over the floating dock. Subsequently, various trips were made to other islands of Bermuda including witnessing the destruction of a reef at the entrance to St Georges by 250 pounds (approximately 150 kg) of gun cotton. Their stay alongside ended on 12 April, when they moved back to moor in Grassy Bay once more, sailing from there the next morning on passage for Portsmouth, on an east-north-easterly course. On Friday 16 April, as on every Friday, the crew were exercised in 'general quarters', firing at a target with the main guns, sometimes with blank ammunition, sometimes purely as a drill without the guns actually being fired. In order for this exercise to take place, the gun deck was cleared of the mess tables, the magazines and the shell room were opened and dummy cartridges sent up to the guns, and fire hoses were rigged ready for use. The guns were loaded and run out in preparation, and occasionally one round would be fired. The gundeck was then restored to mess use, with dinner half an hour later than usual on the days when there was live firing. Reginald Bacon's comments, quoted in the first chapter, on the efficiency of the Navy and the little amount of interest given to gunnery are evident in these inadequate levels of gun drill.

For the first days of the passage there was little wind, but on 18 April it increased, from the south-west, so all sail, including stun sails, was set and the screw was lifted from the water. The wind increased overnight, so much so that at 4:30 a.m. a squall carried away the fore top gallant mast, and split four sails. The squall was followed by heavy rain, then the wind died away; so the next morning, whilst repairs to the mast were undertaken they carried on under steam. This continued for three days,

---

25 Jonathan Coad Support for the Fleet 277–280

before the wind made sailing possible once again. As they neared England on 26 April, all boilers were fired up for a speed trial over a 12-hour period between midday and midnight. The average speed achieved was 12 knots, some 3 knots less than her published maximum.

Four days later they were less than 300 miles from Land's End. On 1 May, Bishop Rock lighthouse on the Isles of

HMS Bacchante *(Author's collection)*

Scilly was sighted, and at 4:00 p.m. the next day they anchored at last off Spithead. The next day the princes' parents, the Prince and Princess of Wales, and George and Eddy's sisters, the Princesses Louise, Maud and Victoria, were brought out to *Bacchante,* which fired a 21-gun salute as they approached.

Bacchante moved into Portsmouth harbour on 4 May, going into the dockyard for a refit and repairs which took until 12 June, allowing time for the crew, including Rosy and the other midshipmen to take leave. On this return to his mother after a 10-month separation, she was bound to have noted a vast change in her son. He had gone away at the age of 15 from Britannia Royal Naval College. The college itself would have been a major change in his life – but a ship of the Royal Navy was an entirely different environment. Life in the gun room, sleeping in a hammock, being one of a small number of midshipmen on a ship among hundreds of men, the majority of whom were of a type that he would not otherwise have come across, would without doubt have caused him to return a man after leaving as a boy. He had seen and experienced things that a person ashore could not have done; the only experience he had not yet had was to have been in a naval battle.[26]

Bacchante's refit was completed in mid-July, when Rosy rejoined, and after loading ammunition whilst at Spithead, she sailed to spend the summer exercising with the Combined and Reserve Squadrons, which were commanded at the time by Rear Admiral Hood. From Spithead she sailed to Berehaven in Ireland, a very large natural harbour between Bere Island and Bantry Bay. On 22 July the fleet sailed, and although the midshipmen's minds were on their half-yearly examinations, they would still have been assisting in the preparation of the ship's watch bills and making up their logs.

The Reserve Squadron, consisting of eight elderly ironclads including the *Warrior,* was manned by coastguardsmen who served for six weeks every

---

26 The author, who himself went to sea on his first trip at the age of just 16, also for 10 months away, writes from experience.

summer, each man serving every other year. The comment was made by a member of the royal family that the Reserve Squadron

> is only dangerous as tending to lull the shore going Englishman into a false belief he has a Navy adequate to his defence. Capital for electioneering purposes is apt also to be made out of their existence. They make an imposing show in the ports of Ireland or Scotland, on water as well as on paper, but [their] apparent strength is show and nothing else.

This comment is very frank; had it found its way into the popular press, the government would have been highly displeased by comment so critical being aired, no matter how young the writer.

The age of the fleet is apparent, as they normally proceeded in a rigid formation at a steady 4 knots, carrying out various evolutions for exercise purposes, whilst *Bacchante* was deployed as a lookout, separate from the ironclads' exercises.

These exercises were the subject of criticism from Captain Charles Fitzpatrick, in a lecture that he gave at the Royal United Services Institute three years later, when he described those naval officers who advocated the use of sails as 'lumbering up the nautical express with old mail coach paraphernalia'. He saw the real danger as a diversion of effort and resources from the study of modern naval warfare:

> Evolutions aloft are so attractive and so showy; there is so much swagger about them, our Admirals have always so highly commended and attached so much value to the smart shifting of topsails or topgallant sails, and so many lieutenants have worked their promotions out of the successful cultivation of this sort of seamanship in their ships companies, that we seem to have lost sight of the fact that it has nothing to do with fighting efficiency in the present day[27]

The combined fleet had, whilst exercising, sailed to Vigo, in Spain, where they lay for four days. They sailed on 5 August, except for *Warrior* which had an engine fault. Two days later, as the wind was favourable, the 13 ships made sail (although still proceeding under steam) 'a rare sight in the present day' but furled them later in the same day. Sail drill in competition with the other ships remained an important feature:

> It is still part of the routine of everyday on-board a man of war when weather permits. This drill consists in taking in as rapidly as possible every

---

27 Peter Padfield Rule Britannia 191

sail that the ship can carry; the vessel may be seen with every sail set alow and aloft and in three or 4 minutes all will be taken in except close reefed top sails that would be carried in a gale of wind … Sail drill is therefore not only useful for a gymnastic exercise for the men, but also as a training for them in readiness, handiness and general smartness.

They arrived back at Spithead on 12 August and anchored until the next day, when they made a two-hour passage to anchor off Cowes, on the Isle of Wight, where they remained for the next week. Whilst they were anchored there the *Himalaya* of the P&O Line passed, carrying troops for the Afghan war, as did HMS *Jumna*, carrying the Rifle Brigade to India. Their stay off Cowes again coincided with Cowes Week and so was marked by parties and other festivities. The week over, *Bacchante* returned to Portsmouth where she lay alongside until 11 September, preparing for her next cruise with the Detached Squadron. On 9 September she was visited by all the Lords of the Admiralty, and four days later moved out to Spithead to take on ammunition ('powder and shell').

The planned cruise of the *Bacchante* was much more extensive than the previous one and would see her away from Portsmouth for nearly 18 months. In that time she would travel into the Southern Ocean, visiting South America and the United States and Canada, China, Japan, Ceylon (Sri Lanka) and Australia, and then return by way of the Mediterranean.

But first, she sailed from Cowes to Vigo to await the training squadron, of which she was to be a part, rather than her previous cruise alone. She stopped off at Portland, after practising various evolutions, including firing her Whitehead torpedoes with practice warheads – and recovering them after the exercise, in view of their cost of £500 each, or over £60,000 each today, in the early 21st century. After a leisurely passage, mainly under sail with light winds drifting them across the Bay of Biscay, they arrived at Ferrol on 27 September, where they stayed until 9 October before making the short passage to Vigo, where they arrived two days later for a visit that lasted until the end of the month, awaiting the arrival of the remainder of the squadron. The first to arrive, on 23 October, was HMS *Carysfort*, followed the next day by HMS *Cleopatra*. The flagship of the squadron, HMS *Inconstant*, was next to arrive. She was a large steam frigate, with a top speed of over 16 knots under steam and 13 knots under sail. The flag officer commanding the squadron was Rear Admiral the Earl of Clanwilliam, whose flag was saluted by the *Bacchante* with an 11-gun salute. Shortly after his arrival he signalled to the rest of the squadron that they would be sailing on 31 October. *Inconstant* had arrived in a gale which continued to blow until the day they sailed, by which time it had moderated to a steady breeze. This was short lived, for a westerly gale picked up, which stayed with them for two days on their passage south-west to Madeira, which was reached after a week's passage. Waiting for the squadron there was HMS *Tourmaline.* Now fully assembled, the squadron sailed for St Vincent in the Cape Verde Islands, so that the fleet could take on coal bunkers. The *Bacchante* loaded 300 tons, coming out to her in lighters, towed by tugs, from the shore; the operation took 12 hours to complete. Happily for the squadron the mail ship *Neva* arrived with 'our mail and many parcels [marked] *not to be opened until Christmas*'. When all the other ships had completed coaling they sailed on 20 November for Montevideo in the estuary of the River Plate, a passage which was to take over a month as they completed it under sail except for the first four days. They arrived there on 22 December.

They crossed the equator on 29 November, and the ceremony of crossing the line was marked on *Bacchante.* Some 230 of the crew and all the midshipmen underwent the ceremony, ruled over by King Neptune who was described as 'the captain of the quarterdeck, sturdy, thickset and hairy'. All those to be operated on

> were sent between decks and brought up one by one, blindfolded, and presented to His Majesty with a few words from the senior member of their mess, descriptive of the character they each bore in the ship. Neptune, then, after exchanging a few observations with his new acquaintance, gave directions as to which of the four various sized razors was to be employed. They passed on, and mounting the ladder, sat down in a chair on the platform for the operation. The barber was accompanied by 'the doctor' with pills in readiness and his attendant with 'smelling salts' in case anyone should require his assistance, which was given quite gratuitously and freely offered to all. This was all over in half a minute, when they found themselves covered with soapsuds, tipped over backwards off the platform into the water in the sail [the lower stunsail had been rigged up to form a tank, then filled with seawater to a depth of approximately 5 feet (approx. 1.6 metres)], through which they were passed on by the six 'bears' [all first class petty officers] getting more or less ducked on their way out … there was ducking in all its forms and under every modification of splashing and immersion: there was the duck courteous, the duck opiate, the duck direct, the duck upright, the duck downright, the shower duck and the duck and drake. The gambols and skylarking were concluded by noon.

The remainder of the day was clouded by the death of an AB who fell from the rigging on to the forecastle head, dying instantly. He was buried at sunset. His body was carried, under a Union Jack, to the quarterdeck through a guard of marines with arms reversed, followed by the captain and officers, bareheaded, to where the crew were assembled. After the funeral service, performed by Canon Dalton from the Book of Common Prayer, his messmates committed his body to the deep. This was followed by three volleys fired in the air by the marines.

During this time *Bacchante* was towing *Tourmaline,* having had her under tow for the last four days over a distance of some 450 miles. The tow was cast off the day after they crossed the equator; no mention of the reason for this tow was given.

The remainder of the passage continued without incident. The daily routine of a deep sea passage in a steady breeze under sail gave the opportunity for Canon Dalton's two charges to indulge, in their journal, considerations of the circulations of the winds and currents in the ocean through which they were passing at a leisurely pace. Target practice was also undertaken by the squadron, but as *Bacchante* had 'expended her quarters ammunition' she sailed on while these evolutions took place. On 22 December they arrived off Montevideo, Uruguay, where they anchored in 4 ½ fathoms (8 metres) of water. This position at anchor, 3 miles off the town, was the closest that they could approach because of the shallow waters of the Plate; it was noted 'there is only one foot of water under our keel, the *Inconstant* has but half a foot'. The width of the estuary at that point is 63 miles from Uruguay to Argentina. (The date of their arrival coincided almost exactly with the date, 59 years later, of the scuttling of the German pocket battleship *Graf Spee* in the shallow waters off Montevideo, after the Battle of the River Plate.) They would stay there until 8 January.

Three days after their arrival they celebrated Christmas Day, with the morning service on the upper deck, singing 'On Jordan's bank the Baptist's Cry', 'Hark the Herald Angels Sing' and 'While Shepherds Watched their Flocks by Night', accompanied by the ship's harmonium; the service was led by Canon Dalton. Afterwards all the officers, including the midshipmen, dined together and ended the meal joining in a singsong; the ship's company then relaxed.

But two days later the atmosphere on board was not in the least relaxed, as the admiral commanding the squadron, Rear Admiral the Earl of Clanwilliam, embarked on *Bacchante* to inspect the ship. This included the crew being mustered by 'open list', each officer and man, on the calling of his name, passing before the admiral. He then inspected the ship, above and below decks. Evolutions and exercises took place in the afternoon. The following evening, after a day recovering from their exertions in front of the admiral, all the officers and midshipmen of the squadron went ashore to a garden party, hosted by the British residents of Montevideo. This started at 5:30 p.m.; at 10:30 p.m. the party ended and the officers and midshipmen left, to spend the night at the Oriental Hotel, which was completely filled by this invasion of British naval officers, to the extent that the midshipmen slept in the sitting rooms. The next day they were then all taken by train to the end of the line, 130 miles into the country towards Brazil. The railway had been constructed with British funding but because of the instability of the Uruguayan government, additional British funds had not been forthcoming to allow the construction of the railway to the Brazilian border. During their return journey to Montevideo a fox was presented to the flag captain of *Inconstant,* which accompanied him on the next passage 'but never renounced his natural habits and made sad gaps in the admirals hen coop and occasionally among the Marines boots'.

On New Year's Day 1881, Rosy went to Buenos Aires with another midshipman from one of the other Royal Navy ships also anchored off Montevideo at the time, to join Princes George and Eddy, who had gone up previously with the Captain of *Bacchante.* From Buenos Aires they travelled by train across the pampas, which was described thus: 'the general effect is similar to that in passing over the Cambridgeshire fens … though of course there are no Cambridgeshire dykes'. Leaving the train at Villa Nueva, they were taken to the Estancia Negretti, owned by an expatriate Englishman, who had built a large European style single-storey house on his estate in the middle of the pampas. The immaculate lawns were surrounded by trees, including willow, Scots fir and poplar, as well as local eucalyptus and gum trees. The flower beds surrounding the lawns were planted with English flowers including varieties of geranium and roses, and the kitchen gardens produced English vegetables and fruit. Whilst there, a game of polo was arranged between the guests in which Rosy played. The ponies used were all trained polo ponies, accustomed to the twists and turns involved in polo. Rosy, who had not been aboard a horse for some time and was not accustomed to those twists and turns, was thrown, suffering concussion, from which however he had recovered before the return trip.

After a week away the party arrived back on board *Bacchante* three days before they were due to sail. On the day before their departure the British minister, who had very recently become engaged to the consul's daughter, gave a ball in honour of the squadron. During the ball an urgent telegram was received, which was handed to the minister. As Lady Wemyss commented 'whether owing to the confusion caused by the Royal entertainment or mayhap "loves young dream" he slipped it into his pocket where it lay forgotten'.[28]

When he eventually read it, it contained urgent orders for the squadron to sail not for the Falkland Islands, but to the Cape of Good Hope in South Africa, to take reinforcements to the Army there, who were starting the attack on the Boers, by providing a naval brigade. It was too late: the squadron had sailed. A gunboat, HMS *Swallow,* was sent out in pursuit. The squadron sailed unwittingly

---

28 Lady Wester Wemyss Life and Letters, 29

on, reaching the Falklands two weeks later. For the last ten days of the passage through the Southern Ocean, gale force winds had blown and, after the warmth of Uruguay, the temperatures had dropped by an unwelcome 20°F. The squadron anchored off Port Stanley in line astern. At 1:00 p.m. the next day *Swallow* arrived with the telegram from Montevideo. Within the hour the admiral ordered the signal 'Prepare for sea immediately; Squadron to go to Cape of Good Hope with all dispatch' to be made. It was a passage of over 3,500 miles and it took just over three weeks.

This had upset the arrangements made by the Governor of the Falkland Islands for all the officers of the squadron to dine ashore with him; however in the well-used phrase, the exigencies of the public service took precedence and the meal was enjoyed instead by the officers of HMS *Swallow*, and HMS *Garnet* which had accompanied the squadron to the Falkland Islands.

The plans for the cruise were all changed. Gone were the passage through 'the Magellan Straits, … the Andes, Cuzco and Titicaca, … The hopes of seeing Cotopaxi and Chimborazo & Quito, the Galapagos as well as … Vancouver Island and British Colombia in the spring.'

The quickest way to reach the cape would have been to have used the engines throughout; however the ships burnt coal at a rate that precluded that option. The most coal-hungry was *Inconstant*, as her engines were of an earlier type than those of the other ships in the squadron. Coal had to be used carefully, to allow for its use in special circumstances and manoeuvring in confined waters. The average speed for the passage was just over 7 knots, although on 1 February with the wind on *Bacchante*'s quarter, her best point of sailing and with stunsails set, she made 12 knots. The squadron continued under sail until 11 February, by when all the ships had sufficient coal stocks to reach Simon's Town under steam. Five days later, Table Mountain was in sight and they anchored in Simon's Bay. They were greeted by the Dutch ensigns flown by some of the Dutch residents of Kalk Bay, showing their support for the Boers.[29]

Simon's Town had been a Royal Naval base since the Napoleonic wars, and the Navy had inherited the base from the Dutch East India Company. It was developed after that time due to the strategic importance of its location on the cape sea route. This declined somewhat after the opening of the Suez Canal in 1869, but due to its position was still on a par with Gibraltar. This decline reversed after the squadron's visit, and in the 1890s it was built up to serve the larger and more powerful ships that were joining the fleet.

The squadron's immediate need was to take on coal and provisions so as to be

---

29 Kalk Bay is today a delightful village, with a promenade of shops and cafes facing the sea, where the author purchased his two volumes of Mahan's Life of Nelson.

ready for any deployment that might be required. They remained at anchor until 26 February, when *Bacchante* steamed round to Table Bay for a ten-day stay, taking the opportunity on her return passage to Simon's Town to exercise the guns using a target dropped overboard, 'expending their quarter's ammunition'. She was to stay there for the next month.

Whilst *Bacchante* had been at anchor in Table Bay, the British Army – which had not received any reinforcements from the squadron in the form of a naval brigade as had been the original intention – was defeated in battle on 27 February. The Boer farmers of the Transvaal fought a British force led by General Colley at Majuba Hill, causing the British to retreat down the hill. Over 90 British soldiers were killed and 134 wounded. The losses included General Colley, who was hit in the forehead by a Boer marksman. In April, as the squadron left South Africa, the Gladstone government entered into negotiations with the Boers, represented by Paul Kruger, following the peace which had been negotiated on 21 March. In August the Pretoria Convention was signed between the British and the Boers, which gave the latter independence within the territory of the Transvaal and was considered to be the result of the British defeat at Majuba Hill.

3: *BACCHANTE*: THE CAPE TO COWES

The squadron eventually sailed on 9 April. The original plan for the route of the squadron had been rewritten because of their time in South Africa, and their next destination was now Melbourne, due east. It was a long passage, over 5,200 nautical miles, and it took five weeks at sea almost entirely under sail, as for the majority of the passage the wind was from astern as they were in the latitudes where the westerly winds blow uninterrupted round the world, frequently at gale force.

Inconstant's captain, Charles C P Fitzpatrick, had strong views on the use of sail at that time. He noted:

> Sending steamers which sail badly to make long sea passages under sail is inconsistent with the spirit of the age … it is a waste of time and both officers and men know this and it disgusts them. The men read much more than they used to and they know quite well that a high state of efficiency in shifting topsails will be of no use to them in wartime.[30]

Despite these comments he was a very skilled sailor, and one officer who served under him described him as 'probably the most able seaman in the Navy as regards the management of sails. He could work the *Inconstant* just like a yacht'.[31]

On 12 May they were in heavy weather, in winds of storm force 10. By 10:30 p.m., of the few reefed sails that were set, the fore topmast staysail split, and shortly after the ship broached – she fell off her course then swerved violently

---

30 Peter Padfield Rule Britannia, 191

31 Peter Padfield Rule Britannia, 191

up into the wind and lay to with her head to the wind. As she would not answer to the helm, it became apparent that there was a problem with the steering gear. When daylight came the next morning, it was seen that although the rudder itself was amidships, the tiller in the captain's cabin was hard over to starboard and the rudder head had been twisted by approximately 20 degrees. The fact that her rudder was amidships accounted for her behaviour in staying head to wind. The remedy was to alter the chains connecting the tiller to the rudder, so that some movement could be made, to allow limited steering. She eventually and slowly responded to the helm and was able to proceed under steam for the nearest land in the south-western tip of Australia, at King George's Sound, nearly 400 miles distant, using the sails to help her keep on course. The next day the wind had dropped somewhat, to gale force 8, which made progress easier. Preparations were made using spare spars to provide a jury rudder should the main rudder fail, but by 15 May Australia was in sight and they steamed up to the entrance of Princess Royal Harbour, from where they could see the township of Albany in the distance.

As they entered, they tried out the jury rudder to establish whether it would have been effective. But even in the enclosed waters it had little effect on their steering, so it was as well that it had not been needed in the conditions in open water. They were to remain at Albany for nearly a month.

The disappearance of, and lack of contact with, *Bacchante* naturally caused considerable worry in the remainder of the squadron; in Lady Wemyss' words: 'Intense anxiety was caused by nothing being heard of her for some time. Great, therefore, was the relief when it was learnt that she had arrived safely at Albany ... and was lying at anchor in St Georges Sound.'[32] The intense anxiety was also felt on board by Canon Dalton, who endured 'much heart-searching'.[33] As *Bacchante* was in open water, with no obstacles to run into, she was in fact in no great danger – but to Canon Dalton, not in any way a seaman despite his previous voyage on *Bacchante,* the experience was not one for him to be other than fearful of.

Divers had been working on the rudder since the day after their arrival and the ship's trim was being changed by moving as much weight forward as possible, to lift the stern and expose the rudder so that it could be removed. Sufficient weight was moved to lift the by stern 4 feet (just over 1 metre) to enable the pins holding the rudder to be removed. It weighed over 6 tons, so it was an exercise in the seamanship skills of the crew to remove and raise it with no recourse to external assistance. A spare spar was rigged to project over the stern and extra

---

32 Lady Wester Wemyss Life and Letters, 29
33 Denis Judd Life & Times of George V, 32

rigging was set up for the mizzen mast to support it. An exercise of this sort was, and is, extremely rare, and for Rosy and the other midshipmen it was an experience that was recorded with a detailed sketch in their journals and added to the knowledge that they would need as officers to be able to deal with any eventuality that might arise during their future seagoing careers.

The rudder, once it was removed, was taken ashore – in itself no mean feat, in view of its weight – to be given a temporary repair by the ship's engineers to enable them to make the passage to Melbourne, where a permanent repair by a shipyard could be made. The repair proved adequate for the purpose and after it was re-shipped *Bacchante* was able to reach Melbourne without incident where she arrived on 18 June, accompanied by *Cleopatra*, which had been diverted to Albany to accompany *Bacchante* on her passage across the Australian Bight should any assistance be required. Once the rudder had been unshipped and taken ashore by the dockyard that had acquired the contract to do the repair, *Bacchante* stayed in Hobson's Bay with the remainder of the squadron, which had already arrived. She remained in Melbourne, awaiting the completion of the repairs to her rudder after the remainder of the squadron sailed on 8 July. Once the repairs had been completed, she then sailed to Sydney, arriving there on 28 July, after a two-day passage. At the end of the month, the squadron, still in Sydney, marked the promotion of their flag officer in command, the Earl of Clanwilliam, to vice admiral with a gun salute. They eventually sailed from Sydney on 10 August, for a short and leisurely passage under sail northwards to Brisbane. *Bacchante* had been given a young kangaroo in Sydney, and it caused amusement on board as it 'is very tame and comes out in the dinner-hour and affords great fun as it goes springing along up and down the deck'. They anchored off Brisbane in Morton's Bay.

The squadron stayed at Brisbane for three days. On the second day of their stay, Brisbane declared a public holiday, shops and offices were closed and a large crowd of people went to Morton's Bay to see the squadron. Six excursion steamers did a good trade with trips round the ships, their passengers watching the evolutions that were taking place on board. On the following day many of *Bacchante*'s officers and midshipmen were invited to breakfast at Government House, after which they went, 'a party of 20 or 30 of us in all, some on horseback, some in buggies, for the Ministerial Picnic at Enoggera'. This, again, was an example of the experiences which Rosy and his fellow midshipmen, together with the officers, experienced as a result of having Princes George and Eddy on board.

They sailed the following day for Fiji, making a slow passage in light winds, taking two weeks, which took them to within a few miles of the International

Date Line at 180° East. At the end of August, there was very little wind for nearly a week, the sails were flapping idly and the ships were at some stages completely becalmed. As they approached Fiji some three days later with the wind now steadier, the squadron furled sails and steamed through the passage in the reef into the port of Levuka, which is on the mountainous, tree-covered island of Ovalau.

The squadron's visit was greeted by a visit to the flagship by the island's chieftains to present a whale's tooth to the admiral, as a 'sign of honour and peace, to welcome a distinguished stranger … the chiefs [passed the tooth one to another] finally laying it at the Admiral's feet, when the flag lieutenant picked it up and presented it to the Admiral'.

After a week in Fiji, *Bacchante* took *Tourmaline* in tow and sailed out through the channel with the rest of the squadron. Once they were out at sea, the towing hawser parted, so rather than reconnect the tow, the squadron made sail to take advantage of the south-east trade wind. They were making the long passage to Yokohama, Japan, which was to take them nearly 6 weeks, a distance of 4,300 miles with only eight days of that time not under sail. For all but the last few days, the thermometer was over 80°F (30°C), both air and sea temperature, and the winds were light, on one day resulting in a day's run of only 22 miles. On 21 September they closed Pleasant Island which lies just south of the equator – and was named by a humourist, apparently, for its unpleasant climate. The flagship sailed close to the island, and two canoes went out to greet her. In the evening when the flagship had rejoined the squadron, she signalled 'A civil war on the island. An escaped convict is king. All hands constantly drunk: no fruit or vegetables could be obtained. The present island king wants a missionary. He was evidently hungry.' They resumed their passage, crossing the equator shortly before midnight. On 24 September it was noted that the kangaroo which had been presented to the ship in Brisbane was well, and so were the wallabies. However, it was announced that the admiral was not well, having succumbed to pleurisy whilst in Fiji, and was confined to bed where he stayed for the whole passage, only recovering very shortly before they arrived at Yokohama. Sadly, a fortnight after the report on the good health of the kangaroo it slipped overboard unnoticed and was lost at sea.

Japan was sighted on 20 October and the following day they arrived in Yokohama where, already at anchor, there were three ships of the Navy's China station, together with American, Russian, French and Japanese warships. They stayed until the end of October. Japan had only started welcoming foreigners 20 years previously, but it was noted in the journal that Christian churches were active in the country including the Russian Orthodox Church, and the Roman Catholic and Protestant Churches, the latter two having gained over 80,000 converts within the previous 10 years. Before that time, any Japanese who turned to Christianity would have been threatened with death.

On 26 October the officers of the squadron were invited to attend a review of Japanese troops by the Mikado. The officers were in full dress uniform, and on their arrival were greeted with ponies to ride for the review. These ponies were very lively and 'there seemed every likelihood of a general capsize of naval officers in one direction and their paraphernalia in another'. One of the medical officers' steeds was particularly frisky, kicking and bucking, whilst careering around the parade ground, lashing out in various directions including at a naval captain, leaving a hoofprint on his leg as he sat on his horse. The pony continued on its own erratic way, with, by now, the rider hanging on manfully,

> and with his cocked hat over his nose, was like nothing so much as a rat looking out through a bunch of scarlet geraniums, and with his sword waving up in the air like the stiffened tail of a tawny lion, continued his equestrian exercises until it was time to dismount and light a cigar and over that to observe that he never enjoyed anything so much in his life before.

On 31 October, the last day of their visit, all the warships in the anchorage dressed ship, with flags flying from yardarms and masts as the Mikado was making a visit to *Bacchante.* At 10:30 a.m. the crews of all the ships manned the yards, and every ship of the two British squadrons, the Russians, Americans and Japanese fired, in turn, a royal salute of 21 guns, which would have continued for over 20 minutes. Fifteen minutes later the Mikado arrived at *Bacchante*'s gangway, to be met by Admiral Willis, the flag officer of the China Squadron, Admiral Lord Clanwilliam still being unwell and confined to his cabin. The Mikado was accompanied by three Japanese princes and seven senior politicians and naval officers. He inspected the ship and watched some gun practice before lunching on board, then leaving after a visit of 3½ hours. As he left he again received a 21-gun salute from all the ships in turn. It was a remarkable occasion; once again the presence on board of the royal princes gave the entire ship's company an experience they would be unlikely to forget.

The following day the squadron sailed for Kobe, arriving on 4 November. After a short stay, they sailed on. On 16 November a target was launched to allow for gun practice and 'a quarters ammunition' was fired; this included 20 rounds for each rifle, each man firing at a small target, with little purpose and no attempt at accuracy. The Nordenfeldt[34] guns were also fired. The journal is caustic in its comments:

---

34 Nordenfeldt guns were an early type of machine gun with 12 revolving barrels, which had been developed as a defence against small torpedo boats.

this 'quarters expenditure of ammunition' is, as at present managed, an absolute waste and to a stranger fresh from the shore, it appears one of the greatest absurdities imaginable. By the present system no single man becomes a better marksman and the only result is a great waste to the country. Everyone appears to have but one object – haul the shot up from the magazine and pitch it overboard and get the thing done quickly in order to make the requisite official entry in the log 'expended quarters ammunition'.

They were now on passage to China, to the port of Wusung, a week's passage past the Korean peninsula and across the Yellow Sea to the mouth of the Yangtze River on which Wusung lies. At its mouth the Yangtze is 70 miles wide. *Bacchante* steamed past Wusung for a further 3 miles, to anchor off the telegraph station. The heat of the passage from Fiji to Yokohama was long astern, as the night-time temperatures were down to nearly freezing point and ice formed on the decks overnight. Their anchorage was within easy reach of Shanghai, and a gunboat of the China station, HMS *Foxhound*, acted as a ferry for their stay, taking officers who wished to visit Shanghai on a daily basis. Shanghai was, and is, a major port; in 1880 close to 3,000 British cargo vessels, steam and sail, with a combined tonnage of over 2 million had visited the port. Ships of all other nationalities together amounted to only two thirds of the British numbers.

After a short stay the squadron sailed on to Amoy, 430 miles southwards along the Chinese coast, for a two-day stay. Amoy had been the site of an action by HMSs *Wellesley* and *Blenheim*, with seven other British warships, in 1840; the town had been bombarded for four hours without causing visible damage to any of the fortifications and with very small loss of life. After the Chinese had surrendered, it was occupied by British troops. Forty years later there was a British consulate, and an English clubhouse, serving a European population of about 200, who were principally English. The majority of these were merchants in the tea and sugar trade of Formosa (now Taiwan). The value of this trade in 1880 was £7 million per annum, equivalent today to £820 million.

Continuing their passage southwards along the Chinese coast, the squadron arrived at Hong Kong in the late morning of 20 December, to moor among the eight Royal Naval ships in harbour, together with warships from the American, French, German and Russian navies. It was to remain there until New Year's Eve. On arrival *Bacchante* started on a series of repairs which went on until just before she left, including bending on a complete new set of sails and painting the gunroom (the midshipmen's accommodation). Stores and provisions for the next eight months were also taken on board.

Hong Kong had been ceded to the British in 1842 when it was little more than a village. By the time the squadron arrived, nearly 40 years later, it had grown into a city of over 160,000 people with an important port, home of the China Squadron.

On Christmas Eve the afternoon was taken up with the squadron regatta and *Bacchante*'s gig, with Prince George as coxswain, won the race for gigs manned by naval officers by two lengths. Christmas Day was, as tradition expected, celebrated with a service of Holy Communion on the quarterdeck led by Canon Dalton, with appropriate hymns played by the ship's band. Afterwards all the ship's officers went round the crew's mess decks, which were decorated with greenery, flags and Chinese lanterns.

On the day before they sailed, the new sails were bent onto the yards, unfurled and then furled properly and securely to the yards. In the evening all the officers and midshipmen of the squadron attended a ball at the city buildings given by the English residents in honour of the admiral of the squadron and his officers. Dinner was eaten in the theatre with the governor of Hong Kong, the admiral and senior officers seated at a horseshoe table on the stage; the junior officers and midshipmen were seated in the balcony from where they could look down on their seniors. This was followed by dancing, which ended early the next morning.

Bacchante and *Cleopatra* sailed on 31 December. The remaining ships of the squadron were to sail via the Cape of Good Hope, with the intention of meeting *Bacchante* and *Cleopatra,* whose passage would take them through Suez and the Mediterranean, at Gibraltar. The admiral, Lord Clanwilliam, who was being repatriated due to his continuing ill-health, was not fit enough to continue with the squadron.

The two ships were now on passage for Singapore, a week away under sail. On 8 January it was Prince Eddy's birthday, so the two princes and the other midshipmen dined with the captain. The next day they arrived at Singapore for a five-day stay and then sailed on to Ceylon (now Sri Lanka), sailing through the Malacca Strait between Malaya and Sumatra, then passing the Nicobar Islands before sailing west across the Bay of Bengal to pass round the southern point of Ceylon and arrive at Colombo in the afternoon of 25 January, making fast to a buoy inside the breakwater. This was to be a longer stay, of nearly two weeks.

As was customary in virtually all of the ports at which they called, the princes went off on visits, in this case through the island, staying at the governor's residence. The night before they set off on their journey round the island, the officers and midshipmen from *Bacchante*, *Cleopatra* and *Ruby,* an elderly wooden gunboat which was also in port, were invited to dinner at the officers' mess of the 102nd Regiment before proceeding to a ball given by the Colombo Club for the officers of the three ships, which was attended by about 300 people. The evening culminated in Scottish dancing 'in which one of our naval officers, sprightly, though past middle age, gained much applause for the energy and fire with which he executed its several figures and whoops'.

Bacchante's normal harbour routine had been added to by the ship's cricket team, supported by the remainder of the ship's company, taking part in a series of cricket matches against several local teams – and losing most of them. On the Saturday night before they sailed, the officers and midshipmen of both ships were invited to a ball held by the governor, attended by 500 people. As it was Saturday, the ball ended before midnight.

On the following Monday morning, 6 February, *Bacchante* slipped her mooring at 9:10 a.m. and steamed out of the harbour, followed by *Cleopatra*. Outside the harbour the two ships dropped their pilots and sailed on passage to Suez for the transit of the Suez Canal. Their track would take them across the northern Indian Ocean, passing Aden, then through the narrow Bab-el-Mandeb before steaming up the Red Sea to Suez. These were waters with which Rosy was to become very familiar in his later career.

Their passage across the Indian Ocean in February was aided by the north-east trade wind which, as they were sailing nearly due west, was abaft their beam the whole way to the Red Sea. On 17 February, Aden was sighted on the starboard side 25 miles away, the loom of the lighthouse clearly visible as the evening drew on. As they passed through the narrow straits of Bab-el-Mandeb the wind had veered round to a southerly direction so was virtually behind them again for the start of their passage up the Red Sea. Their speed through the straits was helped by the current that flows into the Red Sea from the Indian Ocean. But by 24 February the favourable wind had died away, so they steamed on, past Jeddah, passing the lighthouse on Daedalus Reef three days later, and the next day passing the Brothers Reef which was to have a lighthouse erected in the following year.

On 1 March they arrived in the Gulf of Suez. The ship was prepared for the Suez Canal transit, a temporary bridge for the pilot erected by spars being rigged across the ship, secured to the head of the davits, to give him the necessary visibility to con the ship through the canal. It was at this point that the two ships parted company and *Cleopatra* returned to the China station, leaving *Bacchante* to sail on alone.

Ferdinand de Lesseps, the creator and engineering genius in charge of the canal, who was still in Egypt and living at Ismailia, had arranged for the canal to be kept clear for *Bacchante* to pass through on the following day, as he had done when the Prince of Wales had passed through on HMY *Osborne*. However it was decided that *Bacchante* could not delay the transit for 24 hours, so she carried on, entering the canal at 11:00 a.m. The top speed of 5 knots permitted in the canal made controlling the ship difficult, especially with the limited depth and width of the canal. Before arriving at the Bitter Lakes, they had to make fast to the bank – 'gared up' as described in the journal – to allow a convoy of six ships to pass in the other direction. The amount of traffic passing through the canal had grown rapidly since it had opened in November 1869, and by the time *Bacchante* was making her transit 8,000,000 tons of shipping was passing through annually, of which 6,000,000 tons was flying the British red ensign. After the convoy had passed, *Bacchante* resumed her transit, entering the Bitter Lakes, then on to Lake Timsah, eventually anchoring off Ismailia in the evening.

The next morning the two princes, with three officers, three midshipmen and Rosy, went ashore as guests of the Khedive of Egypt, to travel overland across the country and rejoin their ship at Alexandria.

The next morning *Bacchante* weighed anchor and steamed on until the evening, when she gared up again for the night, before arriving at Port Said at 10:30 a.m. on 4 March. She had taken 46 hours to transit the canal, of which only 15½ hours had been under way, the remainder at anchor or moored to the bank. She steamed through Port Said and on to Alexandria, arriving the next day.

The princes' party had travelled up through Egypt, visiting the pyramids at Giza (several pages of the journal are taken up with a detailed description, with sketches, of the great pyramid). They then stayed in Cairo overnight, before going by train 230 miles south to Siout (now Asyut), where they were to join the Khedive's yacht, which was to take them up to the first cataract of the Nile. The passage up the Nile was spent sitting on deck observing the passing scenery and the local people who had come to the bank to see them pass. After 11 hours they moored at Geergah: 'So ends our first happy sunny day on the Nile, when merely to breathe the air, dry, light and warm as we sit under the awning on deck is a delicious pleasure.' It was not only a pleasure, but also a complete change and a rest from life on *Bacchante*.

After a night alongside they sailed a further two hours up river to Bellamieh, where they went ashore and rode by horse and by donkey to Abydos, 'the land of Osiris'. The donkeys were large and powerful with a comfortable gait, so the party rode them bareback, in the Egyptian manner. They reached their destination by noon, for a visit to the Temple of Sethi, father of Rameses II. The party inspected the temple and then after lunch, followed by a brief snooze, moved on to the temple of Rameses II, which was dedicated to the god Osiris; all that remained of the walls of the temple were the foundations and bases of the walls. They returned to the yacht in the late afternoon, swam in the Nile and ate dinner. The next day they sailed at 5.30 a.m. in the cool of the morning before sunrise. They travelled on until the early afternoon, when they arrived at Beramsur where again they took to donkeys to visit Dendereh, riding through fields of wheat, with distant views of the hills of Libya far away ahead of them to the west. The temple was imposing, with 24 huge columns supporting the roof of the first hall, but the carvings of the god Athor at the head of each column had been destroyed by the Christian Copts.

Their trip continued the next day with another early start to sail up to Luxor to visit Karnak and the tombs of the kings. The party went ashore in the morning for their first foray to visit local temples, before setting off in the afternoon on donkeys for Karnak to spend time in the Temple of Ama-Ra. On their return on board in the late afternoon, the Bishop of Limerick, who was staying at a local hotel, joined them on board for dinner. The next morning they set off to visit the Tombs of the Kings, stopping in the middle of the day to have their lunch sitting in the tomb of Rameses IV. After a second day inspecting the tombs, this time enjoying their lunch reclining on rugs in another tomb, they returned to the yacht to continue their passage upriver. With two brief stops to inspect yet more tombs they arrived in the evening at Assouan (Aswan) which was the head of the navigation. After an inspection of the local sites, they started their return to Cairo, by now 600 miles away to the north, on 17 March.

They made good progress down the river, but on the next day ran aground on a sandbank. Despite determined efforts, laying out an anchor to try and free them, the yacht's crew failed to pull them off. A coastal steamer which had been following them downriver tried unsuccessfully to pull them off, resulting in her also becoming stuck on the sandbank. There they stayed until the next morning when, with the help of Egyptian sailors, the anchor was again laid out, this time with a heavy hawser and tackles. This tactic succeeded, and they were hauled off after 18 hours aground. Later that day they took the ground again, floating off shortly before midnight with the aid of 70 men from the local village who had been in the water pushing since late afternoon. They arrived back at Siout next day; a train was waiting to return them to Cairo.

They arrived in Cairo late in the evening and the next morning went to the Khedive's palace to thank him for his hospitality and kindness to the group during their stay. After sightseeing in Cairo the next morning they took the train to Alexandria. The Khedive's help was still very much in evidence, as they were met at the station by his carriage which took them to the port, and then they were taken to the *Bacchante* in state barges, the party resting on a large blue and gold velvet sofa with a heavy silk canopy to keep off the sun.

They stayed in the Alexandria area for a further two days, then sailed on 26 March for the short hop across the eastern Mediterranean to Jaffa (in Syria then, but now in Israel). Shortly after they sailed, they passed Aboukir Bay, the scene of the Battle of the Nile, one of Nelson's great victories. *Bacchante* arrived off the coast at Jaffa and anchored to allow the British consul at Jerusalem to board, who took the princes ashore on a tour through the country, visiting sites in the Holy Land, before completing their tour in Beirut.

After they had left, *Bacchante* weighed anchor to sail to Malta for a refit, returning to Beirut to meet the princes on their arrival there on 6 May. They sailed the next morning in company with HMS *Monarch* for the passage to Athens, a five-day trip under steam as the winds were very light and variable. They passed Cyprus on the day they left, and the following day they passed between Crete to port and Karpathos to starboard. They arrived at Piraeus on 11 May, passing through the narrow entrance flanked by two large pillars, and moored on the southern side of the harbour next to a French ironclad, *La Galissonnière*, which had arrived at Piraeus after participating in the French invasion of Tunis.

Shortly after they arrived the Greek king boarded, greeted by all the naval ships of different nationalities in port by manning yards and firing 21-gun salutes. The King and Queen returned to *Bacchante* the next day with Prince Eddy, who had stayed with them overnight, and stayed on board for some time to visit Prince George, who was in his bunk with headaches and fever. Happily, he recovered the next day so went ashore to join his brother, who had returned to Athens. They returned to the ship a week later with the King and Queen and some members of the Greek royal family including Prince Andrew, the father of the present Duke of Edinburgh.

They sailed from Piraeus for Suda Bay, on the northern coast of Crete, on 21 May. This was in order to meet the Mediterranean Fleet, which was at anchor there. After *Bacchante* arrived and anchored, she joined the fleet's routine as ordered by the flagship, remaining there until the end of the month. During their stay, the fleet regatta was held; on the first day *Bacchante*'s boats secured a first in one race and a second for the gig manned by a gunroom crew, with Rosy in the bow and Prince George as coxswain. The racing on the second day, which was held in a flat calm, brought more successes with three more wins, including the last race, for all comers, over a 3-mile course with the ship's launch with 20 oars, double-banked.[35] It was an easy win, with *Bacchante*'s launch showing a clean pair of heels to the rest of the field.

After the regatta, on the following day, the captain of HMS *Inflexible*, Captain [then] John Fisher, who Rosy and the princes would encounter again whilst studying at Portsmouth and who would become the most influential man in the Navy in the early 20th century, invited the officers and midshipmen from *Bacchante* to see over his ship. *Inflexible* was designed to take heavy punishment,

---

35 'Double-banked' is the term for two men pulling on each oar – a total of 40 men rowing.

with an armour belt amidships protecting a central core, which was itself protected by cork-lined chambers. This protected the engines, boilers and the magazines below decks, above which were two twin gun turrets mounting 16-inch guns. The overall visual effect was not elegant: 'She had, it was universally agreed, the ugliest profile of any ship afloat.'[36] Later in the year, at the bombardment of Alexandria, when her 16-inch guns fired 88 shells, the concussion from the guns caused major damage to her upper works and destroyed all her boats.

On 1 June, *Bacchante* left the Mediterranean Fleet for the passage to Corfu, four days away under steam as the winds were against her throughout. They reached port on 6 June, for a two-week stay, largely spent playing cricket, shooting game and visiting the island which had been a British possession until 1864. They then proceeded to Palermo, in Sicily, for a short visit. It was noted in the journal that since the princes' previous visit 'the whole place looks cleaner, especially the priests; they now have quite new and glossy coats and hats; their ways and manners are like those of English clergymen past middle age.' From Palermo they sailed on to Cagliari, on the southern end of Sardinia, for a brief stop, before sailing on to Valencia in light winds, the passage of under 500 miles taking a week, equating to an average speed of 3 knots. As the harbour in Valencia is about 5 miles from the town and *Bacchante* had anchored outside the port, the midshipmen did not go ashore; instead they were sitting their half-yearly examinations. These examinations carried on for some weeks. On their return to England the papers were sent to be marked at the Royal Naval College, Greenwich, together with the papers of all midshipmen in the Navy at that time. The maximum number of marks over all subjects that could be awarded was 2,600, and the results were published in March 1883. On the *Bacchante* four of the midshipmen scored very highly, Rosy achieving a score of 1,572. The examiners' report stated 'The *Bacchante* now stands first in order of merit of the ships of the Navy … The sum of her percentages is unusually high … The whole of her eight midshipmen are in the first 34 [of the fleet]'.

From Valencia they steamed on to Gibraltar, arriving on 4 July and anchoring at 7.30 p.m., to stay there for 10 days. A week after their arrival there was a rowing regatta in which *Bacchante*'s boats again acquitted themselves well, with one win and two thirds from six races.

They sailed on 26 July for Portsmouth. As this was the last leg of the cruise and the ship would pay off when they arrived, she sailed with her paying-off pennant, 500 feet long (150 metres) streaming out to leeward, its end supported by a gilded bladder floating on the water. It had been planned that she would sail most of the way home and so she had not taken on coal at Gibraltar, but the

---

36 Conrad Dixon, Ships of the Victorian Navy 66

weather conditions were so poor and the winds such that she had to tack out into the Atlantic. It thus became necessary to take on coal, so they made course for Ferrol for that purpose, anchoring there on 1 August, spending all night and the following morning taking on 154 tons. They sailed at 1:30 p.m. under steam and by 8:00 a.m. the next day they were halfway across the Bay of Biscay, steaming at 10 knots. On 5 August they arrived at Swanage Bay, where they met HMY *Osborne*, on which Rosy was to serve as a lieutenant a few years later. On board the royal yacht were the Prince and Princess of Wales with their daughters, who came on board and then returned to the *Osborne* with the princes. They were to rejoin *Bacchante* after she had arrived in Cowes Roads, where they stayed for a week, with parties and receptions ashore and afloat, culminating on 12 August when Queen Victoria visited the ship. Four days later *Bacchante* sailed into Portsmouth and made fast alongside the jetty, where she was officially paid off on 31 August, and the crew left the ship.

4: SUB-LIEUTENANT TO FLAG LIEUTENANT

After *Bacchante,* on 1 September 1882 Rosy was appointed to HMS *Northumberland,* under the command of Captain G F Durrant. She was an elderly ship, one of a class of three large armoured frigates built in 1866. After delays in the building process and further delays caused by the ship's builders, Millwall Ironworks, going into bankruptcy while the ship was launched, resulting in the liquidators seizing her once afloat as an asset of the company. Eight months passed before the Admiralty could take possession of her. One of her early tasks was to accompany HMS *Agincourt* in towing the floating dock to Madeira, on the first leg of its voyage to Bermuda (see Chapter 2). She had originally been built with five masts but despite this could only make 7 knots under sail. The class were described by one senior officer as 'the dullest performers under canvas of the whole masted fleet of this day and no ships ever carried so much dress to so little purpose'.[37]

Northumberland was part of the Channel Squadron, six elderly ironclads whose main role was principally to inspire public confidence in the Navy, although their effectiveness as warships was limited by their age. At the time that Rosy was on board, the second-in-command of the squadron was Rear Admiral the Hon. E R Fremantle, who was an enthusiastic swimmer and had awards for life-saving. One such award was given for his rescue of a man whilst he was in command of HMS *Doris.* A man had fallen overboard, and Fremantle, who was in his bath at that time of the morning, jumped from the stern to save him. However, *Doris* had already picked up the man and, not realising Fremantle's actions, had carried on her way. The ship next astern rescued him, causing considerable surprise to the officer of the watch as he boarded, on being faced with a captain with no clothes on. He was restored to the *Doris* clad in a towel. Her crew were equally surprised,

---

37 Admiral G A Bullard The Black Battlefleet, 26

as they had not realised that they were sailing on without their captain. Although it is not recorded, it could only have been the subject of considerable hilarity to the crews of both ships. Normally, however, the life of the Channel Squadron was not exciting. The ships sailed or steamed slowly, undertaking exercises and evolutions between periods alongside at the various ports along the Channel. It was a boring appointment. But better was to follow.

Rosy was appointed to her on 12 September; however, at the time she was in Port Said, with the other ships of the Channel Squadron, under orders to return home after their involvement in the Egyptian campaign of the time. So Rosy was sent to Gibraltar aboard HMS *Audacious,* which was en route to the China station, as a supernumerary midshipman. He waited at Gibraltar for five days until 16 October, when *Northumberland* arrived with the Channel Squadron. He joined his ship, and she set course back to England, but on arrival at Plymouth she went immediately into Devonport Dockyard for a refit, and long leave was given to the crew until the end of January the next year, leave of nearly three months. As Rosy did not leave *Bacchante* until the end of August, and was on his way to Gibraltar by the middle of September after being away for nearly 2½ years, the long leave would have been very welcome.

At the end of this period the Channel Squadron had re-formed: it sailed to Lisbon and thence to Gibraltar. It was whilst *Northumberland* was once again in Gibraltar that Rosy received his next appointment. In order to take it up he was transferred to a store ship, HMS *Wye,* which was homeward bound from Bombay. She arrived in Portsmouth on 16 May, and Rosy took up his appointment on HMS *Canada,* his last as a midshipman.

She had been built in 1881, and came into service in May 1883, a few days before Rosy joined her. She joined the North America and West Indies station, where she was to remain for the next three years, although Rosy was only on her until September 1883. She and her five sister ships were designed to have a long cruising range, and were fitted with a three-cylinder compound engine, and for sailing a three-masted barque rig.

Rosy found, amongst the other midshipmen in the gunroom, that Prince George had also just joined. For the first time George and his elder brother were separated, the latter remaining at home to be coached for entry into Cambridge. The instructions for George's appointment included the comment that he was 'to be treated in all respects and on all occasions, *while on board ship* [author's italics] in the same manner as the other officers of his rank with whom he is serving'.[38] Because of the seniority that both he and Rosy had gathered, Rosy was first senior midshipman and George was second senior midshipman.

---

38 Denis Judd Life and Times of King George V, 26

Canada sailed from Plymouth on 19 June, bound for Madeira and Halifax. After a four-day stop at Madeira she sailed on to Halifax, taking nearly a month for the passage, most of which was under sail. She arrived at Halifax on 1 August, where she stayed for over two weeks before sailing for St John in Newfoundland and other ports in Labrador. She then sailed for Quebec, arriving there on 23 September. The Governor General of Canada, the Marquess of Lorne, and his wife received the officers and midshipmen 'with much kindness and hospitality'.[39] As the Marchioness of Lorne was Queen Victoria's daughter, Princess Louise, and Prince George's aunt, it is conjectured that the warmth of their welcome exceeded that which would have normally have been extended to Royal Naval ships visiting Quebec.

Whilst there, Rosy passed his seamanship examination with a score of 960 marks out of a possible 1,000, and on that same day, 24 September, he also completed five years' service, was promoted to sub-lieutenant, and was immediately reappointed in that rank to HMS *Canada*.

On 23 September *Canada* had sailed for Bermuda for a refit to enable her to be ready for service as the senior officer's ship of the Barbados Division of the West Indies Squadron. Whilst at Bermuda, Rosy spent much time at Government House with General and Lady Galway, the parents of his friend Henry Galway. The refit was eventually completed in early December and on 14 December *Canada* sailed for St Kitts. Early in the next year, 1884, she joined the Commander-in-Chief West Indies and the remainder of the West Indies Squadron for a round of visits to the islands in the Caribbean. This continued until 8 March when *Canada* left the squadron to sail to Barbados and thence back to Bermuda for a second refit at the end of April. Refit completed, she returned to Canada, arriving at Halifax on 13 May. She then stayed in Canadian waters until mid-July, eventually sailing for the UK on 19 July.

On 6 July, however, Rosy had received a telegram from his mother summoning him home to his brother's wedding, which was to take place on 28 July. Maternal summons or not, it would appear that he did not make the event, as *Canada* did not reach the Isles of Scilly until 31 July; and after the Prince and Princess of Wales had boarded the ship off the Needles, to be landed at Cowes on 2 August, she eventually arrived at Portsmouth on 9 August. Rosy was discharged from her books officially on 18 August.

Three days before the telegram from his mother arrived he had sent a telegram to the Admiralty applying for permission to attend Greenwich Royal Naval College, and was to travel home at his own expense. However, as the *Canada* was about to return home this plan did not materialise. On his return, he was

---

39 Lady Wester Wemyss *Life and Letters*, 32

entered on the books of the shore base HMS *Excellent* 'for studies'[40] so that he could attend the Royal Naval College at Greenwich for the studies to enable him to be promoted to lieutenant in due course.

Whilst at Greenwich he stayed with his mother at her London home on the Chelsea Embankment. He was among friends at Greenwich, as Prince George and others of his term at Dartmouth were also starting their studies for lieutenant. His studies at Greenwich carried through into 1885, when the results of his examinations for the lieutenant's certificate were sent to him. He then moved, with the cohort from Greenwich, to take courses at HMS *Excellent* at Portsmouth, which at that time was commanded by Captain John Fisher. He passed his torpedo course in May and his gunnery course in June. Moving to the Royal Naval College in Portsmouth, he continued his studies into the autumn when he passed his pilotage examinations. It appears that the young officers studying in Portsmouth were as high-spirited as are most students as:

> an incident took place about which the Admiralty papers have now been destroyed. From the entry in the register is, it appears that Mr F.J. Proctor, editor of Chat (a Portsmouth paper founded in October 1884) was assaulted by certain Sub-Lieutenants studying at Royal Naval College Portsmouth. Mr Anthony F Gurney (the late Captain Gurney who died on 30 August 1909) was fined five pounds by the civil power; and the Commander-in-Chief, Admiral Sir Geoffrey Phipps Hornby, apparently took a dim view of the disorderly conduct of the Sub-Lieutenants. Instructions were given for all leave to be stopped and amongst others who were sent an Admiralty letter, dated 16th July 1885, expressing their Lordships grave displeasure, was Mr Wemyss).[41]

After completing his studies at HMS *Excellent*, in October, his next appointment, still as sub-lieutenant (although he had passed his examinations for lieutenant, promotion was not immediate, and in Rosy's case did not come until 1887) was to HMS *Hecla*, a torpedo boat depot ship, which he joined on 9 October at Portsmouth.

Hecla had been acquired as a merchant ship hull, the *British Crown*, in 1878 before launching, to carry mines and torpedoes and act as a depot ship to six torpedo boats. She was therefore completed to make her fit for those particular requirements. Her planned annual routine was to be stationed at Berehaven, in Ireland, in the summer, and go to Malta for the winter, whilst at the same time running training courses for torpedo men. In service she was somewhat

---

40 Churchill College Archive WYMS1/2

41 Churchill College Archive WYMS1/2

unreliable and was not a good sea boat; two years before Rosy joined her and only five years after launching, in the summer of 1883, she was out of service due to the number of defects that had developed, and in any sort of bad weather she shipped green seas over her decks. Immediately prior to Rosy joining her she had spent a further two months in dock undergoing more repairs.

She sailed on 5 November for Malta, stopping at Gibraltar en route, and arrived at Malta to have yet another refit. She had joined the Mediterranean Fleet, considered to be the most prestigious in the Royal Navy at the time, which was then commanded by Lord John Hay. After her refit she sailed from Malta to Suda Bay in Crete, accompanied by three torpedo boats, at the start of February 1886, calling at Syracuse and Zante on the way, arriving two weeks later, as the commander-in-chief and the remainder of the Mediterranean Fleet also arrived. The importance of the Mediterranean command was underlined by the new commander-in-chief who assumed command whilst there. Lord John Hay had been appointed First Sea Lord, and his successor was Prince Albert, Duke of Edinburgh. He was second in line of succession to the throne behind Prince George's father, the Prince of Wales. Albert was a career naval officer and had joined the Royal Navy in 1856 at the age of 12. He was promoted to captain ten years later and given his first command, HMS *Galatea*, in 1867. He achieved flag rank nine years after that. When he was appointed Commander-in-Chief of the Mediterranean fleet, he flew his flag on the battleship HMS *Alexandra*. Captain Percy Scott noted that 'as a Commander-in-Chief the Duke of Edinburgh had, in my humble opinion, no equal. He handled a fleet magnificently and introduced many improvements in signalling and manoeuvring [and] took a great interest in gunnery.'[42] He was promoted to Admiral of the Fleet in June 1893 and left the Navy two months later on the death of his uncle, the sovereign Duke of Saxe-Coburg and Gotha, which title he assumed, and took his place as the head of the duchy.

After Suda Bay, the Mediterranean Fleet was blockading ports on the coast of Greece as war was threatened between Greece and Turkey. This followed the refusal of Prince Alexander of Bulgaria to accept the appointment of Governor of Eastern Romania for a limited term of five years only. The Greek government, in support of his decision, was supplying arms to Bulgaria. This was opposed by the British government, amongst others, to prevent war breaking out.

After her blockading service off the Greek coast, *Hecla* returned to Malta, taking mail and passengers for the fleet. On her arrival there on 20 June she was ordered to return home in order to participate in the major naval display for colonial and Indian visitors on 23 July at Spithead, which was attended by Queen Victoria in the royal yacht.

---

42 Capt P Scott 50 Years in the Royal Navy, 61

The remainder of the summer was spent in home waters with a fleet of torpedo boats, until the beginning of September when *Hecla* returned to Portsmouth for yet another three months in dock.

She eventually sailed for the Mediterranean on 10 December eventually arriving, after being weatherbound in Le Havre for some days, in Malta on 28 December. In January 1887 she sailed in company with HMS *Polyphemus* for torpedo trials. When those were completed, after returning to Malta, the two ships then sailed to Argostoli in Cephalonia, to join the Mediterranean Fleet and the commander-in-chief. Whilst on passage there, Rosy's promotion to lieutenant was confirmed, and he was reappointed to *Hecla* in that rank.

The assembled fleet then proceeded on its summer cruise round the Mediterranean, calling at Naples, Civitavecchia, Barcelona, Corfu, and Venice and other Italian ports. By early October *Hecla* was back in Cephalonia, where she was joined by the troopship HMS *Humber*, which had come out from England to take invalids and others from the Mediterranean fleet needing to return home. Rosy joined her for the passage, arriving back at Portsmouth on 10 November 1887.

Lady Wemyss commented of Rosy's time in Malta on *Hecla* that:

> Malta was very gay in those days, the presence of the Duke and Duchess of Edinburgh, the latter greatly beloved by all naval officers, lending it much animation. To him [Rosy] it remained his favourite station for he loved the climate, the life, the island, its inhabitants, English and Maltese, and was never so happy as there.[43]

On 4 October, whilst Rosy was on passage to Cephalonia, he was appointed to the royal yacht, HMY *Osborne*, to take effect from that day. It was more than a month later, after arriving in Portsmouth on 10 November, that the log of *Osborne* noted that Lieutenant Wemyss had joined from *Humber*.

Osborne was one of two royal yachts, a paddle-steamer smaller than *Victoria and Albert,* the principal royal yacht; she mainly carried the Prince and Princess of Wales and their children on short passages between Osborne House and the mainland, around the United Kingdom and to the nearer Continental ports.

Three days after Rosy had joined her, she sailed to Flushing to embark the Princess of Wales and her daughters, Princesses Louise, Victoria and Maud, to return to England, landing them at Port Victoria on the Medway, before returning to Portsmouth. She then lay alongside in Portsmouth until March of the next year, when she was next called into service.

---

43 Lady Wester Wemyss Life and Letters, 34

The Officers of HM Royal Yacht Victoria and Albert *(Churchill Archive)*

During the winter only one lieutenant was required to be on board, so Rosy was able to indulge in his love of hunting, a passion shared with his eldest brother Randolph who had been master of three different packs of foxhounds: one in Scotland, the Burton Foxhounds in Lincolnshire, and the Craven in Wiltshire. Rosy was hunting principally with the Blackmore Vale Harriers, and sometimes with other packs in Dorset including the Seavington Harriers. Whilst hunting was a great pleasure for him, Rosy at that time felt he had more to offer; although he had a very pleasant life – indeed, easy in his present post – he had ambitions to do more. All his ancestors had represented Fife in Parliament, and he seriously considered following in their footsteps before abandoning the idea, although it was to surface again some years later.

In March, after the winter break, *Osborne* accompanied the *Victoria and Albert,* with the Queen on board, from Portsmouth to Cherbourg, to enable her to go to Florence. On her return she travelled first to Germany, to visit Emperor Frederick, during his short reign, then rejoined the *Victoria and Albert* for the crossing from Flushing, again accompanied by *Osborne*, and was taken to Sheerness. The two ships then returned to Portsmouth.

In the summer the Prince and Princess of Wales and their daughters, Princesses Louise, Victoria and Maud, joined *Osborne* at Portsmouth for the trip across the Solent to Cowes, for Cowes Week. This was a busy week for the royal yachts, and *Osborne* was anchored off Cowes for that period. The summer of 1888 was quiet because the Court was in mourning for Emperor Frederick of Germany, who had died just three months after becoming emperor on the death of his father, Kaiser Wilhelm I. At the end of the week the royal party were returned to Portsmouth, arriving on 13 August.

For a young lieutenant, there was not much in the appointment to improve his knowledge of seamanship or to advance in his profession. After returning from Cowes *Osborne* went alongside in Portsmouth for a further six weeks before crossing again to Flushing to collect the Princess of Wales and her daughters, who were returning from a visit to Austria, and take them to Port Victoria in Kent, a round trip of just five days.

After the winter alongside, which again would have given opportunities for Rosy to spend time hunting in Dorset, in March *Osborne* accompanied the *Victoria and Albert* to Cherbourg for the Queen to visit Biarritz. Five days later they returned to Cherbourg, to return her to Portsmouth. May provided a different route, as *Osborne* sailed from Portsmouth to Stranraer for Prince Albert Victor (known to Rosy as Eddy after their time on *Bacchante*), to be taken to Belfast, where he was to undertake several royal duties. On completion of those he re-embarked and was returned to Holyhead. *Osborne* then returned to Portsmouth until the end of June, when she accompanied the *Victoria and Albert* to Antwerp. The Shah of Persia boarded the *Victoria and Albert* and was then taken to Gravesend, escorted by *Osborne,* for his state visit to London. On disembarking the royal yacht he travelled up to London on board the steamer *Duke of Edinburgh*, accompanied by the Prince of Wales.

Rosy and other officers of Victoria and Albert; *had he transgressed? (Churchill Archive)*

46

Cowes Week of 1889 was very different from the event the previous year. Kaiser Wilhelm II, who had succeeded Frederick, was the first German emperor to visit England. He had been appointed an Honorary Admiral of the Fleet and was accompanied by a number of officers, including Count Herbert Bismarck. On 2 August *Osborne* was joined by the Prince and Princess of Wales, their daughters and Prince George, Duke of Cambridge (the head of the British Army). They were greeted on their arrival by *Osborne*'s commanding officer, Captain the Hon. Hedworth Lambton, and Prince George, who had arrived on board earlier in the day, undoubtedly to Rosy's great pleasure.

In the afternoon *Osborne* sailed to the Nab light, in company with the Admiralty yacht *Enchantress,* the Trinity House yacht *Galatea*, and *Firequeen,* the Commander-in-Chief Portsmouth's yacht, to lead the Kaiser's squadron of nine ships, including SMS *Hohenzollern* (the royal yacht), SMS *Irene* (commanded by Prince Henry of Prussia), two ironclads, SMS *Kaiser* and SMS *Deutschland*, and two frigates, SMS *Preussen* and SMS *Friedrich der Grosse.* All 13 ships, led by the *Galatea,* sailed to Osborne Bay off the Isle of Wight.

The date for the Naval Review had been set for 3 August, but gale force winds and thick misty rain caused it to be postponed until Monday. However, Kaiser Wilhelm and Prince Henry of Prussia visited the Prince and Princess of Wales on *Osborne* that afternoon. On Bank Holiday Monday, although the public display arranged was abandoned, the weather cleared sufficiently during the morning to enable the official review of the fleet to go ahead, and the Kaiser, Prince Henry and the Prince and Princess of Wales embarked on *Victoria and Albert* for the event.

The next day it was, *Osborne* who was the host for Kaiser Wilhelm, Prince Henry and the Marquess and Marchioness of Lorne (Princess Louise), to watch the start of the Queen's Race in the Royal Yacht Squadron regatta; she then sailed Sandown Bay to review the Royal Naval fleets gathered there ready to sail on manoeuvres. On the following day *Osborne* escorted the German royal yacht, SMS *Hohenzollern*, to Portsmouth to enable the Kaiser to attend the Aldershot Military Review.

On 8 August, all the officers of the royal yachts were present at Osborne House for a display given by the crews of the German ships for the Queen. This was the finale of the visit, as the German Squadron then sailed for their home port.

The remainder of August was taken up with *Osborne* transporting the Princess of Wales and her daughters to various destinations.

Rosy's time on *Osborne* was coming to an end. Rear Admiral Richard Tracey, second-in-command of the Channel Fleet, had asked the Admiralty to appoint Sir Charles Cust as his flag lieutenant. Cust was a good friend of Rosy's, as they had been at Dartmouth, Greenwich and Portsmouth together. When Tracey was advised that Cust had been nominated for appointment to *Osborne*, to accompany Prince George who was also appointed to her, he asked that Rosy be appointed as flag lieutenant in Cust's place. Captain Lambton of *Osborne* agreed to this change. The appointments all took place on 18 September, the Admiralty instructing that Rosy was to join *Anson*, Tracey's flagship, without waiting for Charles Cust to join *Osborne*. The Commander-in-Chief of the Channel Squadron was Admiral Baird, who was a cousin of Rosy's mother. Admiral Baird had various idiosyncrasies which included only ever wearing socks that he himself had knitted. He was very Scottish in his tastes, especially with regard to his food, with a particular fondness for haggis.

Admiral Baird flew his flag in *Northumberland,* the elderly battleship in which Rosy had sailed in 1883 as a midshipman. She had helped to tow the Bermudan floating dock to Madeira 20 years earlier – the high point of her uneventful life. The other ships of the Channel Squadron at the time were HMS *Iron Duke* and HMS *Monarch*, both very slow, elderly battleships, and HMS *Curlew,* a small gunboat only three years old. Except for the *Anson*, the fleet looked good on paper; it had no aggressive ability, but showed the flag for the Royal Navy in home and near-European waters for decorative purposes.

The haste for Rosy's appointment was caused by the imminent sailing of the Channel Squadron on an autumn cruise which had been agreed some weeks previously. It was to sail on 25 September for Copenhagen, Kiel, and Karlskrona in Sweden, returning to Portsmouth at the end of October.

After the visit to Copenhagen which they reached at the beginning of October, the squadron sailed to Elsinore (Helsingborg), at the northern end of the Sound (Øresund), the strait separating Denmark from Norway, so that the King of Denmark and Emperor of Russia could visit the squadron. This was at the request of the Prince of Wales, who was at the time visiting the Danish royal family. On 4 October the Danish king and queen and the royal family, the Emperor and Empress of Russia with their royal family, the Prince and Princess of Wales with all their family, including Princes Albert Victor (Eddy) and George, visited the *Northumberland* and the *Anson*. It could be guessed that in the throng, Rosy may have been able to have a short chat with George.

The next port of call, Kiel, was to enable the Kaiser to inspect *Northumberland* and *Anson*, in his uniform of Admiral of the Fleet. Various events followed his visit, including, at his invitation, a dinner at the German Admiralty in Berlin for both admirals and their staff, to which, as flag lieutenant to Rear Admiral Tracey, Rosy was included. The dinner was hosted by Admiral von der Goltz and was attended by the Kaiser.

After the visit, Admiral Baird wrote to the Admiralty to bring to their notice 'the very cordial nature of the welcome extended to the Squadron by German officers generally; numerous interchanges of hospitality prevailed throughout. The Petty Officers of the squadron were also entertained onshore by the German Petty Officers.'[44]

The squadron then sailed to its last port of call, Karlskrona, the main naval base of the Swedish Navy, which, being located near the southern tip of Sweden, has the significant advantage over many Swedish ports of being ice-free in the winter. Their welcome was again warm, with a banquet for the admirals and officers on 19 October, and a ball on the following night. This kind of social activity – flying the flag in friendly countries to cement friendships – was the main *raison d'être* of the Channel Squadron, and it continued until the start of the First World War.

After Karlskrona, the squadron sailed back through the Great Belt, the passage between the Danish islands of Sjælland and Fyn, to England; Rear Admiral Tracey's division sailed to Plymouth, and the commander-in-chief's to Portsmouth.

Anson arrived at Plymouth on 30 October, and the crew headed off for a period of leave. As Rear Admiral Tracey went on leave for three weeks, Rosy, his master absent, would also have had leave for that period. There is no record, but given the time of year and the proximity to Dorset, it would be reasonable to suggest that part at least of his leave would have been spent riding to hounds. Leave over, on his return they prepared, following orders from Admiral Baird, for a winter cruise which started in the middle of December. The squadron sailed first for Arosa Bay, in northern Spain, for various exercises including minelaying and torpedo net defence, before sailing on to Gibraltar, arriving there on 2 January 1890. The squadron then sailed for exercises in the Mediterranean, returning to Gibraltar on the last day of the month. Rear Admiral Tracey then telegraphed to the Admiralty, asking for Lieutenant E S Alexander to be appointed as his flag lieutenant. It appears that this appointment was made following a request from Admiral Fairfax, the Second Sea Lord, to enable Rosy to be appointed to HMS *Undaunted* (which at the time was in Devonport) on her arrival in Gibraltar on 11 March. The squadron had been to Port Mahon, which had been a major naval base in the 19th century, during February but had returned two weeks before *Undaunted* arrived. He was to spend the next 3½ years on board.

---

44 Churchill Archive WYMS1/2

5: LIEUTENANT TO COMMANDER

The appointment to *Undaunted* was a plum appointment; a new ship, with a famous captain. *Undaunted* was a brand-new ship, an armed cruiser built on the Tyne by Palmers of Jarrow. She had a top speed of over 20 knots, an armament of two 9.2-inch guns, one forward and one aft of the superstructure, and ten 6-inch guns mounted in casemates on each side. She also had smaller guns and six torpedo tubes. She was the first ship Rosy had joined that did not have masts rigged for sails.

She was commanded by Lord Charles Beresford, one of the major figures of the Navy at the time. He was an old friend of the Wemyss family, and this would almost certainly have had some part in Rosy's appointment.

Towards the end of the 19th century the British public had started to take an interest in their Navy. A Naval Exhibition was held in 1891 at Chelsea, which included 'displays by seamen and marines with battles on a lake and numerous exhibits by ship builders and engineering firms. In five months it was visited by 2 ½ million people'.[45] The Channel Fleet sailed around Britain, slowly, and the Admiralty supported the creation of the Navy League in 1895, which published a journal entitled *The Navy*, aimed at the younger generation. Beresford was a keen supporter of the Navy League. He was a much talked-about figure, very popular within the Navy, who referred to him as 'Charlie B'. He had been promoted to commander at the very early age of 29, five years before the age at which Rosy attained the same rank, which was in itself considered an early age. Beresford cut a commanding figure and had been elected to Parliament by his Irish constituency at the age of 28.[46]

---

45 Captain John Wells *The Royal Navy: A Social History*, 39

46 As the younger son of the Marquess of Waterford, he was eligible for election to the House of Commons.

The Beresford family estates in Ireland, at Curraghmore, extended to 100,000 acres and employed 600 people. Like Rosy, Beresford was very keen on hunting, with his family's own pack of hounds which hunted on the family estate, to the extent that he had broken ten bones whilst out hunting and, still, in common with the remainder of his family, hunted six days a week when he could.[47]

Despite being popular within the Navy, he had a talent for antagonising his superiors, and this came to the fore with his dispute with Sir John Fisher later in his career. His parliamentary career was a major part of his life. During his 30-year career in the Navy, from 1878 to 1909, he spent under 9 years at sea and 14 years in Parliament, and on his retirement from the Navy was elected as MP for Portsmouth, which he retained until promoted to the House of Lords in 1916. Whilst serving at sea he had a good reputation, as the ships that he commanded were 'happy ships'. His aristocratic lineage had given him a more liberal perspective than many of his contemporaries in the Navy, and he would not accept the huge differences in lifestyle that existed between officers and men in that period. Charlie B, as he became known in the country as well as in the Navy, became a favourite with the public and spoke out about the need for a strong Navy. He had been appointed to *Undaunted* following an appointment as Fourth Sea Lord, assisted by the Prince of Wales, with whom he was a close friend. In an echo of our modern times, his 'secret memorandum' concerning the state of the Navy – which was, in his view unprepared for war – leaked into the press, and his fellow sea lords decided he should return to sea. He had also been involved in an affair with Lady 'Daisy' Brooke, which had ended, as many affairs do, very messily, including incriminating the Prince of Wales. He was better out of the way, on *Undaunted* in the Mediterranean.

The time spent on *Undaunted* followed the pattern of the movements of the Mediterranean Fleet at the time. There were no major crises raging, nor any hotspots for the Navy to deal with, so the two years passed comfortably, Rosy getting to know and enjoy Malta even more than he had previously done. The social life, the climate and the sporting activities made for a wonderful life for young, single and eligible lieutenant – although matrimony for young officers was not encouraged. He entered into all the sports on board, as did the captain, who pulled the stroke oar in rowing regattas. Rosy discovered a talent for entertaining at onboard shows by a ballet dancing routine 'going through all the steps of a "premiere danseuse" in the lightest possible manner with his eyeglass firmly fixed'.[48]

In May 1892, he achieved command for the first time on Torpedo Boat Number 21, for training purposes, for which he had been proposed by Beresford,

---

47 Robert K Massie Dreadnought, 502

48 Lady Wester Wemyss Life and Letters, 38

who had recognised Rosy's leadership qualities. Lady Wemyss commented 'He often declared that Wemyss with 20 men could do what another with 200 would fail to accomplish.'[49] Under Beresford's command, *Undaunted* had achieved a reputation for being the smartest ship at the time in the Mediterranean Fleet (whether that was also reflected in her gunnery skills is not known). When her commission was over, she was cheered by every ship in the fleet as she left. They had left only a short while before the collision between *Camperdown* and *Victoria* off Tripoli in June in which the commander-in-chief, Sir George Tryon, died, together with large numbers of his crew.

In January of 1892, Prince Eddy died of influenza, making Prince George second in line to succeed to the throne after his father, the Prince of Wales. In the same month that Rosy achieved his first command, Prince George was created Duke of York and took his seat in the House of Lords. He followed that, the following year, by marrying. His wife, Princess Mary of Teck, 'had been engaged to Prince Eddy but had been left "delicately stranded" by his premature death.'[50] Prince George's naval career had come to an end.

On Rosy's return to England, he went on leave. He had spent the majority of his time on leave since his sister's marriage to Lord Hugh Grosvenor at their home in Northamptonshire or with his mother in Scotland. His mother had not been happy; Randolph, Rosy's eldest brother, had not made a success of running the estate and had become involved in speculative and unsuccessful ventures, which had had a detrimental effect on the estate's finances, which his mother had managed to build up before he took over. She had to suffer still further, for in December 1894 her eldest daughter died suddenly during the marriage celebrations of her sister-in-law to the Marquess of Cambridge. (He was the brother of Princess Mary, and he later became the Duke of Teck.) The effect of her daughter's death proved fatal. She retired to Wemyss Castle and after a stroke died on 11 February 1895.

Rosy was serving on HMS *Empress of India*, part of the Channel Squadron, off the coast of Spain, when he was told of her final illness. He came home as quickly as he could, but arrived after she had died. She was buried in the family burial ground in Chapel Gardens, overlooking the Firth of Forth. The deaths of his mother and sister in such a short space of time were huge blow to Rosy. He had been particularly close to his mother. He dealt with the double loss by subsuming himself in hard work. He returned to *Empress of India* to resume his appointment.

Shortly after his return the captain of *Empress of India*, Adolphus F St Clair, left the ship for his next appointment, to the Coast Guard, on 25 April. Clearly he had been in poor health, as he died in London only two weeks later.

---

49 Ibid 37

50 Dennis Judd Life and Times of George V, 44

In June the Channel Squadron sailed to Kiel for the opening of the Kiel Canal. Started in 1887, its main purpose was to give German warships a short cut to the North Sea from the Baltic, without having to sail through the narrow Kattegat and Skagerrak between Sweden and Denmark. It was a great success and was widened 12 years later to accommodate dreadnought-sized battleships.[51] Kaiser Wilhelm was immensely proud of the canal, believing it to be one of the greatest accomplishments of his reign. The Channel Squadron was under the command of Vice Admiral Lord Walter Kerr, on *Royal Sovereign* with his second-in-command, Rear Admiral Allington, flying his flag on the *Empress of India*.

In Kiel, in addition to the German fleet and the Channel Squadron, there were ships from the Austrian, Italian, French, Russian, American, Swedish, Norwegian, Dutch, Portuguese, Spanish, Turkish and Romanian navies. All the German princes and grand dukes were present, together with representatives from many of the royal families of Europe. Although the Kaiser had described the canal as 'a symbol of peace', the fact that its main purpose was to expedite the movement of German naval ships to the North Sea made his words seem somewhat hollow. On 20 June, he boarded the German royal yacht, SMS *Hohenzollern*, which Rosy had last encountered at Cowes whilst serving on *Osborne*, and sailed through the canal from the Baltic end at Brunsbüttel to Kiel, at the head of a long line of ships carrying the various dignitaries. At Kiel, as the royal yacht arrived, Kaiser Wilhelm stood alone on the bridge, wearing his uniform of an Admiral of the Fleet of the German Navy with his decorations and medals on his chest glinting in the sunshine. (He had also been awarded the honorary rank of Admiral of the Fleet in the Royal Navy.) He later attended a dinner in his honour on *Royal Sovereign*, the flagship of the Channel Squadron.

In 1894 an Admiralty committee was formed to review the progress made by the reform of the executive officer structure which had been started in 1870 by Hugh Childers, the First Lord of the Admiralty at the time. The intention of the reform was to ensure that there were enough officers in each rank should there be a general mobilisation for war, to enforce an age for compulsory retirement and maintain a healthy promotion process. With regard to the last reform, lieutenants could anticipate up to 17 years in that rank before promotion to commander (this was before the rank of lieutenant commander was created, in 1914). However to show a lieutenant's seniority he wore a half-stripe between the two stripes of his lieutenant's braid after eight years in that rank, which was to become the braid of a lieutenant commander. Rosy achieved this in 1895 whilst on *Empress of India*.

At the end of yet another commission leisurely showing the flag around the United Kingdom and the near Continent, Rosy joined HMS *Alexandra* as flag

---

51 It was increased to a size large enough to allow the battleship Bismarck to pass through in 1940.

lieutenant to Rear Admiral Seymour for a three-month period. She was the flagship of the Reserve Fleet at Portland; her only point of interest was that she was by 1895 the last British battleship to have her main armament below decks, a design that had been superseded decades before. Rosy's appointment coincided with the annual fleet manoeuvres in that year. At the end of that period, his next ship was HMS *Astraea,* a brand-new second-class cruiser. She was one of a class that included HMS *Fox*, which he was to encounter as one of the ships of the Red Sea Patrol in 1916. He joined her as the first lieutenant, second-in-command, on 5 November 1895.

By 1896, relations between England and Germany were deteriorating, and the telegram sent by Kaiser Wilhelm to Paul Kruger, the leader of the Boers in the Transvaal, congratulating him on repelling the Jamieson Raid, which has been organised from the British-controlled Cape Colony, further inflamed the tensions between the two countries. It was in the light of this increasing tension that Rosy next met Kaiser Wilhelm. *Astraea* had joined the Mediterranean Fleet and in early April 1896 was in port at Syracuse, on the southern coast of Sicily. Early in the morning of 7 April the German royal yacht *Hohenzollern,* escorted by a cruiser, entered the port. Soon afterwards the Kaiser was seen leaving the royal yacht in one of its boats, and on *Astraea* it was assumed that he was going to visit the elderly Italian battleship *Francesco Morosini*, the flagship of Rear Admiral Gualtiero. However, it was suddenly realised that he was in fact heading for the *Astraea*.

At that time in the morning the captain was still below, and the upper decks were being scrubbed and holystoned. Before the crew could be fallen in or a proper party to pipe him aboard arranged, the Kaiser was aboard, wearing his uniform of a Royal Naval Admiral of the Fleet – delighted, as he thought, to have caught one of Her Majesty's ships by surprise. As first lieutenant, Rosy was on deck; he greeted the Kaiser and tactfully hinted that the Kaiser, as a British admiral, was most probably aware that admirals did not come on board before morning divisions had taken place. This defused the potentially awkward situation and the Kaiser, disarmed, became very pleasant, had a tour round the ship and later invited the captain to lunch aboard the royal yacht.

The next British national event was carried out on a scale that made the Kaiser's opening of the Kiel Canal seem small by comparison. In 1897 Queen Victoria's reign of 60 years was marked by Diamond Jubilee celebrations. It started on the morning of 21 June with a huge event in London, with a procession from Buckingham Palace to St Paul's Cathedral, involving troops not only from Great Britain but from all over the Empire. A procession of 17 carriages carried the royal family and leaders of countries in the Dominion escorted by troops from the Household Cavalry and cavalry regiments through the streets lined with troops and thronged with people eager to see the Queen. The service was held outside the western end of the cathedral, as the Queen's arthritis prevented her from climbing the steps, and she stayed inside her coach for the entire service. Five days later the Diamond Jubilee Naval Review took place at Spithead, off Portsmouth, the traditional location for naval reviews. The Royal Navy's fleet included 21 battleships and 46 cruisers, and totalled 165 ships, although it was noted that some of the ships present had been brought out of reserve and were so old as to have muzzle-loading guns. Also present were warships from other navies from throughout the world, together with major merchant ships. The fleet was to be inspected by the Prince of Wales as the Queen was now too frail to board the royal yacht, *Victoria and Albert*.

The review also was the occasion of an unofficial display of new technology, as the launch *Turbinia* raced through the lines of the assembled ships at speeds of up to 34 knots. She had been designed by Charles Parsons who, although not a naval architect, had created a beautiful-looking craft, and one which contained the steam turbine engine that Parsons had designed initially to improve electric power generation. The impressive speed of *Turbinia* was taken note of in the Admiralty, and within a very few years the first two ships to be fitted with Parsons steam turbines were two new destroyers, HMS *Cobra* and *Viper,* which in service had a top speed of over 33 knots. The next ship to be fitted was the battleship HMS *Dreadnought* in 1906.

Rosy was of course aware of the impending Diamond Jubilee, and was also keen to gain promotion to commander. If he could achieve this, he would have spent only 11 years as lieutenant, six years below the average. One way to achieve the rapid promotion he desired was to serve on the *Victoria and Albert,* as service on the royal yacht more or less guaranteed promotion on completion of the appointment. He therefore approached his friend Mark Kerr (whose words provide the Encomium at the start of this book), with whom he had been at Dartmouth. Kerr was at the time first lieutenant on HMS *Cambrian.*

Rosy's application was successful, and he was advised of his success whilst *Astraea* was at Lemnos, an island he was to get to know very well when he was stationed there during the First World War. He was to relieve Lieutenant Christopher 'Kit' Cradock, who had just been promoted to commander. (Cradock later lost his life in command of the British squadron at the Battle of Coronel.) By the time that Rosy joined her, the *Victoria and Albert* was an elderly ship – over 40 years old and of wooden construction, with a paddle-wheel propulsion system. She was reserved for ceremonial duties, and was painted black with a gold stripe along her hull and masts of sufficient height to fly the oversized ensigns flown on ceremonial occasions. Although imposing in appearance, she was not by the end of the century, fit for deep sea voyages. Some years before,

HMY Victoria and Albert *(Churchill Archive)*

when she was at that time on a rough passage, and the Queen was on board, the captain asked her if the porthole lids to her cabin could be closed. She was very keen on fresh air so was not prepared to permit this. On being told that the sea could come in she is reported to have replied 'the sea will *not* come in'. On this occasion she was proved wrong, as a sea *did* go in, and the captain, on running down to her cabin, found her in an armchair with her steward holding up her legs while seawater was rushing back and forth in the cabin.[52]

Her captain at the time, Rear Admiral John Fullerton, had been in command since 1884 and would continue to be so until 1901. He had further promotion to vice admiral in 1899, and on retirement in 1904 was promoted again, ending his career as Admiral Sir John Fullerton. He had two children: his daughter Judith married a naval officer who rose to become Admiral Sir Sidney Meyrick; his son, Eric, joined the Navy, and rose to become Admiral Sir Eric Fullerton. For good measure Eric married one of the daughters of Admiral 'Jacky' Fisher. To have three admirals in one family in two generations is a considerable (if unplanned) achievement.

Service on *Victoria and Albert* was very easy, and Rosy rented a cottage 'Mainsail Haul' on the Hamble, so that he could spend his spare time in the summer sailing on *Margaret*, a shared Solent One Design. This class had been designed in the early 1890s and was 41 feet 6 inches long (12.6 metres) with a cutter rig and a gaff-rigged mainsail; it was adopted as a racing class by both the Royal Yacht Squadron and the Island Sailing Club.

Rosy's promotion to commander was announced on 1 August 1898, as his time on *Victoria and Albert* came to an end and he returned to normal Naval

---

52 Lady Wester Wemyss Life and Letters, 44

service. After a short spell on *Minerva*, a frigate, which would be under his command when he was Commander-in-Chief East Indies, he spent a weekend in January 1899 at York Cottage, on the Sandringham Estate in Norfolk, with Prince George and Princess Mary, Lady Mary Lygon (who was a lady in waiting to the princess), Derek Keppel and Helene Brielse. In the summer he was appointed to HMS *Niobe* as commander;[53] she was at the time attached to the Channel Squadron. A first class cruiser, launched two years before Rosy was appointed to her, she was completed in November 1898. She was one of a class designed for trade protection duties on a worldwide basis, with a range of 2,000 miles at close to her top speed of 20 knots. Armed with sixteen 6-inch guns, when launched she was better armed than any comparable ship of a foreign navy, and had a crew of 677. It appears, however, that she had a problem with her propulsion system, as a question was asked in the House of Commons to the First Lord of the Admiralty on 14 April 1899 as to:

> whether, since completing her 60 hours trials, HMS *Niobe* has had another breakdown, and what was the nature of the accident; whether he can state what is the total number of breakdowns which have occurred on the ship since delivery by contractors.

The answer given was that although she had passed her contractor's trials and the three-hour full speed trial on commissioning satisfactorily, there had been subsequent defects which had been remedied, and a fresh 60-hour trial was carried out with a satisfactory result.[54]

The Boer War started on 11 October, and five days later *Niobe* received orders to sail to Las Palmas to await further orders. Rosy wrote to Lady Constance Butler[55] from *Niobe*; the letter that he started in October was sent from South Africa at the end of November:

> HMS Niobe, Channel Squadron, Monday, October 16, 1899.
>
> You can imagine how delighted we all were last evening when at four o'clock we got a signal telling us to prepare for sea immediately. The Captain went off to see the Admiral and came back with the news that we were going to Gibraltar and Las Palmas and there await orders. It isn't actually the Cape but it's well on the way there and I am in hopes we shall go on there ...

---

53 Out of the 30 officers on Niobe, 20 had fathers who were themselves officers in the Royal Navy, including five admirals and seven captains.

54 Hansard, 14 April 1899, vol.69, cc1123–5

55 She was then 20 years old, 15 years younger than Rosy, and one of the great beauties of the time. She was also a keen yachtswoman who sailed at Cowes and had very probably met Rosy when he was sailing Margaret.

Even if we get no further than Las Palmas it'll be something as I expect the transports will keep us pretty busy there and even that small thing will be better than doing nothing in England. It's extraordinary to think of the mobility of the ship and the strength to the country it means. There were we last night just going to evening service at 4:15 p.m. and 6 p.m. we were steaming out to sea, a powerful ship and nearly 700 men! We heard rumours of a British victory on Saturday evening but no confirmation of it, so you can imagine how eagerly we are all waiting to get to Gibraltar and hear some news.

November 3, HMS Niobe, Las Palmas, Canary Islands.

We have been here for a fortnight very nearly. Our news of the war is scanty and comes principally through Spanish sources so that it isn't very reliable, but this latest of two battalions being captured is too awful if it's true, but I can hardly believe it. And here we are all this time lying here and doing nothing except cheering the transports as they go through … The Captain has just sent for me and told me he has received orders to go to the Cape! Hurrah – we shall be off tomorrow I expect. It will be ripping steaming down to the Cape.

Monday, November 20 HMS Niobe.

We're nearly at the Cape now. We hope to arrive there on Saturday and we are all expecting to hear of a big Boer defeat. The whole Army Corps or at any rate two thirds of it is ahead of us so that I'm afraid we can hardly expect any of our people to be landed … We have just passed a transport with mules – poor brutes, I expect they have a pretty bad time of it at sea, and the horses of the cavalry regiments too. One transport we saw at St Vincent with a squadron of lancers on board had lost about 20 horses out of 120 – a big percentage.

Saturday, November 25.

We have made the land and shall be at anchor by 3 p.m. I hope. Well, in an hour or two we shall know what's been going on and what is to happen to us I suppose. I hope it may be something and not fiddling about doing nothing.

Tuesday, November 28. Simons Bay, Cape of Good Hope

We arrived here just after a Naval Brigade had landed and on Sunday we got the news of the fight at Graspan. Our men suffered most severely, but thank God behaved with the greatest gallantry and have received the

Queen's congratulations. I think I'd do anything in the world for that. I think we are certain either to go up to Kimberley from here or perhaps go round to Durban and take charge of the defences of that place. I don't mind which, but anything to be doing something. There is no doubt but that the authorities are still a little uneasy as to the state of the Colony for all along there has been a very great chance of a general rising, for it is certain that the whole place is a hotbed of disloyalty. However, the fear of that must get less and less every day for they have lost their chance. Had they risen at once, on the outbreak of war, it would have been a real bad business. We have not been able to take advantage of our successes purely I think through the unfitness of the cavalry horses. Not anybody's fault, but from the fact of their being brought into action so soon after a three week's voyage.

All those poor fellows who have been killed in the Naval Brigade were pals of mine – but, after all, it's the best way of coming to one's end, isn't it?

No news has been received from Ladysmith for nearly 10 days now. But they are all right, I think, and Buller should relieve them soon. The Naval Brigade saved the place. They arrived there with some heavy guns just one hour after the enemy had commenced bombarding the place and got their guns into action immediately, and silenced the Boer artillery. Hedworth Lambton is in command.[56]

Niobe was involved in the rescue of the transport ship *Ismore* which had grounded on Columbine Point, to the north of Table Bay. The rescue effort was successful, as all on board, including all the troops and 20 horses, were saved. Otherwise, they remained at anchor in Simon's Town. His next letter to Lady Constance Butler started on 20 December and is confined to comments about the progress of the war and the frustration of being inactive. However, in early March, *Niobe* was dispatched to Walvis Bay on the west coast, to protect it from a threatened attack. Rosy landed at the head of 120 men and three guns, and spent a week happily building defences, digging trenches and mounting the guns, before handing over to a detachment of the Royal Artillery. They then returned to the Cape of Good Hope until the end of March when *Niobe* sailed for St Helena with Boer prisoners, arriving on 10 April and landing the prisoners.

From then until the middle of August *Niobe* remained at anchor off St Helena. Rosy's letter continued with descriptions of the island and the comment in May that 'life is a bit monotonous here' followed by a further comment the next month that it's 'dreary, dreary work being here'.

Eventually:

---

56 Lady Wester Wemyss Life and Letters, 45–47

August 12 HMS Niobe, St Helena.

At last we have got definite orders and we shall be back at Plymouth on about 10 or 12 September. I can't tell you how delighted I am at the idea of leaving this place, but all the same there lingers in one's mind the sort of regret at coming home before the war is actually over. I had a sort of wild hope we might have been sent to China, but it seems that life isn't in our way, except getting home, which is always nice. But I suppose it's only human that one should chafe at being inactive when there is so much going on all over the world. We're awfully behind here with our news and all we know is that the King of Italy has been assassinated, that the Duke of Edinburgh is dead and that De Wet is still at large and it seems playing the deuce with our people. Of Chinese news one can have little, except that it is a bad business. But we are quite in the dark as to whether all the Ambassadors had been murdered or not. It's a shocking business altogether. May we come well out of it! They are going to send another 2000 prisoners to this wretched island, so that the ship that relieves us will have the landing of them and their stores and will I suppose have to go through all the fuss and worry with the soldiers that we had to at commencement of our sojourn here. I don't envy them. Well Hurrah! We shall be back soon now.[57]

Niobe arrived at Plymouth on 10 September, when he left the ship. His first trip as commander had clearly been successful, as his commanding officer wrote to him:

I have to thank you very much for the state of good order and discipline you kept the ship in, but also the way you carried out the extra jobs put on us at the Cape and St Helena. I know that often you were poorly repaid by having to fight the soldiers and civilians who instead of meeting us halfway and digging out to get the job through, always threw obstacles in the way and never did a handsturn more than they could help. All these bothers and worries you kept to yourself and only once or twice when things were particularly bad came to me.

His next appointment was to prove both a huge challenge and a huge career boost.

---

57 Lady Wester Wemyss Life and Letters, 54

6: HMS *OPHIR*. OUTWARD BOUND: THE SOLENT TO SOUTH ISLAND

After King Edward VII acceded to the throne in 1901, following the death of Queen Victoria, a proposal involving Prince George, now Duke of York, which had been in the early stages of planning before the Queen died, resurfaced. It had been agreed that he and Princess Mary should visit Australia to open the first parliament of the new Commonwealth. However the new King objected, commenting 'he only had one son left out of three and he will not have his life unnecessarily endangered for any political purpose'.[58] After pressure was applied on the King he relented (rather as Queen Victoria had done when Prince George first joined the Navy). The tour was to take place, to visit not just Australia, but another eleven self-governing colonies and colonial possessions, ending in Canada, and would take eight months to complete.

While Rosy was on leave after his time in *Niobe* he was sent for by Prince George, who asked for his help in the organisation of the tour and also to become second-in-command of *Ophir*, the ship that had been chosen for the purpose. For the time that he was involved in the organisation, he was attached to HMS *President*, 'for special purposes'.

Ophir was one of the ships of the Orient Line, which was 'taken up from trade', as none of His Majesty's ships had accommodation which was sufficiently large – or comfortable – for the royal couple and their extensive entourage. *Ophir* was one of the company's smaller ships, slightly under 7,000 gross tonnes, a cargo passenger liner, with holds to take refrigerated cargo, and was normally part of the regular Orient Line service to Australia. She had, as did all ships of that company, very comfortable accommodation, more than sufficient for the royal party. On becoming HMS *Ophir*, most of her civilian crew were taken off

---

58 Denis Judd, Life and Times of George V, 72

and the deck and engine room departments were replaced by naval personnel; the stewards and cooks, however, were retained, presumably as the standards of Orient Line in that department were more accustomed to the level of service considered necessary than were the naval cooks and stewards of that time. A Royal Marine band was also included as part of the ship's complement.

The total number on board including the passengers, was 559, according to the Duke of York.[59] After assisting with the initial organisation, Rosy's appointment as commander, or second-in-command, of the ship was onerous. In addition to the normal role of the commander, who was responsible for the smooth running of the ship on a day-to-day basis (with the exception of the engine room) including the discipline of the crew and the ongoing maintenance and appearance of the ship, he had the additional responsibility of ensuring that the duke and duchess and their entourage were unaffected by the normal working of the ship. Working round the passengers was a normal part of a liner's crew's routine; but it was not a function that a naval crew were accustomed to. There were also the pressures of ensuring that the safety and security of the ship and her passengers was paramount, despite pressures from the journalists who were travelling on the warships escorting *Ophir*. One of the two escorts on the first leg of the tour was *Niobe*, the ship that Rosy had just left. *Ophir*'s captain was Alfred Winsloe, who had been the captain in *Niobe* with Rosy; he had been promoted to commodore second class for this appointment, and created a Member of the Victorian Order. It would seem likely that Rosy, in the course of his advice to Prince George during the organisation of the tour, may have suggested Winsloe for the post of captain.

Ophir arrived at Portsmouth from Tilbury on 28 February 1901. There she took on coal bunkers and stores. On 16 March the King and Queen, with the Duke and Duchess of York, arrived on board. The King inspected the ship, and then the royal group lunched on board with Commodore Winsloe. The King and Queen went back to the royal yacht, *Alberta*, and at 4.30 p.m. they sailed, steaming out of Portsmouth Harbour. In front was the Trinity House yacht *Galatea*, followed by the royal yacht, then the *Ophir*. Crowds had gathered on the shores of the harbour to watch the occasion.

> Immense crowds of people lined the shores on both sides and one could see handkerchiefs waving as far as the eye could reach, while several bands could be heard playing; and above all the cheers of the multitude both onshore and on the many boats which accompanied us out of the harbour[60]

59 Quoted in Cindy McCreery 'Views Across the Decks of Ophir', in Royal Studies Journal Issue V, 2018, 57

60 Petty Officer Harry Price The Royal Tour 1901, or The Cruise of HMS Ophir (unpaginated)

Off Spithead the *Alberta* slowed down and came abreast of *Ophir*. Rosy ordered three cheers for the King and Queen, whilst the Duke and Duchess of York watched from a vantage point on the bridge. *Ophir* then set off on passage to Gibraltar in rough and windy conditions.

The weather had improved and there was bright sunshine when they arrived at Gibraltar on 20 March so that, as they entered port, they passed between two lines of anchored battleships and cruisers, which were dressed overall and with their crews manning their yards. They all fired a 21-gun salute in welcome. *Ophir* anchored inside the mole and later in the morning the duke and duchess went ashore in the royal barge, passing between two lines of 12-oared cutters, whose crews stood bareheaded in their boats, the officers in charge saluting. *Ophir* sailed two days later for Malta with a new escort, HMSs *Andromeda* and *Diana*. The short passage to Malta was over on Monday morning, and *Ophir* was greeted by a squadron of destroyers coming out to meet them and escorting them into port.

Commander Godfrey-Faussett[61] described the scene:

> Our entrance into the harbour was a truly magnificent sight. Practically the whole of the Mediterranean Fleet was inside, all dressed with flags, the yards manned, bands playing, men cheering, saluting, crowds of people everywhere onshore, decorations all over the place. [He does not note the noise of over 40 warships all firing a 21 gun salute] … In the forenoon the Governor Sir Francis Grenfell, the Commander-in-Chief, Admiral Sir John Fisher, the Second Admiral Lord Charles Beresford[62] [sic] … and all other swells, naval and military, came on board and made their bow[63]

Later in the day, the royal couple went ashore to take the salute at a march past of naval and military forces. Godfrey-Faussett again:

> There were all told about 4000 bluejackets, a very good show of Marines and about 4000 soldiers. The bluejackets certainly were the best on the whole [Godfrey-Faussett was naturally partisan!]. The first Battalion was led by Lord Charles Beresford's bulldog and the other bluejacket's Battalion was led by a goat. Some of the naval officers rode and they looked very well on their smart little ponies.

---

61 Commander Godfrey-Faussett was an aide-de-camp to Prince George and a contemporary of Rosy at Dartmouth. Godfrey-Faussett wrote a daily journal of the tour of the Ophir, which is included in his archive at Churchill College.

62 Beresford was second in command to Fisher.

63 Churchill Archive BGGF 1/49

The duke and duchess were fully engaged with functions ashore until the day they sailed, on 27 March. Their departure, which was not until midnight, was marked by a floating pageant:

> as the evening drew on weird looking craft began to make their appearance on the water, most of them resembling animals and birds, the best products being a swan and a whale, the Elephant, Crocodile, Seaserpent [sic], Lion, Camel being very good. At 8 p.m., as if by magic, the whole fleet illuminated and in the background 500 rockets descended simultaneously ... It was on the water that all eyes were fixed; apart from the fleet the Ophir was illuminated ... Lined up along both sides of the harbour, outside of the fleet, were the destroyers, their searchlights crossing over us and making an archway reaching to the sky ... At midnight a grand salute of 1000 rockets was a signal for us to depart.[64]

Godfrey-Faussett described the spectacle as:

> the most glorious, magnificent and impressive spectacle I have ever seen or ever will see in this world. It is impossible to give any idea of it ... We all got so excited on board here that ... myself and others climbed up the main rigging, tar, pitch and all in our best clothes to get a better view and cheered for all we were worth. I never saw such a sight – and I don't think it would be possible anywhere else but Malta. There is no doubt the Admiral surpassed even himself in all the arrangements.[65]

The Ophir as Royal Yacht (P&O Heritage Collection)

64 Petty Officer Harry Price The Royal Tour 1901

65 Churchill Archive BGGF 1/49

Ophir's next port of call was Port Said, for the transit of the Suez Canal. They arrived in the afternoon and made fast opposite the Pilot House. Coal for the bunkers was taken on, which started at 10:00 pm, loaded by local labour, whose shouts and cries disturbed the sleep of those on board, and was completed about 4:00 the next morning, 31 March. Two hours later she sailed into the Suez Canal. As they approached Ismailia they were advised that the *Britannic*, a troopship which had on board the Australian Commonwealth Guard of Imperial Troops, had gone aground after a sudden gust of wind had pushed her onto the bank. Some of the officers of *Ophir* were taken by launch to the *Britannic,* including Godfrey-Faussett, who commented that:

> the ship seemed to be in a very uncomfortable and dirty state. There are about 49 officers and 1200 men ... Some of the officers are three in a cabin. There are only two baths between 49 of them. The stewards who we saw in the saloon looked a particularly dirty lot.[66]

After anchoring in the Bitter Lakes overnight they passed through Suez in the morning, then out into the Red Sea on passage to Aden, arriving there on 5 April. Waiting there were the two ships that were to be their permanent escorts for the rest of the tour, HMSs *Juno* and *St George,* at anchor off the port. On the evening of the day that they sailed a dinner for 54 guests was held in the Royal Saloon, which was followed by a reception for about 100 people, the duke and duchess shaking hands with all the guests, including many naval officers from the three ships. After the reception ended and the officers had returned to the escorts, they and *Ophir* sailed at midnight, in Godfrey-Faussett's words 'on our way perspiring to Colombo'.

Whilst on the way to Colombo, Rosy wrote to Lady Constance Butler:

> HMS Ophir. At sea between Aden and Colombo, April 6.

> We have just left Aden behind and are now steaming along with a smooth sea and a nice breeze on our way to Colombo. So far our trip has been most successful, though for the first day or two the Duchess was horribly ill, but she has been very plucky and I think enjoying herself very much. Yesterday, at Aden, was the first really very hot day we have had, for we were very lucky in the Red Sea. I had never been to Aden before and I most sincerely hope that fate may never take me there again. [His hope was to be ill-founded.] I never saw such a place, and the very sight of it was enough to make one perspire. A dull heat, brown everything. At Gibraltar we had one shocking bad day and everything had to be put off, but our

---

66 Churchill Archive. BGGF1/49

reception and send-off from Malta were the two very finest sights I have ever seen. Our literary people on board say that pen and ink can't describe it properly, so you may imagine I can't. Our party on board are extremely pleasant and good-tempered and everything shows signs, I hope and think, of the whole trip been most successful, my only curse being the coaling which you may imagine makes a fine mess of my beautiful white side. If it were not for that, I should be quite happy and contented with everything. We are to be four days at Colombo, so I'm hoping to get away for a couple of them and go upcountry to Kandy which I believe is beautiful.[67]

The passage to Colombo was uneventful; the highlight was a concert given by the crew in the Royal Saloon. They were attired in theatrical costumes supplied by the court tailors on board. As the temperature had increased and was daily in the region of 85°F (29°C) with high humidity it could not have been a comfortable experience for all those in the audience. The programme, of ten items, consisted mainly of songs, with a banjo solo to start, one solo dance and with the finale being given by Petty Officer Harry Price.

They arrived at Colombo, on schedule, on 12 April. The duke and duchess had felt the heat of the Indian Ocean, so their visit to Kandy in the hills above Colombo was much anticipated, as it was hoped that it would be cooler. However, that did not prove to be the case. In their absence, the crew were presented with a delivery of fruit, including bananas, pineapples and mango which was much appreciated as it was a considerable rarity in their normal diet. They were also presented with several cases of tea by the local Planters' Association.

On the morning of their arrival, Godfrey-Faussett was in a complaining mood:

> It was beastly hot. I found it especially hot as I had to arrange about the luggage and servants who had to leave for Kandy by a special train at 10. 45 and they required some driving to get them away.[68]

On the royal party's return from Kandy, they were entertained at the Queen's House in Colombo, to a dinner in stifling heat for 52 people, followed by a reception in which about 500 people were presented to the duke and duchess who shook hands with all of them. Godfrey-Faussett and the other aides-de-camp assisted with the process by keeping the line moving. Following that, the royal party returned to *Ophir*. A firework display and illuminations then took place, although Godfrey-Faussett 'did not think they were up to much'. After the

---

67 Lady Wester Wemyss Life and Letters, 58

68 Churchill Archive BGGF1/49

wonderful spectacle they had seen in Malta, it would be difficult to see a display that came anywhere near it.

Ophir sailed the next morning, 16 April, on passage to Singapore. Godfrey-Faussett had learned to play bridge since joining the ship, and on the evening after sailing he had dinner in the wardroom followed by bridge, at which he lost, not an uncommon occurrence for him. After five days at sea, during which time the heat and humidity increased still more, they arrived at Singapore on 21 April, and made fast to the coaling wharf. After the duke and duchess, with a small party including Godfrey-Faussett, had gone in the royal barge to Johnston Pier, where the official arrival ceremony took place, the coaling started. On completion, in the early evening, *Ophir* left the wharf and moved out to the man-of-war anchorage, where she remained for the rest of the stay. The next morning a team of Chinese painters boarded and gave her a fresh coat of white paint from stem to stern, which would have been a great pleasure for Rosy as *Ophir*'s paintwork had become somewhat less pristine than the standard that he sought to maintain.

On 23 April, the royal party returned by the royal barge. *Ophir* sailed at 2:00 p.m. with their escorts, and, taking a route to avoid the Java Sea with its risk of piracy, went at full speed for the first 50 miles through the difficult waters of the Malacca Strait, so as to reach open water before nightfall. After they reached open water, *Ophir* stopped for a burial; one of the crew had died in Singapore, and it had been decided that the burial should wait until it could take place at sea. The burial service and ceremony were witnessed by all on board, including the duke and duchess and their entourage. The duchess had presented a wreath of white roses and maidenhair fern, which was laid on top of the Union Jack over the body. They were now on passage to Melbourne, and two days later they crossed the equator and King Neptune boarded with his court, making his appearance:

> in a chariot composed of huge seashells, the raw jagged edges edged in rope that had the appearance of belonging to some ships of a bygone age ... The whole lot glided forwards drawn by the Guard of Honour, composed of the biggest Marines in the ship and dressed in all the outlandish costumes possible ... When Neptune accompanied by his wife and the whole of his court reached the fore end of the deck, close to the large tank [which had been built for the purpose] he was received by their Royal Highnesses the Duke and Duchess; after a few words of greeting, Neptune stepped from his chariot and carrying a silver goblet in his hand walked up to the Duchess and sprinkled water on her head ... christening her Queen of the Seas.

Ophir *sailing from Portsmouth, led by*
HMY Alberta, *with the King on board*

Following that the main ceremony started, with the Duke first in line, who seated himself in the chair placed at the very edge of the platform overlooking the canvas tank and was instantly seized by Neptune's barbers and was duly lathered and scraped in the orthodox style and then pitched head over heels into the tank, where he received his baptism at the hands of the sea bears in the tank who gave him a severe ducking amid the laughter of the Duchess and suite and the whole of the assembled ship's company[69]

The remainder of the male members of the suite were then anointed, followed by various officers and men. Godfrey-Faussett commented that 'Rosy Wemyss deserves a lot of praise for the arranging of it all!'[70] Rosy, writing to Lady Constance Butler, noted 'The whole thing was very funny and I was in roars of laughter.'[71]

The first stop in Australia was to be Albany for the escorts to take on coal bunkers, as they were at the limits of their range and had needed to reduce speed to conserve coal stocks.

The next entry in Rosy's letter to Lady Constance Butler added:

We are due to arrive at Albany tonight. The concert came off last night and in spite of the ships rolling I danced. One or two of the men on board here are really extraordinarily talented in various ways and we got up quite good entertainments. I am now trying to organise some tableaux. But it is difficult ... We are well out of the heat now and today is the first full day for

69 Petty Officer Harry Price in The Royal Tour 1901
70 Churchill Archives, BGGF1/49
71 Lady Wester Wemyss Life and Letters, 59

a long time we have not seen the sun. I have again missed seeing my tulips and daffodils at Mainsail Haul which is a great disappointment.

The concert in the Royal Saloon was with a new cast including Rosy who did a sword dance, which he managed with great skill even though the ship was rolling and pitching. They arrived at Albany the next morning, well ahead of the escorts. Another reason for the stop at Albany was to allow Sir Arthur Lawley, one of the party, to land to take up his post as Governor of Western Australia. From Albany, which was illuminated in his honour, he went by train to Perth to be sworn in and then went immediately, again by train, to Melbourne for the opening of Parliament. The escorts arrived as *Ophir* sailed. The weather had become considerably colder as they reached Australia. One of the sights of sailing in the southern latitudes were the albatrosses which followed *Ophir* for long periods of time without any discernible movement of their wings.

On Sunday 5 May they arrived off Port Phillip Heads at the entrance to Melbourne, and were joined by the *Juno*, which had caught up; *St George* had been delayed due to engine problems. When they passed through the Heads, they were greeted by three ships of the Australia Squadron, which escorted them as they sailed up to Mornington to anchor until the next morning, for the arrival at Melbourne.

At 9:00 a.m. *Ophir* raised her anchor and steamed the last few miles, to anchor off Melbourne. After lunch the royal party left the ship in *Hygeia,* an elegant paddle-steamer, which had come out to collect them, to land at St Kilda Pier, to the accompaniment of 21-gun salutes from the warships at anchor.

Godfrey-Faussett described the scene:

> Each of the carriages was drawn by four horses [with] postillions, 2 footmen behind and all in powder[ed wigs] – exceedingly smart it was and all so beautifully turned out, splendid horses – Lord Hopetown [the Governor General] has no equal where horses and carriages are concerned … The procession was a very long one over a distance of 7 miles through the town. The crowds were enormous and most enthusiastic, the streets simply lined with stands and all overflowing with people besides those who stood in the streets and at the windows etc. The triumphal arches were magnificent works of art; they must have cost thousands of pounds and they were very numerous, bunting, decorations, Venetian masts everywhere, the whole of the route 7 miles, was lined with these Venetian masts on either side at about 30 yards apart and each one cost over four pounds!!! The huge arch and pillars on Princes Bridge cost the sum of £8000! The whole cost of the decorations, illuminations and all the rest of it that was done in the city

in honour of the Royal visit was over £110,000 [£13,500,000 at early 21st-century rates]. I had no idea that Melbourne was such a huge town, nor did I think any city in the Colonies contained so many splendid buildings. It opened my eyes considerably. The processing round the town lasted for over two hours and it was 4.30 before we found ourselves at Government House. Their Royal Highnesses rather tired I think after the strain of it all.[72]

In the afternoon *Ophir,* together with *Juno* and *St George,* went alongside one of the piers, to take on coal next day. The crew were allowed leave, and half the ship's company (the port watch) went off on 60 hours' leave, after which the starboard watch had their 60 hours ashore, so that they, too, in addition to the normal distractions of 'Jack ashore' could enjoy the decorations in the town. They went by train to Melbourne from the port, and were delighted that they were allowed to travel free of charge. After both watches had returned, having been warmly welcomed by the people (some of whom would have enthusiastically helped them in their distractions), the ship was opened to the public. She was boarded by huge crowds in the best of spirits. The crew had some difficulty in persuading the crowds to leave in the evening, and many stayed on the pier. They were then to see, at 8:00 p.m., the dazzling spectacle of all the warships illuminated.

On 7 May, the duke held a levee at Government House. Godfrey-Faussett, who was on duty, described the occasion:

> No less than 3500 men were presented and shaken hands with – rather exhausting work for the Duke whose arm got very stiff– the Australian handshake or grip is not a thing to be winked at! They took 2½ hours to go by, some of them very odd looking in curious clothes.

Later in the day the duke returned with Commodore Winsloe, Godfrey-Faussett and another aide-de-camp, to St Kilda Pier where *Ophir* was berthed, to visit some of the foreign warships.

> He went around in the blue State Barge [which had been shipped out from England] and in each ship had to drink sweet champagne and so on and inspect the ship.[73]

Two days later the whole reason for the visit to Australia came to pass – the Opening of the first Commonwealth Parliament. The royal procession went from Government House to the Exhibition Buildings where the ceremony was

---

72 Churchill Archives BGGF 1/49

73 Ibid

to take place; 13,000 people were crammed into the space, with, at one end, a huge dais on which were the duke and duchess, the governor general and his wife with, behind them, the governors of all the Australian states and various officials. The day after the opening there was a Review at Flemington Racecourse, where nearly 15,000 troops went by, including a naval brigade of 1,000 sailors and 300 marines. It was estimated it was watched by over 100,000 people.

The itinerary for the tour had to be changed; due to an outbreak of plague in Brisbane, the *Ophir* was to sail to Sydney, while the royal party went by train to Brisbane. Unfortunately, in Brisbane there was considerable anger that *Ophir* was not going there and that the visiting royal party was considerably diminished in size. If the *Ophir* had gone to Brisbane, because of quarantine regulations she could have been held there for up to two weeks, which would have had a major impact on the timings of the remainder of the royal tour. After their visit, the royal party would travel from Brisbane to Sydney to rejoin the ship there.

After sailing from Melbourne, Rosy wrote to Lady Constance Butler with his impressions of the visit:

HMS Ophir. At sea between Melbourne and Sydney May 19

> I must confess that I'm getting a little tired of seeing every place en fete and amongst the drawbacks is the fact that it is very difficult to get one's washing done, as the washerwomen, like everybody else, are having a holiday while we are in port. Whilst in Melbourne we threw the ship open to visitors for two days from 1 to 5 pm and during those hours on the first day it was calculated that over 12,000 people came on board, and rather more the next day, and a surprising part is that they knew they could only see very little because, of course, all the cabins etc were locked up, otherwise I should think they would have been little or no furniture left. We had great luck with our weather – may it long continue. Lady Katty [Lady Catherine Coke] and Bridget [Mrs Derek Keppel] are on board with us … So last night we danced and had great fun. I have bought a cockatoo which I am trying to learn to talk. At present the only results are awful screeches and some bites in the hand, but I suppose that patience will do something eventually.[74]

Ophir arrived at Sydney on 20 May; they first moored at Garden Island, which was a major Royal Naval base with a full range of store buildings, engineering facilities, offices and a coaling wharf, where she went alongside. The main building on Garden Island was the storehouse, a magnificent building described by Jonathan Coad as:

---

74 Lady Wester Wemyss Life and Letters, 60

a substantial building of four stories, constructed of polychromatic brick with sandstone detailing and granite door thresholds, generously provided with loading bays, each with a wall crane, originally hydraulically powered. Internally … The timber floors are carried on substantial cast iron columns in the building, which is divided by fireproof cross walls.[75]

After coaling, *Ophir* steamed up the coast and anchored in the Hawkesbury River to await the return of the duke and duchess.

The royal party arrived back from Brisbane on 25 May, the day before the duchess's birthday, which was celebrated on board in great style, including the crew being given a special tot of rum, in which they were joined by the duke and duchess.

On the next morning *Ophir* and her two escorts, *Juno* and *St George,* steamed out through Broken Bay, at the mouth of the Hawkesbury River, and southwards along the coast; then, turning to starboard, passed through Port Jackson Heads into Sydney Harbour, escorted by the Australian Squadron, to anchor in Farm Cove opposite Government House. In the afternoon the royal couple went ashore in the royal barge, which had been brought round from Melbourne for their formal welcome to Sydney. Godfrey-Faussett noted that the decorations were 'very good indeed, but not quite so elaborate a scale as Melbourne'. The royal visit ended on 6 June when the duke and duchess returned on board and the three ships steamed out of port to find it blowing hard, causing the ship to roll and pitch considerably, and the duchess to retire to her cabin. They were now on passage for New Zealand.

---

75 Jonathan Coad Support for the Fleet, 296

7: HMS *OPHIR*. THE RETURN: SOUTH ISLAND TO THE SOLENT

Continuing his letter to Lady Constance Butler, Rosy wrote:

HMS Ophir. At sea, Sydney to Auckland. June 9th

We left Sydney two days ago and are now on our way to New Zealand, and with our usual good luck we are having a capital passage. Well, the two big places, Melbourne and Sydney are done and finished and I am not at all sorry … An old man who was born in the village at home [Wemyss] came 4 miles to see me. I felt so touched and was so pleased to see him, though he had left Scotland years before I was born … I went up into the Blue Mountains one day to a place called Katoomba, about three hours by train from Sydney. The scenery was beautiful though no peaks to the mountains. One looked across an enormous valley to the hills opposite, a distance of 60 miles, though it appeared hardly half that distance on account of the extraordinary clearness of the atmosphere. The whole country looked quite blue from the colour of the leaves of the gum trees which are rather like the leaves of an olive. Did you ever read a book called Robbery Under Arms by Rolf Bolderwood? A delightful story of Australian station life in the days of the bushrangers? I remarked to a man up at Katoomba that some of the places up there reminded me of the book, and he told me that those were the places described. I thought myself so clever to have remarked it until it struck me as it wasn't me it was clever but the man who wrote the book.[76]

The passage to Auckland, in the north of the North Island, was not pleasant, as the weather conditions were poor all for the whole distance and the sea was

---

76 Lady Wester Wemyss Life and Letters, 61

very rough. They arrived on 10 June, but first anchored off Devonport to wait for the next day, for the official arrival. Whilst at anchor, Harry Price relates:

> Here we witnessed quite a unique incident; i.e. we perceived a small boat making for the ship, and as it got closer, we saw that a little girl was the sole occupant, she was a white girl and no older than 10 years at the outside; she pulled beautifully [and] came up alongside in grand stile [sic] although a nasty sea was running. One of the side boys went down the gangway to meet her and she gave him a beautiful bouquet and asked him to give it to the Duchess, needless to say it was accepted.[77]

By the next morning the weather had improved as *Ophir* made her way with her escort into Auckland for the official arrival, where the duke and duchess landed in state and processed through the streets to Government House. Godfrey-Faussett was off duty, so was able to go ashore, pausing to hear the duke give a speech announcing the annexation of the Cook Islands. He noted that the town

Interior of the Royal apartments in Ophir

---

77 P O Harry Price The Royal Tour 1901

was 'not very interesting'. Two days after their arrival the royal party and some officials from the three ships, including Rosy, went by special train to Rotorua, some 130 miles south of Auckland. On arrival the duke was addressed by the Maori chiefs and replied through an interpreter: Godfrey-Faussett commented that 'both were couched in very flowery and high flown language'. On the following day the entire party went by carriage in a long procession followed by hordes of reporters and photographers. They saw the hot springs and a Maori village, before travelling on to Whakarewarewa, where the main concentration of hot springs and geysers were located, some spouting up to 50 feet (15 metres) high of boiling water. Godfrey-Faussett and Rosy returned later to sit in one of the hot water pools, lazing for half an hour, before returning for dinner at the Geyser Hotel. After dinner they watched a haka dance, given by five Maori girls, four of whom Godfrey-Faussett noted 'were quite good looking', before walking back 3 miles to Rotorua in the dark over a bad road. They returned to Auckland two days later and sailed for Wellington at 5:00 a.m. on Sunday 16 June, arriving two days later. Their Royal Highnesses landed at 11:00 a.m., going in a short procession of only three carriages through an enthusiastically welcoming crowd. The stay in Wellington lasted for three days, and at 4:00 p.m. on 21 June they sailed for Lyttelton, the port for Christchurch on the east coast of the South Island, arriving there the next morning. The royal party went ashore for the formal reception, going on to Christchurch and then by train to Dunedin in the very south of the South Island. *Ophir* had sailed round to Dunedin, where the royal party returned to her, where she was at anchor, by tug. *Ophir* was rolling heavily in the swell, so the process of boarding was, although perilous, eventually completed without problem. The tug, however, caused considerable damage to the accommodation ladder and other external fittings, so Commodore Winslow ordered it to move away so the luggage could be transferred using *Ophir*'s boats. Once all had been boarded, *Ophir* sailed for Hobart.

Once she had cleared the south coast, the conditions deteriorated further and *Ophir* was rolling and pitching heavily, shipping water on board. Harry Price recollected:

> I think the bakehouse suffered the most; I looked in and found the poor baker up to his waist in water, loaves of bread, buns, dough, bags of flour, dishes baking tins etc. Several men have been injured and the Duchess must have been very ill.

Happily the distance to Tasmania is not great and by the time they arrived on 2 July the weather had abated. *Ophir* anchored until the next morning, when they went alongside and the royal welcome once again was given. Fortunately the duchess had recovered from the effects of the sea conditions. After a three-day stay they sailed for Adelaide, in South Australia. The poor conditions at sea had continued, so, arriving off Port Adelaide they found there was too much wind for the *Ophir* to go over the bar and up the river, so they anchored and the royal party transferred to a local vessel for their arrival, followed over the bar by *Ophir* the next day, when conditions had eased. During their stay the ship's band gave three concerts, and *Ophir* again welcomed the public on board; Harry Price believed in greater numbers than anywhere else they had been. Ashore, the royal party had an enthusiastic welcome wherever they went, including a demonstration by the local schools of 'drills and exercises' to an audience of 24,000 people. They sailed on 15 July to a huge send-off by the people of Adelaide for the next and last call in Australia, at Fremantle on the west coast. Their course took them across the Great Australian Bight, which lived up to its reputation for bad weather conditions; a gale from the north-west on her starboard bow causing her to corkscrew – pitching and rolling at the same time – which is a most uncomfortable motion. The weather continued to deteriorate to the point where it was decided that the conditions were such that they diverted to Albany from where the duke and duchess would travel to Fremantle and on to Perth by train. Once the weather had moderated *Ophir* steamed on to Fremantle. Much of the *Ophir*'s time there was taken up by the bane of Rosy's life, coaling, filling the bunkers with nearly 1,500 tons of coal, creating clouds of coal dust which settled everywhere and which all had to be cleaned away before the royal party returned. The day of departure from Australia was 26 July when, at 3:00 p.m., they sailed from Fremantle on course for the long voyage across the Indian Ocean to Mauritius, with relays of escorts, as the cruisers' range was not adequate for the complete passage at *Ophir*'s cruising speed.

Rosy continued his correspondence to Constance Butler:

HMS Ophir, August 11

Australia is finished, for which many thanks, and also Mauritius and we are due at Durban tomorrow night and I'm quite excited as I hope to see Randolph [his eldest brother] as I haven't seen him for over two years. We had a tremendous send-off from Fremantle, our last Australian place. It was a good place for a send-off as we had to steam about half a mile quite close to quays which were thronged with enthusiastic crowds. HRH stood up on the bridge and gave three cheers for Australia. He has a capital voice and it must have been heard by thousands and how the people did shout! I didn't manage to get ashore at Mauritius as I was too busy on board and so saw nothing of the island for which I am sorry. [Rosy's time at Mauritius was taken up with the coaling procedure and cleaning the ship afterwards.]

Simon's Bay, August 21

We got we got here two days ago and I have been coaling ever since. How I loathe the very word Coal. It plays the deuce with the appearance of the ship and I always have so little time to do it in. We leave here the day after tomorrow and get to Quebec on September 15 and then a good month's peace and then Home. I must say I shall be glad to get home. A most interesting and enjoyable cruise it has been, but I shan't be sorry when it's all over. I am now beginning to wonder if they will promote me on arrival. There are precedents for it and I am in great hopes that they will. The Rubicon is passed when one has attained the exalted rank of Post-Captain and is always pleasant to pass that ... I missed seeing Randolph at Durban – he had gone home with Chesham ... He thinks he will have to come out again in three months time, and if this is so, I suppose I shall miss him in England.

They sailed from Simon's Bay on 23 August, bound for St Vincent in the Caribbean. The temperatures rose as they sailed towards tropical latitudes, and Godfrey-Faussett was

rather anxious about our shirts. No washing done onshore since we were in Perth in July and then very little on board. The capabilities of this ship [sic] laundry are very limited indeed and if one succeeds in getting four shirts washed in a fortnight one is lucky.[78]

Such were the cares of an aide-de-camp!

After an uneventful 10 days at sea they arrived at St Vincent on 3 September. Godfrey-Faussett's entry in his journal on the next day focused on coaling, which started at 7 a.m. The duke and duchess were taken to *St George*, which with *Juno* had rejoined them as their escorts, for the day. The remainder of the royal party joined them, returning at 11:30 a.m. 'Everything filthy dirty. The coaling carried on the next day from 7 a.m. until 4 p.m., despite which, the Duke and Duchess remained on board; most of the rest of us spent it on board the other ships.'[79]

Coaling and cleaning completed, *Ophir* sailed soon after 4 p.m., leaving behind *Juno* and *St George*, for the voyage north, up the eastern coast of North America to Quebec on the St Lawrence River in Canada. Writing during the passage to Quebec, Harry Price[80] remarked on:

---

78 Churchill Archive BGGF 1/49

79 Ibid

80 Harry Price was a petty officer on board Ophir, whose journal provides a view of the tour from the lower deck and provides a counterpoint to Godfrey-Faussett's.

Physics or Physical Drill of which we got plenty and our commander was a regular school of physical culture and never seemed so happy as when he had charge during the drill, especially when he ordered 'knees up'.

The scope of the commander's role was all-encompassing!

They reached Canadian waters on 13 September, and were met by two ships of the North American Squadron, HMSs *Indefatigable* and *Tribune*, carrying mail from Canada and also a French Canadian pilot, who would take them up the St Lawrence River. During the next morning HMS *Quail*, a torpedo boat destroyer (the predecessor of a destroyer), came out to *Ophir* to collect dispatches. To save time, it was decided to rig a boom out from the *Ophir's* side for *Quail* to collect the bag from the end of the boom, whilst steaming at 15 knots. But the lieutenant in command of *Quail* misjudged his approach, colliding with *Ophir's* starboard bow before *Quail's* speed enabled her to pull clear from a considerable risk of being run down, crossing close ahead and making, in Godfrey-Faussett's words 'an extraordinarily narrow escape by a few inches only'.

News reached the ship on 15 September, as they made their way up the river, of the death of President McKinley of the United States of America. Next morning, the duke told Godfrey-Faussett that he was to represent him at the funeral of the president in Washington or New York.

> I am delighted of course – 'twill be ripping to visit Washington or New York and a great honour to represent the Heir Apparent at the funeral of such a big man as the President of the United States. As soon as we arrived at Quebec Sir Arthur Bigge telegraphed to the Embassy at Washington asking when the funeral was to be, and then HRH said he would telegraph again to say that I was coming to represent him and asking that I might be put up at the embassy … When it is over I will rejoin the Royal Train wherever it may be in Canada at the time.

Later that morning *Ophir,* followed by four escorting cruisers, arrived off Quebec, mooring to a buoy in the river. At noon the duke and duchess landed in Quebec, to be taken in a carriage procession to Government House.

> The steepness of the hills in the town of Quebec is terrible – it is difficult to understand how heavy carriages can be got up some of them. The royal carriage was a monster, one of the Royal posting or town coaches I think they call them, sent out from Buckingham Palace Mews on purpose for their [sic] TRH's visit. It was drawn by four horses and postillions[81]

---

81 Churchill Archive BGGF1/49

The next morning a telegram from the British Embassy at Washington, which had arrived the previous evening whilst the royal party were ashore, was read, which advised that the official ceremony in connection with the funeral of President MacKinley was to take place that same day, making it impossible for Godfrey-Faussett to get there in time. 'I am most disappointed.'

The royal party left the ship on 18 September to join the royal train for their tour of Canada, which was to last a month, crossing Canada and eventually arriving at Vancouver before returning to the east coast. Amongst many other places they were to visit were Montreal, Ottawa, Winnipeg, Toronto, Niagara and St John before arriving at Halifax to rejoin *Ophir* for the return to England.

From Quebec she had steamed round to Halifax. On her arrival, Rosy was able to set the crew to work, scraping to remove anywhere rust had occurred and applying red lead paint where appropriate, followed by the top coat of white. After the first day of preparation of the upper works she moved into dry dock; as the water drained out of the dock, the crew, standing on floating pontoons, cleaned the underwater parts as the level descended and then painted the bottom with antifouling. When that was completed, she moved out of dock over the next morning. The crew were given three days' leave by watches, the starboard watch going first. After the leave period she then moved to the coaling wharf and, with the help of sailors from the escorts, a large heap of coal was moved to the bunkers, followed, naturally, by cleaning thoroughly all the new paint which had been coated in coal dust.

Rosy wrote to Constance Butler whilst in Halifax:

HMS Ophir, Halifax, Oct 10

Tomorrow three weeks we shall arrive in England and I'm looking forward to it tremendously. TRH's and all their party are living in a train so far as I can make out but from all accounts seem to be amusing themselves. Poor old Lady Katty could not go as she was too ill, but she has now gone off on a little tour of her own with our doctor to look after her. The ship seems very lonely and dull without them all, but I am getting through a lot of jobs I couldn't possibly have done with all of them on board. We leave here on Monday 21st for St John's Newfoundland and leave there on Friday 25th; we hope to anchor off Portland for the night of Thursday 31st, and to Portsmouth the next day. I hear there are to be great functions there and the whole of the Channel Fleet are to meet us off the South Coast of Ireland and escort us up the Channel. If only we can get fine weather, it will be a fine sight. We have had most beautiful weather here and the climate is perfectly delicious – bright, warm and dry. I had meant to try to have taken a few days leave and gone to Boston and New York, but at the last moment I found that there was so much to do and so much to see that I didn't go. I have been playing a good deal of golf and after years am really getting better I believe. It is a most fascinating and at the same time the most irritating game.

The party all returns tomorrow week and I shall be very glad to see them. It seems ages and ages to me since we left England. How glad I was to get away and how glad I shall be to get back. We had an awful job coaling the other day – 1,800 tons of coal did we have to get in and it was raining most of the time – beastly – however I hope I shall never have to get coal in again.[82]

They sailed from Halifax in bad weather and a snowstorm, escorted by *Niobe* and *Diadem,* with a further escort of six ships of the North American Squadron to take them out of harbour. Before finally leaving Canada they called at St John's in Newfoundland. During the passage there, Prince George invited Rosy to become an Extra Equerry, an honorary post which was accepted with great enthusiasm. Bryan Godfrey-Faussett was invited to become an equerry, which was a great honour, although it would result in his naval career coming to an effective end, as he would be seconded from the Royal Navy for a period of three years.

After two days at St John's they sailed at 7:00 a.m. so as to clear the Grand Banks early in the afternoon. They were now on passage home: Harry Price's journal for their departure day is headed 'Homeward Bound'. He noted:

All the men were in great glee at the prospect of soon being in Old England. Portsmouth was looked forward to with more interest than any place we had been to yet and sea songs, mostly about going home, were the order of the day, and night, 'Rolling Home to Merry England' being the favourite.

In the same vein Godfrey-Faussett noted the distances travelled since sailing from Portsmouth: on *Ophir* 45,657 miles and by train 12,295 miles. He also noted that the royal couple, at public receptions only, had shaken hands with 24,835 people.

On 30 October, which was Bryan Godfrey-Faussett's 38th birthday, the smoke of the ships of the Channel Fleet could be seen in the distance. As they approached, it could be seen that it consisted of six battleships and seven cruisers, the latter including *Ophir*'s escort for much of the

---

82 Lady Wester Wemyss Life and Letters, 64

Signed photographs of Princess Mary and Prince George, aboard Ophir

tour, *St George* and *Juno*. The following day they arrived in the Solent and anchored in Yarmouth Roads. At 5:00 p.m. all the members of the royal suite, the ship's officers and ship's company, were individually presented with a commemorative medallion by the duke and duchess; those of the members of the suite, Commodore Winsloe and Rosy's, were of gold and the remainder were of silver.

The return home for the royal couple was greeted with relief 'that the tour was widely seen as a success … "Thank God that the tour has gone off so well".[83]

On 1 November the Trinity House yacht *Galatea* escorted the royal yachts HMSs *Victoria and Albert, Osborne* and *Alberta*, followed by *Ophir* and

> Soon after lunch we proceeded up harbour, preceded by the *Victoria and Albert*, passed through the fleet anchored at Spithead, the ships being manned … A great reception as we went up harbour. Southsea beach and all the way along black with people who waved and cheered.[84]

After they had arrived alongside, during the afternoon the King and Queen came on board *Ophir*, to be greeted by the royal suite and the ship's company all drawn up on deck to receive them. In the evening there was a dinner party on board the *Victoria and Albert*, including the royal family. From the *Ophir* were their Royal Highnesses the Duke and Duchess, and the royal suite, Commodore Winslow and Rosy. Other guests included the Lords of the Admiralty, led by

---

83 Cindi McCreery 'Views Across the Decks of HMS Ophir' in the Royal Studies Journal No.1, 2018, 80
84 Churchill Archive BGGF 1/49

the first lord, Lord Selborne. Later in the evening, in *Ophir*'s smoking room, Godfrey-Faussett

> saw the Duke speaking to Rosy and then Rosy told me that the Duke had told him that he had spoken to Lord Selborne about him and that he would be promoted to captain on Wednesday … there were other promotions … I am delighted all round. Rosy, of course, is the luckiest as he has only been a commander for about three years. This afternoon he received from the King the MVO.

The next day the royal party and the suite left *Ophir* and travelled to London for a rapturous welcome from the crowds lining the street for the procession from the train to Buckingham Palace.

The last words on the success of the tour are from Lady Wemyss:

> It had ended without a hitch from first to last, but there can be no doubt that this achievement was in a great measure due to the Second in Command. For there had been difficulties; a certain amount of friction, misunderstandings, disagreements which had required all his tact, his knowledge of the world and, above all his imperturbable good temper to everybody. He had done so successfully and in consequence had won golden opinions and was highly spoken of by everyone. It was undeniably the qualities he had shown on this occasion which attracted the attention of Sir John Fisher who [had] just come to the Admiralty as Second Sea Lord.[85]

Rosy had achieved the rank of captain at the extremely early age of 37; he had been made MVO and was an Extra Equerry to Prince George; he was now to go on to a very different challenge.

8: *OSBORNE*

Whle Rosy had been away, the pressure for reform in the Navy, led by Admiral Jacky Fisher, had increased dramatically. Fisher was described by Arthur Marder as

> one of the most interesting personalities of the 20th century. He owed nothing to influence, wealth, or social position but everything to sheer ability, character and perseverance ... he was noted for his sense of humour, storytelling ability, sparkling wit, gaiety, charm and boyish enthusiasm. But In his official capacity Fisher could be arrogant, stern, unrelenting and, when serious mistakes were made, even cruel.[86]

In 1902 he was made Second Sea Lord and Head of Personnel, which is where he wanted to be, and where he could bring in the changes that he fervently believed were essential.

He was to lead the huge changes that shook the Navy, supported by Lord Selborne, the First Lord of the Admiralty. The changes affected all aspects of the Navy, and discussion and descriptions of the changes have filled many books. The aspect that is of particular interest for this book, insofar as it relates to Rosy Wemyss, is that of education. This was coupled with the need to update the rank structure of the officers: as it stood, it did not reflect the changes brought about by the steam engine and therefore change was required to streamline the training so that engineer officers and executive officers would be on the same grade both professionally and socially. Before the changes, the executive officers were found in the narrow band of the top social and economic scale which had become more rigidly applied in the latter part of the Victorian era, and the engineer officers,

---

86 Arthur J Marder *From the Dreadnought to Scapa Flow*, Vol.1, 15

who had entered the Navy from dockyards or industry, were not considered to be gentlemen and so were regarded as inferior. Before steam, officers had understood their ships completely. Now 'the real masters of the Navy were the despised engineers, whose mammas were not asked to tea by other mammas [of executive officers].'[87]

Fisher's proposals were put forward in the name of the First Lord of the Admiralty, Lord Selborne, who put the proposals before the House in 1902. The essence of the 'Selborne Scheme', as it was known, was that the Navy would take boys as cadets at the age of 12 to be educated in general subjects in addition to naval subjects. This would bring together, in training, boys who would know each other from boyhood and create a socially homogeneous body in which all officers, in whichever sphere they might later specialise, would have a sufficient knowledge of engineering for the steam age. Although it was not received with universal approval – 'It was making greasers of us all' was one typical comment – support came from some very senior and influential officers. Captain Reginald Bacon, described by Fisher as 'the cleverest man in the Navy', wrote to Fisher:

> The common cry is that nothing could be more efficient than the present Engineer Officers. This I beg leave to doubt. I know of no body in the world ... who cannot be improved on and the way to improve on the present engineers is to give them common interests with the Executive and promotion to work for ... The new scheme is bound to work and be a success – and it is on the account of the magnitude of the success of the infant that the labour pains are so severe!!! But all will be well if the Admiralty sticks to their guns.

Admiral the Hon. Sir E R Fremantle (whose son, Admiral Sir Sydney Fremantle, would be in command of the First Battle Squadron at Scapa Flow in 1919, when the German fleet was scuttled), also wrote in support:

> I may say that I am entirely in favour of the general entry of offices. In my early days, quite two thirds of our seamanship was fitting rigging, shifting spars and handling sails. This has all gone. Our motive power is now steam and our officers ought to be trained to understand and work the machinery which is used for all purposes ... It was Drake who said he would have the gentleman and soldiers to haul and draw with the mariners and now we executives must not be too proud to grease and gauge with the engineers.

As did Lord Charles Beresford, in April 1903:

---

87 Quoted in William Jameson *The Fleet that Jack Built*, 106

I regret the opposition in the country to the present scheme. I am certain that such opposition is unfounded and unsound and if I had still been in the House of Commons I would have knocked the bottom out of it. We must remember, however that all reforms are opposed, generally by those who are too old, or whose brains are not receptive enough to perceive that 1903 may require different administrations and systems to 1803. A reformer's life is only to be compared to that of an Early Christian, and both, perhaps, receive the honour and respect given to them a trifle late. In 20 years time naval officers will wonder how a steam navy could possibly have been run and administered by an executive who knew nothing whatever about steam mechanical appliances, although every evolution, action and duty could only be carried out by the aid of machines and skilled mechanics.[88]

To this end a new college for the 12-year-old entrants was to be created. A site for the college had to be located, which was found at Osborne House on the Isle of Wight. This had been Queen Victoria's retreat, but since her death in 1901 it had been less used and King Edward VII was very happy for part of the grounds and the stables to be used for the purpose.

A large hall, dormitories, a mess room and quarters for the officers seemed to arise as if by magic, while messing accommodation for the cadets as well as classrooms and laboratories were provided by adapting the existing stables.[89]

The works started on the last day of February 1903, and the first building was occupied on 1 September in the same year.

Rosy had been chosen to become captain of the new college by Fisher, for whom he was the ideal candidate; Rosy's own view of the scheme was that change was urgently needed and that revision of the naval system of education was imperative. In this post he was given the opportunity to train the Navy of the future in the way in which he believed it ought to be trained. He seized the opportunity with both hands.

He was given a free hand to choose the naval staff of the college. His first appointment was William Ruck-Keene, who had sailed with Rosy on *Ophir* as first lieutenant and had been promoted to commander at the end of the cruise. He became commander of the college. (After his time at Osborne he was promoted to captain. His last appointment was as captain of the Royal Naval College Dartmouth, which he held for the latter part of the First World War.)

---

88 Churchill Archive WYMS 1/5
89 Lady Wester Wemyss Life and Letters, 68

Rosy's other early appointments included another officer from *Ophir*, Surgeon Lieutenant Robert Hill, two engineer officers and a carpenter lieutenant.[90] Nine other officers also joined the staff.

The man chosen as headmaster was Dr Ashworth, who had been the senior science master at Harrow, and he, too, was given a free hand to choose his staff for this new venture. All the staff had arrived by the end of August, and spent the following two weeks sorting out timetables and all the necessary details, before 75 little boys arrived in their stiff new uniforms.

Dr Ashworth described the spirit inspiring the college:

> It is difficult for anyone who lived through the first two years of Osborne's existence to speak with due restraint about the zest and enthusiasm which one and all brought to the common stock. It was of course a great adventure in itself – naval and educational – and great issues were involved. But much of it was a direct inspiration and infection from R E Wemyss – anyone who has also shared in other creative tasks will know how much less inspiring they can be with a lesser man as leader. It is common property that he was a born leader of men and that he consciously studied the art which many others succeeded and failed in without taking thought and here was the opportunity of a lifetime.[91]

In the spring of that year Rosy had become engaged to be married to his cousin, Victoria Morier. Her father, Sir Robert Morier, had died in 1893, when he was ambassador to Russia. Her mother had moved to Cannes in the south of France with her daughter. On 21 December 1903, only a few months after her mother had also died, they were married in a quiet ceremony. At the end of his leave they returned from Cannes to Osborne for the start of the new term.

He had written to Victoria earlier in the year:

> July 1903
>
> Today I have been busy hustling these people. As the time goes on I find that these people have not very great ideas on getting things finished and are inclined to think that a day or two does not make much difference. I have to make them think differently and it isn't always as easy as sounds. Two of the Lords of the Admiralty and the C.-in.-C came over today and looked round the whole place. I think that none of them believed that it would be all ready by Monday but I know how the whole job is going and I feel confident it will be all right.

---

90 This rank was created in 1903.

91 Lady Wester Wemyss Life and Letters, 70

Osborne August 1

The King is expected after 3 p.m. tomorrow. Of course I shall have to go on board immediately after his arrival ... Tomorrow I actually assume command, for up to now I have only been working from the Admiralty, but now I shall have command of the Racer as well. All of it is interesting but of course there is lots and lots to do.

August 4

Oh, I have been busy. Well it's all over now, thank God, and well over. I have had much to contend with, as a great many people, most of whom should have known better, had been telling the King that there was nothing at Osborne to open. The consequence was that he said he'd only come privately to see the place. Now for reasons politic Sir J Fisher wanted him to open it, and naturally I wanted it to further his wishes. Well, I got him (the King) to come today and he was astounded and delighted. So much so, that he said it was to be put in the papers and recorded in some conspicuous place in the building that he had opened it and named it. I needn't tell you how delighted I am.

On 15 September, the first day of the new term of the new college, he wrote:

Such a busy day and most successful. We have all the boys in, safe and sound and I must say I am delighted with the parents of them all – nice gentlemanlike boys – every one of them as happy as the day is long ... Luckily today was beautiful and the place looked charming. The parents came with their boys and were all delighted with the place and buildings and well they may be ... Our first day has been most successful. Everything shaken down into place wonderfully and my large family of 75 small boys are a going concern and going well too.

The first term was an undoubted success, only interrupted by many visits, of which Rosy became rather tired. However on 15 December he wrote:

Our last night here ... The cadets are going off tomorrow morning and if it wasn't that it means coming to you, I should be sorry for never has a man been better served than I have been, and never has a man been surrounded by such good and loyal officers. Tonight they entertained me at a feast and gave me a very fine silver salver with all their names on it. I am delighted like to think that they were all really cordial to me and at the present was accompanied by real good wishes ... I send you every sort

Royal Visit to Osborne College (Churchill College)

of good wishes from my officers. I know that in time you will like and appreciate them as I do.[92]

The visitors continued to arrive in the new year – encouraged by Fisher, keen to show off the new experiment – including headmasters of public schools, politicians and foreign naval attachés. The house in which Rosy, and now Victoria as well, lived was a former police cottage which had been enlarged by the addition of a bay window to the front elevation. It was still small, but it was there that Rosy received many of his visitors. Apart from official visitors the newly married couple found themselves welcomed by many people including their nearest neighbour, Princess Beatrice, at Osborne Cottage. His duties were such that they were able to enjoy racing at Goodwood and Cowes Week. At the Easter holidays they went back to Cannes, and in the summer they travelled north to stay at Wemyss Castle.

One of the assets the college had acquired was the former tender from the Royal Naval College at Dartmouth. HMS *Racer* was small, elderly gunboat in which cadets could undergo seagoing training. Built in 1885, she was barque-rigged, but also had a steam engine; she was wooden planked on the exterior, but with iron frames and keel. The officers of the college were also the officers of *Racer*, with Rosy nominally in command.

Although it was a very pleasant life, as the college had settled down and was running smoothly, the Russo-Japanese War had concentrated Rosy's mind on his next step. He had successfully set up and launched Osborne Naval College, and with the war scare in the country he did not want to find himself in a backwater. He needed

---

92 Lady Wester Wemyss Life and Letters, 73

a seagoing command, particularly so as he had missed out on sea time, a certain amount of which is a requisite before a captain can be considered for flag rank.

The appointment of Sir John Fisher in 1904 as First Sea Lord was the start of the next round of profound and controversial change in the Royal Navy. Now he initiated a major shift in ships and equipment. The Royal Navy was spread all over the world, its ships grouped into three commands. The main fleets were the Home Fleet and Channel Squadron, the Mediterranean Fleet and the Far Eastern Fleet. In order to fulfil the needs of Empire a great number of ships of varying types, from gunboats to cruisers and battleships, were required. However, many ships were, in the words of Lord Selborne, who introduced Fisher's further reforms to the Cabinet on 6 December 1904, 'too old to fight and too slow to run away'.[93] He concluded by saying that 'a certain number of ships of comparatively small value have been or will be withdrawn from commission'. He did not say that his intention was to remove 154 ships from the Navy List. The purpose of this was to release officers and men for redeployment to the new ships being built; it resulted in the release of 950 officers and 11,000 men.[94] In addition to the men who were deployed into the ships that were being built, many men were moved into older ships that had been put into the Reserve Fleet. Some of these obsolete ships were, however, scrapped to save money; at the time the saving was £845,000 per annum. Unsurprisingly, this brought forth a wave of protest; although one journalist commented:

> Though the old system of worldwide distribution was popular there was one fatal mistake in it. For lawn tennis, waltzing, relief of distress or ambulance work after an earthquake it was admirable; for war purposes it was useless, because the force was divided and subdivided and largely composed of ships that could neither fight an enemy nor escape him.[95]

In 1905 a Russian fleet, sailing down the North Sea, had mistakenly thought that a fleet of Hull trawlers was, bizarrely, the Japanese fleet and had opened fire, inflicting some damage. This incident, combined with the news of the Battle of Tsushima, caused the British public to fear the onset of war. The Battle of Tsushima was a major battle between the Russian and Japanese fleets. The Japanese fleet, although much smaller than the Russian and with only half the number of battleships, used the latest technology at the time, wireless telegraphy, to position their ships according to the Nelsonian tactic of 'crossing the T' to attack the line of the Russian fleet. It was a complete success: the Russian fleet lost all eight of its battleships and over 5,000 men, whilst the Japanese Navy lost only three torpedo

---

93 Selborne 'Memorandum', quoted in Nicholas A Lambert Sir John Fisher's Naval Revolution, 99

94 Admiral Sir John Fisher, quoted in Nicolas A Lambert Sir John Fisher's Naval Revolution, 112

95 Quoted in Captain John Wells The Royal Navy: An Illustrated Social History 1870–1982, 76

boats and 116 men. It was the first major naval battle since Trafalgar, 100 years before, and was watched by Royal Naval observers on the Japanese ships.

After the Christmas leave of 1904, which Rosy and Victoria had spent at Cannes, on his return to England in January 1905, he spent time in London at the Admiralty sorting out the future of the college. It was finally settled that, after relinquishing his appointment at Osborne, for a short while he would oversee both Osborne and Dartmouth, after leaving HMY *Osborne* as captain, with much sorrow. His successor there was Captain E Alexander-Sinclair, an old and valued friend who Rosy could trust to carry on and build the college ideas and traditions that he had initiated. However, his ideas were not fully endorsed by some of the parents of the cadets. Writing to Sir John Fisher, after leaving, he commented:

> [there is] a tendency on the part of the parents of some of the cadets at Osborne to hope at least that their sons might not become Lieutenants (E), with no chance of commanding ships or fleets, and I have a suspicion that, for this reason, they have in some cases even discouraged their sons in their engineering studies.[96]

Rosy's request for a seagoing appointment succeeded, and after some months in London overseeing the two colleges, with visits to both of them, he was appointed captain of HMS *Suffolk*, which was part of the Third Cruiser Squadron in the Mediterranean Fleet, whose commander-in chief had recently become Admiral Lord Charles Beresford, with whom Rosy had served 15 years before on HMS *Undaunted*. In *Suffolk* he was to succeed (the then) Captain David Beatty, who would achieve particular fame (or notoriety) in command of the battlecruiser squadron at the Battle of Jutland and eventually become First Sea Lord, ousting Rosy from that post.[97]

Suffolk was a heavy cruiser of nearly 10,000 tons displacement. She had come into service only the year before and was heavily armed with fourteen 6-inch guns, mounted variously in twin gun turrets and side casemate mountings. Secondary armament was provided by ten quick-firing 12 pounder guns as defence from torpedo boats. On her acceptance trials she had exceeded her designed top speed, reaching nearly 25 kn. She had a crew of just under 700.[98]

Rosy was delighted with his new ship, and also by the prospect of returning to the Mediterranean and Malta, which he loved so much.

---

96 Quoted in Arthur Marder From the Dreadnought to Scapa Flow Vol.1, 47

97 This will be written of in more detail later in this book.

98 The next HMS *Suffolk*, also a heavy cruiser, and HMS *Norfolk*, were the ships that found the Bismarck in the Denmark Strait in May1941, which ultimately resulted in her sinking – but not before HMS *Hood* had been sunk by the Bismarck.

9: SUFFOLK

From the day he joined the *Suffolk*, Rosy kept a daily journal which gives a vivid, but concise, description of his daily life. The initial entry starts:

> Joined HMS *Suffolk* at Phelerum Bay on Saturday, September 23 – proceeded to Lemnos – joined the Fleet. Left Lemnos on Friday 29th, arrived Smyrna Saturday 30th. Left Smyrna Tuesday sixth arriving Malta Monday, October 9. Made fast to 2 and 2A buoys at Sliema. Tuesday coaling ship.[99]

Rosy had been welcomed at Lemnos by Lord Charles Beresford who was 'charming, most cordial and welcoming and altogether pleasant'.[100] The Third Cruiser Squadron consisted of, as flagship, HMSs *Leviathan, Carnarvon, Lancaster* and *Suffolk*. The admiral in command of the squadron was Rear Admiral Sir Hedworth Lambton, who eventually became Admiral of the Fleet Sir Hedworth Meux. (In accordance with the terms of Lady Meux's will, he had changed his name to benefit from a very large inheritance from her.)

In the first week of Rosy's arrival in Malta, a pattern of his daily life became obvious: he was on board during the day, lunching in the wardroom and later having 'Dinner at Club. Bridge.'

The following week, on 16 October, he noted that at lunch on board 'New cook not v. good'. They sailed on the Tuesday to Genoa where they met HMSs *Renown* and *Terrible. Renown* was to carry Prince George and Princess Mary, the Prince and Princess of Wales, to India, who would be joining *Renown* at Genoa.

---

99 Churchill Archive WYMS 12/1. Unless otherwise noted, further quotes are from the same source.

100 Lady Wester Wemyss Life and Letters, 76

On Thursday Rosy had lunch on *Renown* with her captain, Hugh Tyrwhitt, and noted that it was 'v.g.'. However, dinner on *Terrible* was only 'quite good'. *Suffolk* sailed on Saturday 21 October, waiting outside the port to salute the Royal Standard as *Renown* passed, and then to escort her to Port Said. Later in the day, Trafalgar Day, he noted 'At noon speak to men re: Trafalgar, read out Nelson's last prayer – also prayer after victory – Guard presented [arms]. Played last post'.

They arrived at Port Said on 26 October, and on the next day Prince George and Princess Mary visited *Suffolk* and had tea with Rosy. On the Saturday *Renown* sailed for Suez whilst *Suffolk* took on coal. As captain, Rosy, at last, did not have to have any part in it, and he spent the day ashore in the English Club.

Although a virtually new ship, *Suffolk* had engine problems. Their sailing from Malta to Genoa had been delayed by two hours because of a problem with the port engine overheating; on their return voyage to Malta from Port Said, the starboard engine had malfunctioned, and the next day the engine bearings ran hot.

On her return to Malta, there was no further movement until January of 1906. However, before Christmas, Victoria had joined Rosy at Malta.

In 1906 Malta was Britain's fortress in the Mediterranean: indeed, Joseph Chamberlain, the colonial secretary when he visited Malta in 1900, sent a dispatch to the governor in which he stated that 'the island was held principally as a great fortress',[101] which it was to remain through two world wars. An army garrison, in addition to the naval base, had created a strong British presence on the island and had created an active social and sporting life for those stationed there, the sporting facilities including tennis courts and a racecourse. The fortress and its population were a major benefit to the island, as a third of its local population were directly employed by the British establishment and even more were employed indirectly. Rosy knew the island well from his time on previous ships which had been stationed there, so he would be able to show Victoria the 16th-century forts, churches and palaces on the island. Their social life was busy and living costs were very low, which, as Lady Wemyss commented, meant that: 'Nearly everyone could afford a box at the excellent Italian opera or to enter a pony at the races, an unceasing subject of local interest.' (Rosy had noted that he went to the races on 9 November and commented 'Rather good'). Admiral 'Charley' Beresford and his wife, at Admiralty House, held many social gatherings, which added to the social scene: his 'geniality, high spirits and good humour' gained him great popularity as a commander-in chief with all ranks.[102]

On Monday 12 November Rosy noted 'Commissioned 111 Strada Vescoro, Valletta' and, the following day, 'getting house ready'. On Wednesday he went on

---

101 Quoted in James Holland Blue Water Empire, 123

102 Lady Wester Wemyss Life and Letters, 78

SS *Carolan* to Syracuse to meet Victoria and return with her to Malta to their new home, where they arrived at 3:00 a.m. the next day. Despite that, Rosy was on *Suffolk* later in the morning to take her out for preliminary battle practice; he noted 'not very satisfactory'. He returned in time for dinner at home; the first dinner in their new home. The next day *Suffolk* again went out, to join in the gunlayers' competition. 'Very disappointing results' was his comment.

In January 1906 *Suffolk* sailed on a short trip to Syracuse and Port Augusta, but the engine trials that were the purpose of the trip were abandoned due to bad weather. The engine problems were only part of the problems that Rosy had inherited on *Suffolk*. Admiral Fisher had told Victoria (they had met at Carlsbad, where Rosy and Victoria had gone to try to cure him of the sciatica that he had developed at Osborne) that *Suffolk* was the 'worst ship in the Navy'. He was now finding out that there had been some substance in Fisher's comments. When he joined he had found the officers were discontented and the men unwilling, in addition to the problems with the engines. The latter were beyond his power to remedy, but the officers and crew he could – and did – change, working hard to bring the ship and its crew to the high standards of morale and performance that he required.

The Mediterranean Fleet sailed in February for manoeuvres with the Channel and Atlantic Fleets. On 19 February, in Lagos, Portugal, Rosy noted: 'general drill in forenoon … *Suffolk* about the best'. His hard work in lifting the spirits of the officers and crew was having results. Rosy wrote to Victoria from Lagos:

> A really magnificent sight this huge Fleet coming in – there must be something like 40,000 men in the ships … I don't think from what I hear that either of the two Fleets are so comfortable or well-run as ours. Certainly Charlie is an exceedingly pleasant man to serve under. … Everybody in the Fleet seems unsettled and everybody hates the way that the Admiralty (or rather Fisher) has of not telling anybody anything. I must say it is extremely annoying and is causing much discontent, which is always a pity and in this case I should think quite unnecessary.[103]

This comment bears out Rosy's place in the Beresford camp; the dispute between Fisher and Beresford was starting to escalate. That Rosy was a supporter of Charlie Beresford was hardly surprising, given their similar views, in addition to their similar backgrounds, characters and interests.

After the combined fleet had gone its separate ways after Lagos, the Mediterranean Fleet visited Genoa. On arrival there, on 14 March, Rosy took the midnight train to spend time at their house, Villa Montbrillant in Cannes. He arrived home to find Victoria not well, although she had recovered by the next

---

103 Lady Wester Wemyss Life and Letters, 79

day. On Saturday they visited Miss A de Rothschild for lunch. Rosy commented on her garden 'Very wonderful – but much too artificial – stank of money'. He noted that Victoria was unwell again on the following Monday; she was expecting their first child, due in September. His leave over, he returned to Genoa on the Wednesday noting 'Very sorry to leave Cannes'. On the morning after he returned, he breakfasted with Beresford, before *Suffolk* sailed to Gibraltar, from there to return to Plymouth to recommission.

Whilst in Gibraltar, Rosy went to Algeciras to have dinner with Admiral Sir William May, Commander-in Chief of the Atlantic Fleet, who was living in a hotel there. The Algeciras Conference was still sitting, endeavouring to find a resolution to the Moroccan Crisis of 1904, which had been precipitated in March of that year when the Kaiser visited Tangier. He declared that he supported the sovereignty of the Sultan, Abdul Aziz, which statement challenged the French influence on Morocco. Thirteen nations were represented on the conference, which had started in January 1906, an agreement being arrived at on 30 March. One of the results of the conference was a strengthening of the Entente Cordiale between Britain and France and an increasing level of distrust with Germany.

Suffolk arrived in Devonport on 30 March. There was a week before the ship recommissioned, so Rosy was able to manage a quick visit to Osborne. After his visit he wrote to Victoria:

> Everything there seems to be getting along first rate ... This afternoon they were having the sports so that I saw everybody ... Now that the building there is all finished, they are getting the place very nice and tidy and are beginning to plant hedges etc. It gave me much pleasure going there, though I still find I am jealous of everybody else having anything to say to the place.

On the following day he went to the Admiralty:

> I ... was there practically all day. I saw Lord Tweedmouth [First Lord of the Admiralty], Sir John Fisher and Drury [Vice-Admiral Sir Charles Drury, Second Sea Lord] ... and had a most interesting conversation with the Director of Naval Intelligence. Everybody was extremely civil and couldn't do – or rather offer – enough for me. I thought Lord Tweedmouth a most pleasant man but he gave me the idea of being much torn between the Fisherites and the anti-Fisherites, and no wonder, considering that he can't possibly know enough of the subject himself to be able to form any sort or kind of an opinion. I said straight what I thought and kept nothing back. It's no use having opinions if you are to keep them to yourself.[104]

---

104 Lady Wester Wemyss Life and Letters, 81

The old crew paid off the ship on 8 April, and the new crew joined the same day. Four days later, *Suffolk* left the dockyard and moved out to anchor in Plymouth Sound. The next day the commander-in chief inspected the ship during the morning. In the afternoon Rosy was able to go ashore to meet his elder brother, Randolph, and return with him on board. Randolph was a guest on board for the passage to the Mediterranean.

They arrived at Gibraltar on 18 April, from where Rosy wrote to Victoria:

> I am delighted with my officers and men – the former appear first-rate and the crew seem a fine lot, big and willing, and I see no reason why we should not come right to the top. Powell [the new Commander] is a man after my own heart, energetic, able, good-tempered, very keen and very quick and handles the men well. So that everything looks very promising; … We are hard at work all day drilling, etc, and I have no doubt but that we shall get the ship into a very great state of efficiency. The officers are all keen and energetic and as a natural consequence so are the men.

Soon after *Suffolk* had arrived in Malta, on 22 April, she sailed with the Cruiser Squadron for Phalerum Bay, off the Greek coast near Athens. This was to be in a more strategically convenient location, because of the dispute between Britain and the Ottoman Empire over the administrative border between the Hejaz, controlled by the Ottoman Empire, and the British-controlled area of the Sinai peninsula and the Governate of Jerusalem, which had brought the two countries closer to war.[105]

Suffolk stayed in Phalerum Bay with the remainder of the squadron, whilst *Minerva*, the flagship, with Rear Admiral Lambton on board, steamed at full speed for Port Said. Rosy noted 'From what I gather they seem to think there is at least a possibility of the Turks invading Egypt by the Suez Canal. Personally I think all that nonsense.'[106]

After a few days *Suffolk* was dispatched to Crete, where a general election was to happen and the civil authorities feared major unrest. However, on their arrival they found that any disputes had been peacefully resolved. Rosy wrote to Victoria:

> May 13 Suda Bay Crete
>
> I arrived here at noon and am awaiting a carriage to take me up to Canea to go and see the Consul-General Esme Howard, with whom I was at school. There are two Russian ships, a French ship and an Italian, all junior

---

105 www.jstor.org/stable/260181? Journal of Contemporary History Vol.14 1979 677–692. <Accessed 12/12/2020>

106 Lady Wester Wemyss Life and Letters, 82

to me, so that I am in command of quite an international fleet … So far as I am concerned I am 'all on my own' as they say, and so to speak my own master which is always something. The country here is charming just now – masses of wild flowers and there are some beautiful trees in the valleys and magnificent mountains. Altogether a beautiful island and enormously improved since I remember it last.

May 21

I got to Candia on Saturday and on Sunday morning landed my men [he had embarked 50 English and 40 Russian troops] in Suda Bay as previously arranged to try and keep order. But a calmer or quieter population or less excited election I never saw and we had absolutely nothing to do. So this morning I re-embarked the men and am now steaming away towards Athens.[107]

As the crisis had abated, the squadron returned to Malta. Rosy's hard work with the crew continued to pay dividends, as it improved to the point where he commented 'I haven't but the slightest doubt but that very shortly we shall be the smartest ship on the station'. His pride in his ship and the satisfaction he found in creating an efficient ship with a happy and contented crew are very apparent – even to being the best in the fleet at coaling which, given Rosy's comments when on *Ophir* about coaling, are ironic.

After two weeks in Malta, when Rosy and Victoria were able to spend time together, the whole fleet sailed for its summer cruise, visiting Spain and then carrying out combined manoeuvres in the Atlantic before calling at Gibraltar. Whilst there, in conversation with other officers, Rosy had an opportunity to gauge the current opinion about the First Sea Lord:

I have come to the conclusion that Sir J Fisher and his Board are playing the very deuce with the Service. Not in the way of the new Scheme of Entry, for with that I cordially agree, but with his dispositions, appointments and his way of ignoring all precedence and valuable experience. The state of unrest all through the service is very serious, I can't help thinking. The fact that clever, able and energetic as he (Sir J.F.) is, he is, as we all know, absolutely unscrupulous and the way in which he is blending his own and the Service's interest to the detriment of the latter is now becoming very apparent. I quite allow that he has done an enormous amount of good but alas! I am afraid he is suffering from what the Bluejacket calls swelled head and having got an enormous (too much) power into his own hands, he has taken the bit between his teeth and nothing seems able to stop him in his mad career of

107 Lady Wester Wemyss Life and Letters, 84

perfectly unnecessary reforms. It is a very serious matter and may become really dangerous. I am extremely sorry that Sir William May is to go to the Admiralty. I am much afraid he will only be a puppet in Sir J.F.'s hands.[108]

There were changes in the squadron, with two senior officers leaving; Captain Warrender went, which made Rosy the senior captain of the cruisers. Rear Admiral Lambton was to leave at the end of the year, to be replaced by Rear Admiral Barry, who Rosy knew from when they had sailed together on *Astraea* in 1895, when Rosy was first lieutenant and Barry was captain. Beresford was also close to leaving, as he was moving to take command of the Channel Fleet.

On 30 August Rosy, who had been given a month's leave so as to be present for the birth of their child, arrived at Lausanne, in Switzerland, where the baby was to be born. She arrived on 17 September and was named Alice. When he returned to Malta at the end of September, Beresford gave Rosy permission to take *Suffolk* to Cannes in November for the christening.

Rosy and Victoria were very moved by the interest and affection shown in the new arrival by *Suffolk*'s crew; Rosy wrote to Victoria on 7 October:

> How charming of the officers to send the child a bowl and spoon. Of course I am touched and quite delighted. What a delightful thing for her to have in after years. I think a christening from the ship splendid [this had been presented by the warrant officers]. I am quite at a loss how to thank them, it makes me feel quite shy.

In addition to those gifts the midshipmen had presented an egg cup and spoon. Victoria wrote:

> The *Suffolk* arrived at Cannes on November 17, and the christening, which took place a few days later, assumed an almost purely naval aspect – the *Suffolk*'s chaplain, Rev. V. Baker, performed the ceremony, the church was decorated with flags and crowded with delegations from the ship's company which stood godfather, represented by the Commander, who afterwards cut the christening cake with his sword.109

It was the first visit in 40 years by a Royal Naval ship to Cannes, and the ship was given a warm welcome including a mayoral reception. Visitors to the ship, which was opened to the public, came by special trains from all around the neighbouring area.

---

108 Lady Wester Wemyss Life and Letters, 86
109 Ibid 88

On *Suffolk's* return to Malta she and the fleet remained in port until February 1907. In January Beresford had relinquished his command. The fleet went out to mark his farewell as he sailed from Malta. Sadly, Rosy was not on *Suffolk's* bridge for the occasion; on the previous day he had been walking in the dockyard by Number 4 dry dock, when a board gave way. He fell 60 feet to the bottom of the dock. Those who saw it happen were sure that he had been killed by the impact, so were more than surprised when he was picked up from the bottom of the dock, with his uniform torn to shreds, but apparently unhurt and with his monocle still firmly in place. He was severely bruised but miraculously not more seriously injured, and was laid up for several days to recover.

After the February manoeuvres, in which *Suffolk* once again suffered but acquitted herself with distinction, she returned to Malta. Further repairs were required, so *Suffolk* went into the dockyard. On the following day, 7 March, Rosy sailed for Marseilles on a French ship, en route to Cannes. It was not a pleasant trip: 'heavy weather – horrid ship – <u>very seasick</u>!' He arrived home on 11 March and had two weeks' leave before returning to Malta at the end of the month. In April *Suffolk* and *Lancaster* sailed to Toulon to meet the royal yacht, HMY *Victoria and Albert*, which had arrived there to embark the King and Queen. *Victoria and Albert* was the latest in the line to bear the name, and had replaced her elderly predecessor, on which Rosy had served as a lieutenant. (She turned out to be very long-lived, serving as a depot ship in Portsmouth in the Second World War before being scrapped in 1954.)

Whilst at Toulon, Rosy wrote to Victoria:

April 6

We are to meet the Fleet at 11 am off Cartagena. The King embarked last night and I suppose that the Queen has arrived this morning. Everybody admires the *Suffolk* enormously and certainly she is looking uncommonly well. The Commander of the *Victoria and Albert* told Powell [*Suffolk's* commander] that he had never known that it was possible to get a grey ship to look like that.

April 8

Such a fine sight this morning when the Yacht met the Fleet. We had left early and joined the Admiral before the Yacht passed in between the lines and as she came through all the ships fired a salute and then the King of Spain came out in his yacht and joined us.[110]

---

110 Lady Wester Wemyss Life and Letters, 90

From Cartagena, the *Victoria and Albert* travelled to Malta, Palermo and Naples, where the King left to return to England. The Queen and Princess Victoria stayed on board the royal yacht and, escorted still by *Suffolk* and *Lancaster,* went on to Athens. Rosy wrote to Victoria after they had arrived:

May 14, Athens

I dined at the Palace last night – a large dinner of about 80 people. A decidedly fine room and the table was strewn with rose leaves – rather pretty. After-dinner Prince George, Prince Andrew[111] and I retired behind a window curtain and smoked cigarettes! The whole proceeding had rather an *opera bouffe* appearance. Certainly there is an amusing side to these small Courts.

May 16 Athens

Yesterday we went to Tatoi. Prince George drove us out there in a motor-car. … Tatoi itself is charming. The house rather like an ordinary, rather ugly, very comfortable middle sized country house planted down in the middle of a pine forest through which have been made miles and miles of roads and paths … The party consisted of all the Royalties, all the Queen's people, Keppel, one or two officers from the Yacht and myself. We had luncheon outside under some trees and very pleasant it was. I sat next to the Queen of Greece. What an agreeable woman, so simple and present and cordial and hospitable.[112]

After Athens, *Victoria and Albert* and *Suffolk* returned to Corfu, where once again Rosy was at a lunch with the King and Queen of Greece. From Corfu they returned to Naples, where the Queen and Princess Victoria left the ship, and *Suffolk* returned to Malta until the end of June. On 26 June the fleet sailed for its summer cruise and manoeuvres to the eastern Mediterranean, which included a stop at Haifa. Rosy did not enjoy the extreme heat there, and wrote:

I cannot think what on earth the C-in-C brought us to these parts for. I dare say that at another time of the year when less hot one could take an interest in the surroundings but it's too hot now for anything of that sort to be enjoyable.[113]

In mid-July *Suffolk* had her annual inspection by Rear Admiral Barry, Flag Officer of the Cruiser Squadron 'and extremely satisfactory it was – quite first rate.

---

111 The father of HRH Prince Philip, Duke of Edinburgh

112 Lady Wester Wemyss Life and Letters, 91

113 Ibid 93

The ship looked absolutely beautiful. Barry had to say that never had he seen a better – all the drills too went like clockwork. I am so pleased for Powell's sake.'[114] Despite past repairs and refits *Suffolk*'s engines were still a persistent problem, to the extent that on her return to Malta she went into the dockyard for two months for work on the boilers. This gave Rosy the opportunity to take some leave, and so he went to Villars in Switzerland to join Victoria and their baby, Alice. It was a relief to him to escape from the heat and breathe the mountain air. They moved on from Villars to the Italian lakes, which neither of them had visited before and thoroughly enjoyed. He returned to Malta to find that the repairs were far from complete, so travelled to Rome to rejoin Victoria for a further holiday, touring through Italy, before returning to the ship on 1 November. Although the works were progressing, *Suffolk* was not ready for sea trials until the end of January when she sailed out on a short cruise to ensure that the repairs had produced the desired result.

Beresford's successor as commander-in-chief was Admiral Sir Charles Drury, who had been Second Sea Lord, and was a complete change from his predecessor. As Victoria wrote: 'There was no concealing the fact that since Lord Charles Beresford's departure all the life and go seemed to have gone out of the Fleet, while his successor was showing himself inferior in every way.'[115]

In December 1907, HRH the Duke of Connaught was appointed High Commissioner of the island and the arrival of he and the duchess brightened an otherwise dull winter. In the new year, Rosy's time on *Suffolk* was coming to an end. They sailed to Palermo for target practice, followed later by a short cruise to the Greek Islands, before returning to a series of farewell parties, for he had a great many friends on Malta, both English and Maltese. On 13 April *Suffolk* sailed out of Valletta harbour for England, cheered out of port by the fleet.

---

114 Ibid 94

115 Lady Wester Wemyss Life and Letters, 95

10: HMS *BALMORAL CASTLE*

On arrival at Plymouth, the crew paid off *Suffolk* and Rosy took the first train possible to Cannes for leave at home with his family. He had written to Victoria 'What a happy time we shall have in May. I am feeling like I used to feel at school before the beginning of the holidays and ticking the days off the calendar.'

In the two years while he had been in the Mediterranean, Fisher's reforms, which Rosy had been aware of from a distance, had gathered pace. In addition to the changes in education, of which Rosy approved, there had been many other changes. This caused friction between the Cabinet and the Admiralty: Fisher fought hard to try to prevent cuts in the Naval Estimates. However Asquith, who became prime minister in April 1908, wrote:

I have very little confidence in the present lot of Sea Lords who chop and change as the mood suits them. Our naval supremacy is so completely assured having regard to the sketchy paper programme and inferior shipbuilding resources of other powers that there is no possible reason for allowing ourselves to be hastily rushed into these nebulous and ambitious developments.[116]

His view was not unreasonable: an article in *Dresdner Nastrichter* on 5 February 1906, translated and with a footnote by the Director of Naval Intelligence, on the recent naval manoeuvres in the North Sea (or, as the article says, 'German Commercial Seas') noted that:

the great sea manoeuvres which have been taking place this year [are] to educate the English fleet ... for an eventual fight with Germany – the most likely, nay, the only adversary that may be seriously considered as the possible one.

---

116 Quoted in Nicholas A Lambert Sir John Fishers Naval Revolution, 136

It continues by discussing the dispositions and composition of the fleet, particularly noting the arrival of *Dreadnought*, and concludes:

> England herself ... who is far ahead with her fleet, equal to the united forces of the three most powerful sea Powers of the second rank. What could Germany ... do in comparison with this mighty power. The answer to this question can only be a humiliating one for us and this bitter acknowledgement of the truth must spur on every German patriot.

The Director of Naval Intelligence commented:

> This paper shows a very just appreciation ... of the danger Germany will incur if she ever ventures to dispute the command of the sea with us. It is a wholesome sign and tends to peace[117]

Asquith's quote shows clearly that he disliked, and was suspicious of, the Navy. That he was able to comment on the naval superiority as he did reflected on the revolution in battleship design created by the launch of HMS *Dreadnought*. The creation of this 'all big gun' class of battleship was, it was claimed by the Admiralty, 'a leap forward of 200% in fighting power'.

At the beginning of February 1908 the Cabinet had decided to reduce the Navy Estimates by £1.34 million. After a campaign by Fisher, using the press to embarrass the politicians, the cut was reduced to £900,000. The following month, during a debate on the Navy in the House of Commons, Asquith incorrectly described the second ship projected to be built in that year's programme as a battlecruiser. This gave Fisher an opportunity; never one to miss a trick, he had the designs for the 15,000-ton armoured cruiser with 9.2-inch guns amended to a 19,000-ton battlecruiser with 12-inch guns. As the prime minister had thus described the projected ship, he could not retract.[118]

Rosy's next step, which he very much desired, would have taken him to the very centre of the changes in the service. He very much wanted to be appointed as naval secretary, private secretary to the First Sea Lord. This did not happen: Rosy wrote, in later years, of events in 1914. He had been summoned to the Admiralty for a meeting with the First Lord of the Admiralty – Winston Churchill – and as he was about to leave:

> I was in the Naval Secretary's room after bidding goodbye to the First Lord [when] Lord Fisher came in. I had not spoken to him since the year 1908,

---

117 Churchill Archive WYMS 2/1

118 Nicholas A Lambert Sir John Fisher's Naval Revolution, 142

when he had proposed to me to become Naval Secretary, at the same time adding that such an appointment would be a gross job since there were many men senior to me who ought to be preferred; plainly intimating that the price I should have to pay would be absolute subservience to his views. I had indignantly refused to accept the post under those conditions though it was the one I most coveted at the time and from that time there had been no communication between us. When, therefore, he came towards me with outstretched hand the situation was not without its embarrassments.[119]

Rosy was all too conscious of the fate suffered by those who opposed Fisher. He was conscious that future appointments could well be unforthcoming, and indeed that he could be forced into a corner and leave the service. Fisher believed in the Three Rs: Ruthless, Relentless and Remorseless. Those who opposed him he threatened 'Their wives should be widows, their children fatherless, their homes a dunghill'.[120]

At the time Rosy was so angry that he contemplated resignation from the service. Prince George wrote to him on 7 May from the Jockey Club at Newmarket:

My dear Rosy,

... You must really get this silly idea out of your head about leaving the service, as you think you may not have your sea time in when you arrive at the top of the tree. What ever they promise or do not promise I am sure the Admiralty, whoever they may be at that time, would allow you to count the extra year you remained on at Osborne, provided you do not refuse a ship when offered to you. It may be a bore at this moment if you had to go to sea again at once, but in 2 ½ years you will probably be an Admiral and then all would be well. If offered a ship you must accept ... You would be miserable if you left the service really and now you are so near the top it would be madness to think about it ...

Believe me, most sincerely yours, George[121]

Fortunately the Second Sea Lord, Sir Francis Bridgeman, had known Rosy when Bridgeman was second-in-command of the Mediterranean fleet under Beresford and Rosy was in command of *Suffolk*, and Bridgeman was able to help. However before his next appointment, Rosy had to deal with a personal tragedy; his elder brother Randolph died on 17 July, and as an executor and a trustee

---

119 Lord Wester Wemyss The Navy in the Dardanelles Campaign, 16

120 Arthur Marder From Dreadnought to Scapa Flow, Vol.1, 84

121 Churchill Archive WYMS 2/8

of his will he spent the summer and autumn dealing with Randolph's estate, travelling many times to Wemyss.

This took his up his time until September, when he undertook a series of war courses in Portsmouth, until 15 February 1909, when he was appointed to command the battleship HMS *Albion*, part of the Atlantic Fleet – which, he noted, 'does not come up to the *Suffolk* in any way'. He remained on *Albion* until August, and after leave in September was appointed as Commodore, Devonport, and in command of the Royal Naval Barracks, with the rank of commodore second class. It was an appointment with no real challenges, which gave him the time and opportunity to visit friends locally and enjoy shooting on the Mount Edgcumbe estate. Then in February 1910 he and Victoria went to their home in Cannes for some leave. However, only a few days after their arrival he received a telegram from his old friend Prince George, now the Prince of Wales, who, with the Princess, was to be travelling to South Africa to open the first Parliament, asking Rosy to take command of the ship that was to take them there.

The ship that had been chosen was the *Balmoral Castle,* a ship of the Union Castle Line which had come into service in February 1910 before being taken up for service in August of the same year. She was the first ship of the line to be fitted with wireless telegraphy. Union Castle ran a regular service to South Africa; a ship of that line would have been the obvious choice for the purpose, and one of their latest ships, with the best standards of comfort and equipment, was the candidate chosen.

Rosy had returned from Cannes early, leaving Victoria there, to start the arrangements for the forthcoming trip. This, with his ongoing command at Devonport, together with regular visits to London to plan the royal visit, kept him fully occupied. In May he had travelled to London to meet Victoria, on her return from Cannes, when, on the morning after he arrived, on Friday 6 May he heard of the illness of King Edward VII. He had been suffering from a severe attack of bronchitis; despite that, on that day he smoked a large cigar, enjoyed a light lunch, but then had a series of heart attacks. Two days before that Prince George, when he visited his father, had noted that 'his colour was bad and his breathing fast'. During the afternoon, as the King's condition worsened, Prince George was able to tell his father that his horse, Witch of the Air, had won at Kempton Park. That good news was the last the King heard, as he slipped into unconsciousness and died at 11:45 p.m.[122]

Rosy had been appointed an ADC to the King in April and this, coupled with his position as equerry to Prince George, involved him in the immediate aftermath, helping to deal with the telegrams that flooded in to Marlborough

---

122 Denis Judd Life and Times of King George V, 89

House, where the King had died. For the funeral, he was attached to the Duke of Mecklenburg-Strelitz, who he had to meet at Dover and escort to London. On 17 May the coffin, which had been lying in state at Buckingham Palace, was taken from there to Westminster Hall for the public lying-in-state. Rosy walked in the procession behind the coffin with the other ADCs. Two days later he was part of the funeral procession from Westminster Hall, partly by train, to St George's Chapel, Windsor. The procession was made up of British and foreign royalty, representatives of all the Dominions, Colonies and overseas possessions, and of virtually every foreign country in the world, nearly all in uniform, only the sombre clothes of President Roosevelt of the USA providing a contrast.

On the day after the funeral George, now King, had told Rosy that he could now not go to South Africa, so his place would be taken by Prince Arthur, Duke of Connaught, and the royal tour would now start in October.

During 1909, a campaign to remove Fisher as First Sea Lord gathered pace. An enquiry into Admiralty policy was the last straw. In this Beresford took his part. He had ended his seagoing career in March 1909, and his departure from Portsmouth and arrival in London was marked by huge crowds. At Waterloo, as he stepped onto the platform, he was greeted with cheers and the crowd sang 'For He's a Jolly Good Fellow'. It all underlined the esteem in which he was held, not only by the officers and men of the fleet, but also the general population. No longer in active service, Beresford planned an attack on Fisher. After a prolonged campaign his attack succeeded. On the King's birthday, 9 November 1909, Fisher was created Baron Fisher of Kilverstone and he resigned as First Sea Lord, the resignation to take effect on 25 January 1910, his 69th birthday. The news was announced on 2 December, together with the announcement of his successor, Sir Arthur Wilson. Fisher's departure was timely. His methods of command had been a major factor in the breaking of the spirit of unity in the Service, and the Navy needed a period to recover and cease the internal wrangling.[123] He had nevertheless accomplished much:

> A tornado of energy, enthusiasm and persuasive power, a man of originality, vision, and courage, a sworn foe of all outworn traditions and customs, the greatest of British naval administrators since St Vincent, Jackie Fisher was what the lethargic Navy had been in dire need of. His five-year tenure of the post of First Sea Lord was the most memorable and the most profitable in the modern history of the Royal Navy.[124]

Sir Arthur Wilson had been promoted to Admiral of the Fleet in 1907, but as there were no seagoing commands he retired to his home in Norfolk and was

---

123 Arthur Marder From Dreadnought to Scapa Flow, Vol.1, 205

124 Ibid 206

the same age as Fisher when he reluctantly agreed to become First Sea Lord. His selection was universally accepted with enthusiasm. His record as a seafaring officer and his steadfast refusal to become involved in the schism that had split the Navy gave him a steady platform to take on his new role.

In his earlier career he had won the Victoria Cross in the Sudan, and had been employed at sea in the highest commands continuously for six years until 1907. Arthur Marder described him as:

> Sturdily built [with an] athletic figure … His blue eyes always gave one the impression of being a little screwed up as though from looking in the spindrift whipped from the wave tops in a gale … He was extremely reserved and unbending, self reliant, untroubled with nerves of any sort and hard as nails physically … He was also kindly and human, and not lacking in humour … To the blue jackets he was 'old 'Ard 'Art' since he worked all under him as hard as he worked himself.[125]

His character did not lend itself to the role of First Sea Lord as he would not delegate work, and was obstinate and reserved to the point of secretiveness. Although a superb leader at sea and revered throughout the fleet, he was not a success ashore. In that he was not alone: many others were cut from the same cloth.

In September Rosy and Victoria went to Southampton for him to commission *Balmoral Castle* and take her to Portsmouth, where, on 11 October, the Duke and Duchess of Connaught, with their daughter, Princess Patricia, and a large suite boarded the ship. They sailed that afternoon with HMS *Duke of Edinburgh* as escort. There had been much competition for appointments to *Balmoral Castle*; Rosy had, as he wrote to Victoria, received 'Applications … [which] continue to arrive in shoals'. Those who had been picked he approved of, as he continued '[I am] greatly pleased with all the officers'. Three of these officers, Lieutenants Marriot and Bevan, and Secretary Paymaster Hugh Miller, were to remain on his staff for the whole of the forthcoming war, and became much valued friends.

Balmoral Castle crossed the equator on 22 October, and he wrote to Victoria:

> This morning we have been crossing the Line and playing at Neptune and I must say a most excellent piece of fooling it was … There is a childishness and simplicity and absolute lack of vulgarity about the blue jacket which is really extremely refreshing. Everybody was much amused and the whole thing went off without a hitch. In the evening it being Trafalgar day I read

---

125 Ibid 212

them a short lecture and spoke a few words on the subject which I trust were taken in.[126]

Four days later they arrived at St Helena, where the governor was to be invested with the order of the KCMG. This was undertaken on the deck of *Balmoral Castle,* with appropriate pomp and circumstance, with all the officers in full dress, a guard of marines and the ship's band. Rosy concluded his account of the occasion to Victoria 'I was much pleased with my little stage-managed business.'

They arrived off Cape Town on the last day of the month to find a thick fog off the port. Rosy was on the bridge throughout the night:

Last night at 11 p.m. just as I was going to bed we ran into a thick fog which we never got out of until we were actually alongside the wharf this morning. I got up close to the land and anchored at 5 a.m. not knowing for certain where I was. I remained on deck until 6.30 hoping for it to clear up to see where I was, when I turned in never having left the bridge. No sooner had I laid down then I was called to say the fog was clearing. It was cleared enough for me to see where I was when it came down as thick as ever again. However, I had seen enough for me to be able to grope my way to the pierhead and in we came to the very minute I had said I would arrive, to the astonishment of everybody and greatly to their joy for they thought that inevitably all arrangements would have to be put off.

As commodore, he accompanied the royal party ashore, part of the procession to Government House. He commented that:

the Governor-General and Lady Gladstone ... are both agreeable and kindly, but some of the Governor-Generals staff are absolutely and completely incompetent and we have had gently but firmly to take matters into our own hands and run the whole business. Now that we have taken these drastic steps things are going quite smoothly but Monday and Tuesday morning the chaos was awful.

His account continued:

November 6

The opening of the Parliament was really very fine and very well done, very impressive and the speeches all very good ... On Friday night there

---

126 Lady Wester Wemyss Life and Letters, 109

was a big full dress dinner and a reception afterwards. We took charge of the arrangements for the people passing the Duke and Duchess and that was all quite good – but outside! 2000 people had been asked and absolutely no arrangements made at the hall door to regulate the traffic in any way. The Hall is small [with] bad approaches and the consequences were something awful. Of course we only heard of all this afterwards. Huge crowds, jamming and trampling and fainting. Useless ADC's and distracted secretaries, fainting women and at last some of the crowd actually gained entrance through the windows. Eventually the Guard was called out and the people kept back at the point of the bayonet. A most disgraceful event from which these people should surely be punished. The veriest baby would have, I should have thought, taken some steps to keep order and regulate matters.

From Cape Town the royal party, including Rosy, travelled by train to North-Western Rhodesia (now Zambia), then to Salisbury in Southern Rhodesia (now Zimbabwe), where they arrived on 18 November. On the next day:

I went out hunting early this morning and enjoyed myself very much though the sport wasn't very good. The morning and was delicious and I felt 18! They hunt jackals with a pack of foxhounds, but there was little or no scent but galloping over that lonely veldt in the morning air is delicious.

The tour through South Africa continued, arriving at Pretoria on 27 November to a tremendous reception. Government House, where they stayed, impressed Rosy:

[It] is perfectly beautiful … and is a sort of mixture between Dutch and Provencal and seems to suit the surroundings extremely well. Beautiful rooms, spacious corridors, staircase hall and loggia; it is situated on the top of the hill and overlooks glorious stretches of green valleys with fine hills as a background.

The Governor of the Transvaal and Orange River Colonies was none other than Lord Selborne, who, until arriving in South Africa in 1905, had been the First Lord of the Admiralty, and who had introduced Fisher's plans for the reform of naval education which had resulted in Rosy's appointment to Osborne.

Rosy and two others spent the day visiting the zoo in the morning: he remarked on 'a delightful baboon … which turned somersaults in the air on being told to do so'. In the afternoon they visited the Premier Diamond Mine which at that time was 'half a mile long and a quarter mile wide' and employed up to 16,000 people. The tour through Africa was starting to wear on him:

> I shan't be sorry to be on board again, in spite of having enjoyed the trip so enormously, for I am getting rather tired of having no privacy at all and one sees rather too much of everybody.

He was therefore pleased when they sailed from Durban a week later: 'I don't think that anybody was sorry to be peaceably installed on board once more.' Ten days later, as they crossed the equator northbound, after rounding the Cape of Good Hope, 'the Duke got it into his head that he would like to go to Sierra Leone. I told him I had no objection provided he would only stay there the day and come away before Sunset.'

They arrived on 15 December:

> and landed at nine and never, never in my life have I seen such enthusiasm as was displayed … and seldom have I seen such ludicrous contrasts. Addresses were presented at the Town Hall which were read out by the Town Clerk who was in a barrister's wig and gown. The white wig, which by the way was too small for him, gave him the most ludicrous appearance and it was all we could do to hold our countenances. The pomposity, the burlesque and dignity made the whole thing a screaming farce, but their real enthusiasm and genuine good humoured gaiety gave the touch which saved it from being quite absurd.

Sierra Leone was the last port before arriving at Portsmouth. On Christmas Day in the Bay of Biscay, in the evening, a big dinner was held in the wardroom, at which Rosy 'said a few words and really meant everything I said. They certainly have been most extraordinarily kind and thoughtful and nice and the whole trip has been very much pleasanter than I expected it to be.'

They arrived in Portsmouth on 28 December and the duke and duchess disembarked the ship to return to London. It had been a most successful trip, and to mark Rosy's efforts in making it so, he was appointed Commander of the Order of St Michael and St George in January 1911.

The words of Prince George were prophetic, as on 19 April Rosy was promoted to rear admiral, less than three years after receiving Prince George's letter.

11: THE END OF PEACE

Soon after his return from South Africa, he became, as Naval ADC to the King, involved in the preparations for the Coronation of King George V. He was attached to the French Mission, and in addition to meetings at the French Embassy there were rehearsals at Westminster Abbey for the service and at the Royal Mews for the procession. The Coronation took place on Thursday, 22 June.

The King wrote in his logbook his own account of the day:

> It was overcast and cloudy with some showers and a strong cool breeze but better for the people than great heat. Today it was indeed a great and the memorable day in our lives and one we can never forget … May and I left B.P. in the Coronation coach at 1030 with eight cream-coloured horses. There were over 50,000 troops lining the streets under the command of Lord Kitchener. There were hundreds and thousands of people who gave us a magnificent reception. The service in the Abbey was most beautiful but it was a terrible ordeal. I nearly broke down when dear David came to do homage to me as it reminded me so much when I did the same thing to beloved Papa … Worked all the afternoon with Bigge and others [which would have included Rosy] answering telegrams and letters of which I have hundreds … Our guests dined with us at 8.30. May and I showed ourselves again to the people.[127]

It was followed on the Saturday by the Naval Review at Spithead, for which Rosy was on board *Victoria and Albert,* with other members of the court and ADCs. This was followed by a week of banquets, garden parties and other festivities until the end of the month when all the foreign missions returned to their homes.

127 Denis Judd Life and Times of George V, 95

Promoted to Rear Admiral, 1912 (IWM)

In July the Agadir crisis erupted as SMS *Panther* arrived there. This event brought Britain and Germany close to war. The background to this were discussions with Germany over the number of battleships to be built in the following year's programmes. The German response to the British proposals was received on the same day that *Panther* arrived. However, the discussions continued and by the end of September passions had cooled.

Whilst this was occurring, Rosy was on half-pay. He had been offered the command of the Mediterranean Cruiser Squadron, but the post was not available for 18 months. As nothing else of interest was available and a chance to return to the Mediterranean was very attractive, he chose half-pay during the interval. After the summer spent in London, he and his family travelled for a holiday to Martigny in the Vosges, returning to spend the autumn at Wemyss Castle, before leaving for Cannes for the winter. In Victoria's words 'it still retained most of its traditions of courtly seclusion and leisured ease'.

Rosy entered into the cosmopolitan social life with enthusiasm, playing golf, bridge, and joining the Cercle Nautique, which was at the centre of Cannes social life. This was a pleasant interlude, but by the spring he was ready for naval activity and when asked to sit on a committee at the Admiralty he accepted immediately.

In the autumn of the previous year, Winston Churchill had been appointed First Lord of the Admiralty, moving from the Home Office; this was considered a downward step. However, he had gone to the Admiralty as he thought the Anglo-German naval rivalry was more exciting than home affairs.

His appointment did not meet with universal acclaim; within the Navy his reputation for cost-cutting and cheese-paring caused concern. Comments in the *Naval Review* of the time refer to him as 'a windbag', 'a political gambler of the worst kind' and 'a self advertising mountebank'.[128]

When Churchill was appointed, the naval secretary was Rear Admiral Ernest Troubridge. But Churchill wanted (the then) Rear Admiral David Beatty as his secretary, as he had met, and been impressed by, him in the Sudan. Troubridge, who had considerable influence within the Admiralty, had to be found a suitable appointment as compensation. Churchill, without consulting anyone, gave him the command of the Mediterranean Cruiser Squadron, which at that point was shortly to become vacant.

Rosy, who had been offered the appointment earlier and had gone on to half-pay to wait for the vacancy, was outraged. He had heard the news through the grapevine so he wrote to Bridgeman (by then the First Sea Lord, succeeding Sir Arthur Wilson), as it was he who, as Second Sea Lord, had made the offer. Bridgeman's letter in reply was less than clear in its wording, but it became clear that the news was correct. So on 22 July Rosy submitted a letter of resignation. The Admiralty, however, was not prepared to accept it. He had a fine reputation within the Navy, with many friends throughout the service and also in very high places, so at an ill-tempered interview with Churchill Rosy was persuaded to continue his service in the Navy, on the undertaking that he would be offered the first vacant appointment at sea.

---

128 Arthur Marder *From Dreadnought to Scapa Flow*, Vol.1, 252

Lady Wemyss conjectures that had Rosy gone to the Mediterranean the Cruiser Squadron would have been better led than under Troubridge, who had not had a seagoing post since 1908, and that in 1914 the escape of the German cruisers SMS *Goeben* and *Breslau* to Turkey would have been prevented. The Turks would not have entered the war without that support, and the Dardanelles campaign would not have happened.[129]

There was time before Rosy's next appointment for him, Victoria and Alice to travel to the Continent for his annual cure. That year they had set upon Bad *Salzschlirf*, near Frankfurt, which had been highly recommended to them. Victoria's parents had been close friends of Count Goertz, whose castle at Schlitz was nearby. Rosy was delighted by the castle, as the welcome and warm hospitality reminded him strongly of Wemyss Castle. They left Alice with Count Goertz and his daughter, the Countess Elizabeth, to travel through the Black Forest to Lake Geneva to stay at Ouchy. After returning to Schlitz Castle to collect Alice, they returned to England.

Rosy had made a brief visit to the Admiralty from his holiday, at which time he was given the appointment of Rear Admiral of the Second Battle Squadron. He took up the appointment on 29 October, hoisting his flag on HMS *Orion* at Portsmouth, sailing two days later for Berehaven in Southern Ireland.

He wrote:

> Here I am at sea again and at present I seem to have nothing to do. Going out of harbour yesterday I felt like a fish out of water on the breach. Everybody [has] something to do except myself, and as I have never been accustomed to this it feels strange, but when I get some other ships with me it will feel different.[130]

Wemyss Castle, c. 1913 (Churchill Archive)

---

129 Lady Wester Wemyss Life and Letters, 132

130 Ibid 139

When he joined the Second Battle Squadron as rear admiral, Admiral Jellicoe was in command, but he was soon promoted:

> I have just heard from Jellicoe that he takes over as Second Sea Lord on Monday next, so that the command of the Squadron will devolve on me until his successors appointment. He tells me that Bridgeman is resigning through ill health, so I conclude Battenberg moves up to First Sea Lord but this matter I don't know.

> December 13.

> I have just received a telegram that George Warrender is to come in Jellicoe's place. I am glad for he is a gentleman and I can get on with them and I believe him to be an excellent officer.[131]

The departure of Bridgeman caused a major storm. Churchill had suggested that his health was not good. This was not the case, but he insisted on Bridgeman's resignation, which took place on 2 December. Stories began to circulate in the press that his resignation was not on the grounds of ill-health but had been forced upon him, this fuelled in part by a newspaper report that Bridgeman had been seen in Yorkshire fit enough to be riding to hounds three days a week.

Rosy, observing the storm from a distance, wrote on 18 December

> I have been dining with George Warrender. About Bridgeman this is what I hear – that he, Bridgeman, was always away from the Admiralty and never at his work and that consequently Winston Churchill proposed to him that he should resign, whether on the ground of ill-health or not I can't quite make out. Bridgeman did not seem to see it in that light, and declared his intention of returning to the Admiralty, upon which Winston Churchill led the matter before the Cabinet, who insisted on Bridgeman's going. Now you will acquit me of having sympathy with WC, but I must confess in this case it seems to me perfectly right. But what makes my blood boil is a fact that a man – an Admiral – who has arrived at the dignity of being First Sea Lord should behave in such a manner as to allow of his being possible to treating thus.

> Dec 20

> The House of Commons seems to devote itself to nothing but the Bridgeman affair and I think that B. himself will hardly thank Charlie Beresford

---

131 Lady Wester Wemyss Life and Letters, 140

raking the whole matter up by the time it is all finished. Seriously, the whole matter is damnable, undignified and extremely bad for the Service in particular and the general good in general.

Dec 21

I wonder if you have read the Bridgeman debate. It is disgusting reading. They all come out of it badly, to my mind. Winston Churchill, Charlie, Bridgeman, Battenberg – the whole lot, and I'm thoroughly disgusted with the First Lord, his Sea Lords and all my brother officers. I have just had a long talk with Pakenham (Fourth Sea Lord) whose revelations are extraordinary.[132]

it was a relief to go on leave for Christmas at Cannes, to get away from naval politics and the news of the Balkan Wars which were causing rumours of an impending war in the eastern Mediterranean. He spent his leave gardening, playing golf, relaxing and enjoying the amusements that Cannes had to offer over the Christmas season. He was happy to return to *Orion* after his leave; he was on the best of terms with Warrender, the captain of *Orion* he liked; and his flag lieutenant, Bevan, and secretary, Miller, who had both been on *Balmoral Castle* with him, were becoming a close part of his immediate team. He rejoined in February, in Devonport, writing:

HMS Orion Feb.13

This morning I went to see Sir. G. Egerton the new C-in-C. He thrilled me by showing me a letter he had received from poor Scott [the Antarctic explorer] and very nearly the last one he wrote. He never complains, but merely states that it was the unprecedented weather which caused the catastrophe and that he did not consider that he had left any possible precaution undone. He wrote quite quietly, asking Sir George (whom he thought still at the Admiralty) to look after his widow (he already describes her as such) from the Admiralty point of view and then asks to be most kindly remembered to Lady Egerton, and this from a man who it is thought had already been many days without food and one, at least, of whose companions lay dead beside him. It is wonderful in these materialistic days and a great example.[133]

Rosy had had a very high opinion of Scott, and when he was about to leave Osborne College he had tried to persuade Scott to succeed him in command but

---

132 Lady Wester Wemyss Life and Letters, 141

133 Ibid 142

unsuccessfully, as by that time Scott was wholly concentrating on his expedition to the Antarctic.

The Second Battle Squadron spent all spring and summer in home waters, and was off the Scottish coast in September, where at the end of the month he wrote from Cromarty, having played golf at Tain, and enjoyed the glorious landscape round about, his letter ended 'No word yet of who my successor is to be – really too bad of the Admiralty.'

A decision was made soon after that letter as he lowered his flag on *Orion* on 28 October, and his place was taken by Rear Admiral Sir Keith Arbuthnot. The ships of the squadron were about to have a significant change of tone in the way the squadron was to be commanded. Arbuthnot was considered to be a martinet, enforcing rigid disciplinary standards. His methods were noted by Jellicoe as, when he was in command of the First Cruiser Squadron little over a year later, Jellicoe noted that his ideals were too high and, in today's terms, he micromanaged the squadron to an excessive degree. He was killed at the Battle of Jutland in 1916, as the ship on which he was flying his flag, *HMS Defence*, blew up in an explosion which killed all 903 men on board.

After leaving the *Orion* Rosy was again on half-pay and again, as Christmas approached, went to Cannes. It was to be a different Christmas from that of the previous year: the events happening elsewhere in Europe were causing much concern and the atmosphere was subdued.

The political situation in Ulster was also giving great concern at home. Beresford had written to Victoria Wemyss:

> We have not advanced at all towards peace, with regard to the Home Rule Bill. We have evidence that the Churchill plot was an accomplished fact. That he was the moving spirit in the whole question, that he took charge of the Army, the Cabinet and the Government for the time being, that arrangements were made to seize all the strategical points around Belfast by means of the Army, associated with the Navy, and that arrangements had been made to arrest Sir Walter Carson … and the [other] leading people associated in the Ulster uprising. The resignation of the officers brought the matter to a climax.[134]

Rosy had had a letter from a close friend, which also noted:

> Winston … had for some days been not in his office at the Admiralty but in his colleagues office at the War Office. It is unquestionable that a military plot was planned, a coup d'etat to settle the Ulster opposition once and for

---

134 Churchill Archives WYMS, Box 1/2

all. The leaders were to be arrested at the same time. Two men caused the failure of it, [Brigadier] Gough in Ireland and [Rear Admiral] de Chair at the Admiralty. Churchill had ordered the third Battle Squadron to be sent from Spain to Ireland, calling in at Plymouth for the Flag Officer, Vice Admiral Bayley to go to London for orders. De Chair had heard of the plan and went to Jellicoe for it to be stopped. The latter went, perfectly fearlessly, with Battenberg, the First Sea Lord, directly to see Churchill. The orders were cancelled. Bayley, when he had arrived in London, was caught by De Chair, and then by [Rear Admiral] Leveson before he met Churchill, to explain the situation. Bayley, who had until then been fully and enthusiastically supportive of Churchill's idea, instead told him that he absolutely declined to land a single man in Ulster.

The letter ended:

> You ask what impression I have about the younger officers with regard to Ulster: you may rest assured, I think; the Navy, neither officers nor men, intended to be used as an instrument for enforcing the Divine Right of our political party.[135,136]

This view was held not only by naval officers: in an official paper, 'Correspondence relating to Recent Events in the Irish Command', the report from the headquarters of the Irish Command noted that:

> If the duty involves the initiation of active military operations against Ulster, the following numbers of officers by regiments would respectfully and under protest preferred to be dismissed:
>
> Brigade Staff: 2 officers
>
> Fourth Hussars: 17 out of 20 doing duty
>
> Fifth Lancers: 17 out of 20 doing duty
>
> Sixteenth Lancers: 16 out of 16 doing duty.[137]

It was signed by Brigadier Gough, the GOC of the 3rd Cavalry Brigade.

None of this affected Rosy directly, as he was abroad and on half-pay; he and his family stayed at Cannes until May, eventually returning to England in June, when he visited Wemyss, which at the time was uninhabited. He wrote to Victoria in June, from Edinburgh:

---

135 Ibid Box 1/2

136 Churchill Archive WYMS Box 1/2

137 Ibid

I went over to Wemyss. It's very sad to see the place absolutely deserted. I did not go into the house, but all over the place … It was a beautifully bright day and a fresh NW wind which kept away all smoke and made the atmosphere clear and keen, so that everything was at its best. Chapel Gardens was really beautiful and very hot, and I spent quite a long time there sitting on the grass and basking in the sun. I'm going over again tomorrow to go to church … I love going back and seeing all the old people, getting now fewer every year, alas! But it is not an exhilarating experience.

Two days later he wrote 'What an awful tragedy, the Archduke! It may have tremendous consequences I should think.'[138]

The previous October Churchill had proposed to the First Sea Lord, Battenberg, that instead of the customary full-scale summer naval manoeuvres in 1914, a test mobilisation of the Reserve Fleet, which was intended as an economy measure, should take place. Battenberg had agreed to this, and accordingly the orders were promulgated on 10 July and the mobilisation began on 15 July. This was followed on 17 and 18 July by a grand review of the fleet at Spithead. Churchill commented that 'it constituted incomparably the greatest assemblage of naval power ever witnessed in the history of the world'. Those ships that had been mobilised of the Reserve Fleet had added to the spectacle, but their efficacy as fighting units was of a much lesser level than those that were currently in commission. As the events in Europe escalated it was a huge stroke of luck that the fleet was virtually ready for war at the same time.[139]

On the same day that the order to mobilise the Reserve Fleet was given – and events in Europe were changing very quickly – Rosy left to join his family in Germany for their summer holiday. Although hesitating because of the news, he had eventually decided it was safe to go. Victoria Wemyss describes it as a false sense of security. With the benefit of hindsight it did seem a very strange decision to make. However, *Salzschlirf,* to which they had returned for a second year, was peaceful and world events seemed far away. They settled down to enjoy their holiday.

Two weeks after they arrived the text of the Austrian ultimatum to Serbia was published. Victoria Wemyss described the events thereafter in her diary:

Saturday, July 25

We are all getting somewhat disturbed about the Serbian answer … [a mutual friend] tells us at supper that his valet had heard through the personal of a telegram saying Serbia has rejected the ultimatum.

138 Lady Wester Wemyss Life and Letters, 147

139 Arthur Marder Dreadnought to Scapa Flow Vol.1, 433

Sunday July 26

The Austrians have rejected the ultimatum. Austria is invading Serbia. I urge R. to try and see Witte [a Russian diplomat who had firmly stated the previous evening that Russia would not go to war] before his departure and ask him again what he thinks. He does so but apparently Witte has not changed his mind.

Despite his comments

A certain effervescence is beginning to make itself felt. The band plays Deutsche Uber Alles and the Austrian Hymn ... while great tension manifests itself between Russians and Germans, who eye one another with undisguised hostility.

Monday, July 27

Excitement is increasing ... Heinecken (the president of Nord Deutscher Lloyd, the shipping company) tells me that stock exchanges all over the world are in a state of panic ... Baron Meck, the Russian Railway King, just arrived from Moscow, has received a ciphered telegram informing him that mobilisation is in full swing in Russia on the German frontier; this seems indeed grave news.

Wednesday, July 29

It sounds rather ridiculous, but ... we are all getting anxious and beginning to discuss the advisability of leaving. R. telegraphs to Admiral Hood [the Naval Secretary] to ask what he is to do ... R. receives a reassuring answer from Admiral Hood telling him that his return for the moment is unnecessary but to keep himself prepared. Mr. Cloete, the South African, had asked him for his advice. ... adding that everybody looks on him, R. as a political barometer for whilst he remains quietly drinking the waters they cannot believe that war is imminent. R. in consequence shows him Hood's telegram which calms him ... we are beginning to realise the danger of the situation and feel convinced that it is Russia that is pushing to war. The Russians, indeed, hardly deny the imputation. Later that evening I was sitting in a corner of the hall playing patience when Heinecken, who had been out all day, came down the stairs, looking very pale and visibly upset. Silently he placed a telegram before me: 'The situation has become much worse; the Russians are mobilising and the British Fleet are beginning to move'. He then vanished into outer darkness, presumably to the telegraph office. I rushed upstairs to tell R. who, very tired, had gone to bed. While we were talking – a knock at the door, the lift boy with a telegram – from Admiral Hood – 'Return immediately'. We gazed at each other in consternation. The only thing to do, however, was to pack and leave as soon as it was light … they were just finishing our last preparations when dawn was beginning to break … I went to wake the child who murmured sleepily 'Then it is war, Mummy'.[140]

They drove to Frankfurt to catch the 3 p.m. train for Flushing, to then catch the train ferry to England. At every station they bought newspapers, but no mobilisation was mentioned. After an uneventful journey they arrived in London on the Friday morning.

On arrival, Rosy went straight to the Admiralty, to find that he was to be appointed to command the 12th Cruiser Squadron, which was to guard, in conjunction with a French squadron, the Western Approaches, at the entrance to the English Channel.

The information that was being received at Salzschlirf was much better than that which was being received in London. Rosy commented:

On the whole, London was extraordinarily ill informed of the great issues hanging in the balance and the seemingly total misunderstanding what a great European war was likely to be, regarding it somewhat in the light of a Second Boer War or even less … everybody expected that the contest would be sharp and short.[141]

On Saturday 1 August Germany declared war against Russia and France; Rosy went to the Admiralty to see whether the order to mobilise the fleet had been issued:

It came after lunch and I went down to Plymouth accompanied by my wife on the 6.30 train … Bevan, my Flag Lieutenant came with us … [When we arrived there was] great difficulty in finding any sort of conveyance to take us to an hotel, which we eventually reached at 1 a.m. We were the first to arrive, but all through the night were kept awake by the incessant noise caused by hungry and hurried Naval Officers arriving from all parts of the country in every sort of manner.[142]

On the following morning, the reserves were called up and Rosy hoisted his flag on HMS *Charybdis*. She was an elderly ship of an obsolete type, as were the

---

140 Lady Wester Wemyss Life and Letters, 155

141 Ibid 157

142 Lady Wester Wemyss Life and Letters, 158

other ships of the squadron, *Diana, Eclipse* and *Talbot.* All had been built during the last decade of the previous century. They sailed on Tuesday 4 August. Victoria returned to London that evening, and on hearing on her arrival at Paddington station the sound of cheering crowds, realised that war had been declared. At 11 p.m., midnight German time, the Admiralty sent the signal to all HM ships and shore bases throughout the world 'Commence hostilities against Germany.'

Rosy, at sea in the English Channel, wrote:

> A rather disturbed night as I may expect for many a long day. Well, there it is and I am beginning to fear that I shall not find much to do. Guarding the Channel is worthy but if nothing comes this way it will hardly be glorious.[143]

Churchill had ensured that the fleet was in readiness

> Obviously the first thing was to be ready; not to be taken unawares; to be concentrated; not to be caught divided: to have the strongest Fleet possible in the best station under the best conditions in good time and then if the battle came one could await its result with a steady heart.[144]

Within 12 hours of the mobilisation order on 1 August, every ship of the fleet was at her war station or had her orders.

Arthur Marder finishes Volume 1 of his five-volume history of the Navy in the First World War with the following words:

> And so the great war had come at last – the war which Fisher had in 1910 predicted would break out in the autumn of 1914. Armageddon was about to put the fleet to the severest test in its proud and ancient history. On the performance of those 'far-distant, storm beaten ships' depended the destinies of free men.[145]

---

143 Ibid 160

144 W S Churchill, 'The World Crisis', quoted in Arthur Marder Dreadnought to Scapa Flow Vol.1, 435

145 Ibid 436

PART TWO: BELLUM

12: IN THE WESTERN APPROACHES

Alfred Thayer Mahan's 'far distant, storm beaten ships' had been applied to the blockade against the French just over 100 years before Rosy was again blockading the Western Approaches. In an ironical difference, he was now part of a joint blockade operation with the French Second Light Squadron: nine cruisers under Rear Admiral A Royer. But although the Allies might have changed, the conditions had not.

Rosy was initially quite content, writing to Victoria:

> It is wonderful how things are shaking down – my dinner tonight was quite excellent! Plain and well cooked and the steward seems to be a veritable treasure – no difficulties. It appears that he went and helped himself at the stores – I couldn't make out if he actually stole – my eyes are getting heavy again and I must get some sleep.[146]

In the morning the two squadrons met and officers were exchanged to act as liaison, with Lieutenant Commander Erskine Nicholson going to the French flagship, and Lieutenant Fahner joining *Charybdis*.

Rosy was frustrated by the lack of news from the Admiralty; in contrast the French liaison officer was very well-informed. For six weeks the squadron patrolled with little to see initially, but one or two ships started to appear, and on 7 August they met a destroyer which was able to update them with news of the war. One of the aspects of his command which started to grate was that he was always at sea, as when *Charybdis* returned to Plymouth to coal, he would shift his flag to one of the other ships of the squadron. He was always on call:

---

146 Churchill Archives WYMS7/11/1 (i)

I am a good deal disturbed in the night. I have to stay in my clothes always, but I have a very comfortable spring mattress and I'm beginning to quite like it. It's extraordinary how I find I look upon nearly everything from an entirely different point of view to what I did a few days ago. In small things, for instance, a dirty shirt no longer shocks me! I'm very lucky to have a small bar … My cabin, which a short time ago I should have considered bare and uncomfortable, is to me now a veritable haven of peace and comfort.[147]

In September, when Rosy was contemplating whether he might be spending the whole war in the Western Approaches, a signal arrived for the squadron to return to Plymouth, to be replaced by Admiral Bethel's squadron of elderly battleships, in order for the 12th Cruiser Squadron to proceed to Canada to escort a convoy carrying the first contingent of Canadian troops to the Western Front. Rosy was not given much information:

As I so often found during the war my instructions from the Admiralty were of the vaguest and I started from England entirely unaware of the ships of the convoy or their number or indeed anything about them and learnt nothing even on my arrival at Halifax where Admiral Hornby, who I found there, knew as little as I did.[148]

He went to Quebec to endeavour to clarify his orders and was able to see the men who would be going to France:

A magnificent looking lot of men were those who formed the first Canadian contingent – but of course absolutely destitute of any training and nearly so of any discipline. With an ignorance that was truly sublime in its magnitude, General Hughes told me that when his boys arrived in Flanders – and he thought they should land at Calais immediately – the enemy would begin to feel unhappy – the spirit was splendid, but the ignorance colossal.[149]

He also found that when he issued instructions to the masters of the transports, the Merchant Service did not react to them as would the Royal Navy. He had instructed that they keep radio silence once the troops had boarded in Quebec, but:

---

147 Churchill Archives WYMS7/11/1 (i)
148 Churchill Archives WYMS 6/6
149 Ibid 6/6

I began to realise how hopelessly indisciplined were these captains. It was distinctly and energetically laid down from the moment that the troops arrived on board the W/T was to be cut off, but I might as well have whistled – they were at it all day like so many parrots, and when on their arrival at Gaspe Bay [the rendezvous area] I sent for the captains and demanded an explanation of their disobedience of my orders. They were struck dumb with astonishment that I expected my orders to be carried out – one of them even went so far as to say that he had no means of enforcing the order. I soon put that right.[150]

They eventually sailed with the transports arranged in line astern, each line supervised by a cruiser, and once in open water they formed up in three columns abreast. The problems that had arisen in Gaspe Bay had all been sorted out. One problem that arose was that one ship had made a signal to say that it only had three days' provisions on board; this for a ten-day crossing. Rosy went on board himself to find out the reason for this:

I sent for the purser and the captain for an explanation, to be told that there were only sufficient fresh eggs for three day's breakfasts! But of rations I asked? Of ordinary rations we have plenty was the reply. Then why all this fuss I asked – there was no answer but they seemed quite incapable of understanding that fresh eggs for breakfast were not actually necessary.[151]

Once sailed, they had good weather for the main part of the crossing, which enabled the masters of the transports to learn how to keep station in line. Despite the order that all lights were to be extinguished at night, this proved to be virtually impossible to enforce. As they approached the Channel, the weather changed and:

It came on to blow hard and then indeed the station keeping became awful – I think there must have been as much as 30 miles between the leading and the rear ships. One cruiser was stationed astern to act as a whipper-in and a difficult job she had.

He was pleased to arrive at Plymouth, describing it as a beautiful sight. As there were insufficient pilots available for all ships to enter port immediately on their arrival, when Rosy approached with the last batch of ships he found a long line of huge transports stretching back from Plymouth breakwater to the Eddystone lighthouse, awaiting their pilots.

---

150 Ibid 6/6
151 Ibid. 6/6

it was a glorious afternoon, flat calm and the sight of that long line of huge ships filled with troops is one I shall never forget – what a target for a submarine.[152]

One of the masters who was an exception to the remainder was Captain Thomson RNR, who proved to be an exceptionally good ship handler, in Rosy's opinion 'as if he had been on the bridge of a man of war all his life'. He was to meet this officer several times afterwards, including at Mudros. He had been called up for naval service, and Rosy obtained the command of a torpedo boat for him.

While they were returning from Canada on 22 September, the sinking of HMSs *Aboukir, Cressy* and *Hogue,* three elderly cruisers, occurred in the southern part of the North Sea. The loss of life was great: 62 officers and 1,397 of the crews, the latter mainly reservists and cadets from HMC Dartmouth, who previously had been at Osborne and would have been known to Rosy. All three ships were torpedoed by a solitary U-boat, the *Aboukir* first, then the other two which had stopped to render assistance.

Following their return, the 12th Cruiser Squadron had returned to their patrol area in the Western Approaches. The submarine menace was becoming very apparent, and Rosy wrote in his journal:

> Bad weather and protracted monotony were to be my lot for the next three months, both of which combined to make me irritable towards the Admiralty, whose policy I had no means of fathoming. [He had proposed an alternative to the use of cruisers in the Western approaches but for various reasons it was not adopted.] That they realised the danger from submarines to which we were exposed was proved by my receiving orders from them to change my line of patrol – they wished me to confine my activities to a small space between Lands End and the Scillies and gave me orders to that effect.[153]

In his letters to Victoria, his longing to be at home with her is great and his overwhelming love for her shines through, calling her 'Pusscat' and ending his letters with valedictions such as 'God bless you my love, my life, my dear, dear sweetheart, your loving and devoted Tomcat'. He calls their daughter Alice 'Kitten'. He starts one letter 'one passes through horrible moments in one's life – the most horrible of those of parting. I feel as if my heart were being torn out of me and left behind with you – but there it is nothing that you or I can do now can alter it.'[154]

---

152 Churchill Archive WYMS 6/6

153 Ibid WYMS 6/6

154 Churchill Archives WYMS7/11/1 (i)

In his letters he vents his frustration at being stuck in the Western Approaches, in a backwater, when he wanted to be in the North Sea, where, in the autumn, towns on the east coast of England were being bombarded by German ships, and in Scapa Flow the Grand Fleet lay ready for action.

Before the squadron returned to patrol duties, Rosy had, whilst on leave in London with Victoria, gone to the Admiralty to report on the convoy and set out his ideas on future convoys. In his meeting with the First Sea Lord, Battenberg, he had asked for:

> A more roomy and convenient ship better able to accommodate myself and my staff, when he suddenly asked me why I was flying my flag in her [*Charybdis*]. 'Because I was ordered to' was my very natural reply– 'oh' he said 'I thought perhaps you had some sentiment on the subject'.[155]

Discussion then ensued on the operation of the Western Approaches patrol, and it was eventually decided that it should continue as it was, but with the addition of the *Euralyus* and the *Bacchante*, and that he should fly his flag in the former, with his flag captain also transferring to her. This was a distinct improvement as *Euralyus,* of the same class as the *Cressy, Aboukir* and *Hogue* which had been sunk some weeks before, was a much larger, even if still elderly, heavy cruiser. She was to be Rosy's flagship for his next two appointments. On his return to Devonport after his leave, on which he had been relaxing apart from his visit to the Admiralty, he rejoined *Charybdis*, as *Euralyus* was still in dock, completing an overhaul. Nevertheless he was able to write to Victoria:

> Charybdis at sea, Friday morning
>
> [This is] the last time I shall date my letters from this old ship, my darling, as tomorrow I transfer myself and my belongings to the *Euryalus* and I expect to be much more comfortable there in every way. I have felt very cramped here and my wretched staff have had no space to work in at all. They will feel the benefit of the change even more than I. What a happy and delightful six days we spent together – you have made my life so universally and entirely happy that I think I was beginning to look upon such happiness and content as my just due and right and our separations and the conditions of war have brought me up and showed me a very plainly for what a lucky man I am and how grateful I ought to be for all you are to me.

The conditions on his station in the Western Approaches had altered significantly whilst he was away, escorting the convoy from Canada. The U-boats

---

155 Ibid

had made their presence felt, and they were now operating in the Channel and Western Approaches, which made the work of the squadron more difficult, as they could no longer stop and examine ships to thus become a target, nor could they economise on coal by slow steaming or lying stopped. Instead, they were zigzagging and on the move continuously. When the weather conditions deteriorated, Rosy was very glad he was now on the *Euralyus*, which was very much larger, and consequently more stable, than the *Charybdis*, which had left the squadron and been sent to Bermuda. Nor did he have to transfer at sea when *Euralyus* returned to Plymouth to coal, but instead was able to transfer inside Plymouth breakwater. This gave him the opportunity to have breakfast ashore with the commander-in chief. Rosy hoped that he might have gained some of the latest news but 'he appeared to be in the same state of blissful ignorance as to the march of events as I was'.

His restricted patrol area caused him great concern, as he felt that it would be easier for submarines to find the squadron, trace their movements and sink one of the ships. When he was next in Plymouth, he went up to the Admiralty to propose an alternative plan for the patrol, to employ trawlers for the purpose rather than the cruisers. This was not accepted, but he received orders to take the squadron into Plymouth and there await further orders. After a few days, he was ordered to report to the Admiralty for a meeting with Winston Churchill, the First Lord of the Admiralty, who told Rosy that it was:

> proposed to send an expedition out to East Africa for the purpose of capturing the Königsberg which had taken refuge in the Rufiji River– the naval forces on the spot not being of sufficient strength for the purpose … it was outlined that I was to have a brigade of Marines and that the Königsberg, once captured or destroyed, a new station would be formed under my command – acting separately from the South African Station which was then under the command of my old shipmate, Rear Admiral H King-Hall and a rigorous blockade of the Coast established.[156]

Rosy returned to Plymouth in great haste, as his orders were to depart for East Africa within 24 hours, to hand over command of the squadron and to collect whatever of his belongings that he felt he would need, before returning to London. No further information had come from the Admiralty, but he was summoned to a meeting with Winston Churchill at 3 p.m. on the day after he arrived. Whilst he was at lunch with friends on that day, he was called to the telephone and

---

156 Churchill Archive WYMS 6/6

curtly informed by some unknown person at the Admiralty that the East African expedition was off.[157] My feelings can be better imagined than expressed! – No squadron, arrangements for East Africa almost complete and without a command – I repaired to the Admiralty in a towering rage ... After some delay, at last I waylaid Churchill in the passage and accompanied him to his room, and before I could open my mouth to ask for some explanation, he informed me that the project had been postponed, that it that morning had been decided to force the Dardanelles, that the island of Lemnos was to be made the base of the operations, that he wished me to proceed out there at once – the next day in fact – that I should probably be the Governor of the island– and that further orders would follow me immediately – which by the way they never did![158]

The lack of orders irritated him at the time, but when he arrived at Lemnos:

I was glad that I could consider myself a free agent, able to carry out my duties without the handicap of any limitations beyond those of my own conscience. It was a freedom for which I was to be truly grateful in the future.

Later in the afternoon, following his visit to Churchill, he developed a violent toothache, necessitating a visit to the dentist which was arranged for midnight! He left for Lemnos the next day, 17 February, accompanied by his flag captain, Mitchell, his flag lieutenant, Lieutenant Commander Bevan, and his secretary, Paymaster Lieutenant Miller, via Paris, Marseille and Malta.

---

157 An attack on the Königsberg was mounted in July 1915. She had been blockaded in the Rufiji Delta since the previous October, but could not be attacked as she was at least 10 miles upstream, out of range. Monitors, which had a shallow draft and large-calibre guns, arrived from the Mediterranean in July and on the 11th she was so severely damaged that she was scuttled by her crew. (Marcus Faulkner The Great War at Sea: A Naval Atlas 1914–19, 71)

158 Churchill Archive WYMS 6/6

13: MUDROS

During his passage to Lemnos Rosy wrote to Victoria; he had had little chance to tell her of the rapid change and pace of events before he had left:

Paquebot Caledonia, Saturday, February 20

My dearly beloved, at last I can sit down and write to my dear Pusscat and tell her how much I love her and how dreadfully sorry to leave her with the uncertainty of when we may next meet once more – if it were not for that I would be much happier in what I am doing or rather in what I hope to do, than I was in my last job. The monotony, I trust, may be a thing of the past and in front of me lies much hard work in, I believe, what may prove to be by far the most interesting sphere of this world wide war – What a crossing we had – I was awfully sick the whole way across and never was so happy as when I found myself in smooth waters in Boulogne … I was met on landing by a French naval officer who saw me safely through, for as you know I had no passport. It was raining and we found that the train did not start from the Harbour station but from the Gare Central and as no cars of any sort were procurable we had to pick up our luggage and make the best of a bad job and carry it through the mud and slush … on arrival at Paris I washed and refreshed myself at the Buffet du Nord.

Sunday a.m.

We have passed through the Strait of Messina and are arriving at Malta tomorrow morning. I hope I shall find the *Hussar*[159] or some other ship ready to take me on at once – I am impatient to get to my Kingdom.

---

159 She was a torpedo boat destroyer based at Malta.

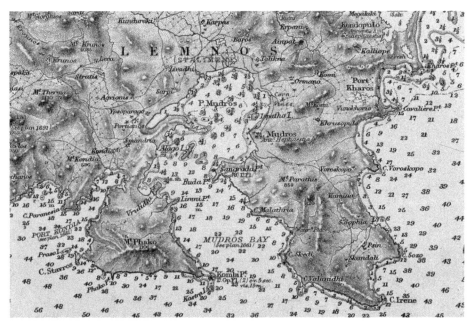

Mudros harbour from Admiralty Chart OCB 1087. UK Hydrographic Office

HMS Queen *(by permission of Glyn Evans)*

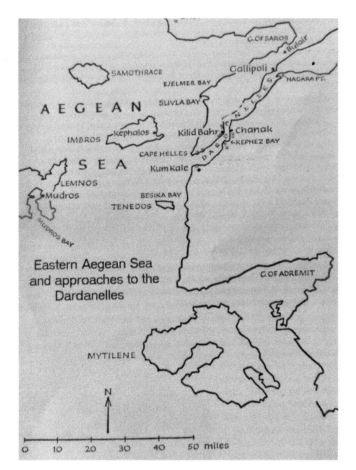

Small scale plan of Lemnos, showing Mudros harbour and the Dardanelles. (By permission of the Institute of Seamanship:Journal Vol.4, No3 September 2009)

Thursday: Lemnos

Arrived here this morning. Yesterday afternoon we got to the fleet off the Dardanelles and I saw the Vice Admiral and had a long chat with him. I shall not live on shore, but onboard the *Blenheim* – much more comfortable and much better in every way.[160]

He would not have known that the day before he started his letter, on passage from Marseilles, that the first naval attack, on four of the forts defending the Dardanelles, had taken place with a bombardment which went on from 10 a.m. until sunset. Despite the heavy fire from the 12-inch guns of the British battleships, little damage was caused as there were no direct hits on any of the guns in the forts, although their magazines had been destroyed.

---

160 Churchill Archive WYMS 6/6

During his long chat with Carden, Rosy had hoped to receive more detailed instructions. However, all he was told that he would not be the governor of the whole island, but only of the harbour and the town of Mudros – not the Kingdom he had written of in his letter – and that 10,000 troops might be expected to arrive shortly; but beyond that there was no information about any forthcoming plans for any combined operations. He therefore took up his post with only 'vague ideas of what I had to prepare for but always hopeful that I should shortly receive some further instructions'.[161]

When he arrived, the large harbour of Mudros was virtually empty, with only a dozen or so ships at anchor. He transferred himself and his staff to HMS *Blenheim*, a destroyer depot ship – but, as Rosy noted, to the disgust of her captain, who now had to find space for an admiral and his staff in the limited accommodation on board.

Rosy had visited the island of Lemnos many times in earlier years and knew it well, but had not seen it with the eyes that now viewed it when he landed on 25 November. For the operation of the port he needed piers, cranes and a supply of fresh water; none of these were available. All that Mudros had to offer was one small pier for the use of the local fishing boats, a huddle of houses and the church. For him to have authority over only the town, rather than the island was a major disadvantage, as he had to consider precautions against:

> Spies, secret agents, mischievous neutrals, babblers and adventurers of all sorts … How this was to be achieved in a harbour, the larger portion of whose shores were not under my jurisdiction, in a town whose inhabitants owed no allegiance to the English flag … was a problem difficult of solution. There was one bright spot – I had received no instructions; I would ask for none and choose my own way to salvation or damnation.[162]

Although Rosy had been appointed by London as governor, his authority, he found, was tenuous, as the island had its own government officials and he had no legal authority to administer Mudros. Greece was in theory a neutral state; if so, its neutrality was being very flagrantly violated. He did not know its attitude to the Allies, and only discovered it as the campaign progressed. In order to deal with the civic side of his duties, he acquired two more members of staff. The manager of the Eastern Telegraph Company, based in Athens, which operated the telegraph service in the wider area was sent to join him. He then acquired a secretary in the form of a civil servant from the Cyprus Civil Service, who had a wide knowledge of the local languages, manners and customs.

---

161 Lord Wester Wemyss The Navy in the Dardanelles Campaign, 19

162 Ibid, 23

On the operational side, of all the pressing problems the most urgent was to ensure the supply of fresh water sufficient for the troops that would be arriving. The Admiralty had taken the advice in the current *Mediterranean Pilot*, the Hydrographic Office pilot book, which stated that water was plentiful. There was indeed water in the hills above the town, but not in Mudros, and the time and labour required to bring the water down from the hills were not available. The problem was solved by water being carried in ships from Malta; every ship that arrived from Malta brought water in her storage tanks, which proved to be adequate for the numbers that were to arrive.

On 1 March, only a week after Rosy had arrived, General Birdwood, the commander of the Australian and New Zealand Army Corps (ANZAC) arrived at Mudros from Egypt, where his troops were encamped. From him Rosy learnt that the number of troops that might be expected was nearly 40,000, four times more than he had earlier been told. On the following day he took the general to meet Vice Admiral Carden to discuss the course of events. Following that meeting and the receipt of other information, Carden telegraphed to London that, if the weather stayed fine he could get his fleet through to Constantinople in about 14 days. Reconnaissance by minesweepers within the first 6 miles had not found any mines, and the countryside in the area around Cape Helles was deserted. However, this state of affairs did not last, as Turkish troops arrived in strength and drove off the British landing parties. The weather changed for the worse, and Turkish howitzers moved into place and were shelling the minesweepers. These ships were North Sea trawlers which had been pressed into service with their civilian crews. They had no objection to sweeping mines but they did object to being shot at, so they had to be replaced by naval personnel.

Back in Mudros, two days after the meeting with Carden the first troops arrived, in the shape of 5,000 Australians. Of these, only 1,000 landed and made a camp, the remainder staying on their transports because of the lack of water. Five days after that, a French general arrived at Mudros and informed Rosy that French troops would be arriving shortly and that he had been told that Rosy would supply them with their various requirements. This turned out to be easier than he had anticipated, as once the areas for the camp were marked out, he was not called on further.

The next contingent to arrive was the Royal Naval Division, 8,500 strong. It had been embarked in a state of confusion and haste, with the men, their stores and their equipment scattered over a number of ships. The commander of the division, Major-General Parris of the Royal Marines, had been told that his troops could be disembarked, reorganised and then re-embarked at Mudros. Rosy advised both him and the Admiralty that there were no facilities to enable this, and so the fleet of transports had to be sent to a port, such as Alexandria, with appropriate space ashore, where the necessary reorganisation could be undertaken. This underlined for Rosy that the preparations for the campaign were not being undertaken methodically; he was able to take from that the state of mind he would find necessary.

His task of organising the base continued, together with collecting with the materials needed to run a large combined military and naval operation, which also continued apace, even though limited by a lack of means and the necessary personnel. He had been able to acquire boats and lighters from Piraeus, but then found that there were no naval personnel to supervise them, and that the Greek seafarers who were hired proved to be unsatisfactory. The Greek naval officer who was in charge of the small naval party in the town accepted the British arrival, as he was in no position to oppose any changes that would be made; initially cold as to the turn of events, he soon became a very helpful ally.

Some two weeks after Rosy's arrival:

> The officer commanding the Greek Garrison at Kastro, in company with the Bishop of Lemnos, paid me an official visit. Now I felt that the success of my administration would depend very considerably upon the terms I might find myself on with these gentlemen. So after many complementary [sic] speeches on both sides, which we all three recognised as meaning nothing at all, I produced some big cigars and large glasses of brandy that I had luckily been able to obtain at Malta and with this help manage to persuade them to follow the line of conduct adopted by their naval confrere at Mudros. Before they left the ship they assured me that not only would they put no difficulties in my way, but would even render me assistance in any steps I should deem necessary to take, so long, be it understood, that they themselves were not called upon to intervene … And for an extra big glass of brandy and an extra large cigar I managed to wheedle out of the Commandant permission to take care of the guns at the mouth of the harbour, a care, I may add, I had already exercised without his permission.[163]

Naval crews had been found for some of the minesweepers, as volunteers had responded to the call to replace the civilian crews. During the night of 13 March a new attack was launched. However, once the trawlers had arrived in the minefield the enemy lit them all up and opened fire. Yet the trawlers continue to sweep until only three remained afloat. The results of their efforts could be seen when daylight came, as mines were floating down on the current; they were

---

163 Lord Wester Wemyss *The Navy in the Dardanelles Campaign*, 33

exploded with rifle fire. But as a result of the losses, minesweeping was from then on done by day, in the hope that enough mines would be cleared for the fleet to attack four or five days later.

At Mudros, Rosy was finding that not having control of the whole island was creating problems. As a result of his meeting with the commandant and the bishop a system of passes was created to restrict access to the area where the camps were located and to the town. The commandant had helped to create the system, but without much result as passes were being issued indiscriminately – and one pass was even issued, knowingly, to an enemy spy. This was just one of the issues by now fully engaging Rosy as he wrote to Victoria:

March 13, 1915

My work seems to be as all-embracing as it is perpetual. From allocating land, adjusting compensation for damages, supplying water, urging lazy people to do some work, landing armies, and organising defences down to the ordinary squadron work, nothing seems to pass me by. Telegrams pouring in in baskets full, messages by wireless telegraphy, orders from England (generally contradictory), requests from all parts of the Mediter-ranean demands for the possible and impossible from every quarter, this will give you some idea of what I had to deal with at all hours of the day and night. Merchant captains and military officers seem to vie with each other in seeing which can be the most tiresome and all the time I know that one small exhibition of temper on my part at the wrong moment may do infinite harm. So you can imagine that I sometimes have a trying time. However, it is all interesting and often amusing, and I am consoled by the presence of a delightful old Colonel of Engineers, who not only works well and quickly but sympathises with me and is as full of humour and spirits as a boy of eighteen. He has been of great assistance to me, and between us we get through a marvellous amount of work in the 24 hours. ... You would have laughed had you been able to see me today settling the dif-ferences between a voluble and excited French Colonel and a stolid and obstinate English Major, both of whom wanted to pitch tents on the same piece of ground, and neither of whom spoke or understood a word of any-thing except his own mother-tongue. Truly I felt that Solomon would have been better fitted to deal with them than I, for each one of them was as much in the right as the other, inasmuch as neither had any claims at all, and both had to be satisfied.... In a few minutes I had both settled on quite new territory each one thinking that I had just settled a dispute in his favour and what 'a damn good fellow' I was on one side and 'aimable camarade' on the other.[164]

---

164 Lord Wester Wemyss The Navy in the Dardanelles Campaign, 35

The lack of information from which Rosy had suffered was also experienced by General Hamilton, who had been appointed on 12 March to command the troops on Lemnos.

> His written instructions, received from Kitchener on the 13th were meagre and not entirely clear. (They struck one of the Dardanelles Commissioners as appearing 'like the utterances of a Delphic oracle'). This much was plain: the scope of the military operations had not been decided and Kitchener still hoped the Navy would be able to force the Straits without military help.[165]

Hamilton was provided to take with him to Lemnos a 1912 handbook on the Turkish army, a pre-war report on the Dardanelles defences and an out-of-date map.

On 15 March the plan of attack was issued, and on the same day Vice Admiral Carden resigned on health grounds. Two days later, Churchill appointed Rear Admiral de Robeck as his successor, promoting him to vice admiral.

Rosy wrote of de Robeck's promotion:

> On March 16, in response to a message from the Vice Admiral lying off Tenedos, I proceeded there in a destroyer and found him ill and obliged to give up the command. The situation thus created was a delicate one, for his departure would leave me the senior officer, since Rear Admiral de Robeck, his second in command of the squadron operating against the forts, though older and senior to me in the Service was actually my junior on the Rear Admiral list.

> Here was I, organising the base, an arduous task inevitably bound to suffer from a change of command, whilst de Robeck was in the middle of a complicated operation, in full possession of and knowing its most intricate details of which I was completely ignorant; yet surely the senior officer's place was with the squadron at the front. I discussed the situation from every point of view with him [Carden] and with Commodore Keyes, his Chief of the Staff, and eventually made up my mind that no other course was open to me except to return to Mudros to carry on my work there leaving the operations in de Robeck's hands … it is hardly necessary to state that I did not come to this conclusion without considerable heart-burning and a bitter feeling of disappointment, but I have no doubt in my mind that under the peculiar circumstances the decision was the right one to take and it had the happy result that for the remainder of the

---

165 Arthur Marder *The Dreadnought to Scapa Flow* Vol.2, 237

campaign de Robeck and I worked together with the greatest cordiality and friendship. And so I returned to Mudros, sore and disappointed I must confess, yet conscious of the correctness of my conduct.[166]

On 17 March, Rosy went to a council of war on board HMS *Queen Elizabeth*, now the flagship of de Robeck – newly created, on Rosy's suggestion, a vice admiral. General Hamilton was also there. Rosy returned to Mudros 'with a clearer conception of the military ideas than I had been yet able to get.'

Kitchener's hope that the Dardanelles would be forced by the Navy was dashed on 18 March, when a naval battle in the Dardanelles resulted in the loss of HMS *Irresistible* and *Ocean* (both battleships) and the French battleship *Bouvet*, and caused severe damage to the *Inflexible*. For the situation to progress it now required the military to be part of the operation. To that end a meeting of the admirals and generals was held on HMS *Queen Elizabeth* on 22 March, and it was decided that any combined action must be postponed until a comprehensive plan had been developed and agreed. As a result of that meeting, Rosy had, in addition to his responsibilities for the base at Mudros, been given the task of the preparation of the naval part of the combined operation. Until that plan had been agreed, Rosy's travails at Mudros continued unabated, as he wrote to Victoria:

March 22, 1915

I have had the very deuce of a time these past few days. Gales of wind that have done much damage. The transports are so helpless and their captains equally so under such circumstances – their boats get adrift etc … What I hate is the amateurs that spring up on every side … Yesterday the French wanted to haul two Italians out of a Greek steamer because they suspected them, probably rightly, of being newspaper correspondents. Imagine the complications which might have arisen. Luckily I was in time to intervene.

March 25

Truly mine is a boisterous kingdom, so far as the weather is concerned I should say, for the inhabitants seem peaceful and law-abiding enough. But the weather! An incessant gale for a week now and it has done much damage … How my heart goes out to the ancient Israelites who had to make bricks without straw! If you could imagine what the fatuous authorities seem to expect from us out here. They seem to think that because we have the use of the harbour from the Greeks and that I am here with the title of Governor and Senior Officer that they have established a base. Good

---

166 Lord Wester Wemyss The Navy in the Dardanelles Campaign, 40

God! I have *nothing*. But we struggle along and truly I am surprised at the results we obtain and lost in admiration at the resources of my people.[167]

In April the task of working out the plans for the combined operations were commencing. The complications of landing an army of 100,000 men with all their guns, stores and supplies, with a limited number of small craft and in the face of an enemy who were determined to stop them, were huge. Once Rosy's plans for all the details of the landings were completed, he also became directly involved as, in conjunction with General Hunter Western's 29th Division, commanding a division of the First Naval Squadron, he was flying his flag on the cruiser *Euralyus* (which was to remain his flagship into his next appointment) with three other cruisers, *Minerva*, *Talbot* and *Dublin*, and three fleet minesweepers.

At a subsequent meeting of the staff, a proposal was put forward by Commander Unwin, an officer on Rosy's staff, for landing men from a ship adapted for the purpose, which could be run up onto the beach; this was probably the first landing ship ever to be used. The proposal was not met by the staff with much enthusiasm, but Rosy saw the advantage that it offered; the shortage of small craft for landing men on the beach was a major problem and this idea overcame that. He therefore gave his consent and Unwin was told that he could 'take any ship I liked in the harbour and fit out as I liked to carry out my scheme'.[168] He chose *River Clyde,* a 4,000-ton cargo ship which had been chartered to the French for carrying military stores. She was released from her charter and went alongside the depot ship HMS *Reliance* to be converted for her new purpose. Unwin asked for volunteers from HMS *Hussar* to man the ship. He chose six seamen, six engine room ratings, the warrant engineer, the ship's carpenter and her surgeon. Midshipman George Drewery RNR became her second-in-command – rapid promotion for a teenager, although on a short one-way trip to a dangerous destination!

All the arrangements were in place by 19 April. Rosy hoisted his flag on *Euralyus* on that day. He noted, 'It was pleasant to be once more surrounded by officers and men whom I had grown to know so well during those weary months in the Channel and for whom I had formed so high a regard.' That morning the date for the attack was set for 23 April, and the first movements would start on 21 April. However, the weather delayed the start for 48 hours with yet another gale, so the preliminary movements started on the afternoon of 23 April. The first transport to leave headed to Tenedos to anchor, followed by *Euralyus*, *Implacable*, *Cornwallis* and *River Clyde*. As they sailed from Mudros, Rosy noted

167 Lord Wester Wemyss The Navy in the Dardanelles Campaign,46
168 Quentin Falk Mr Midshipman VC 4

the change in the harbour from when he first arrived, when he had found it virtually deserted. Now it was crowded with

> vessels of every description, men of war, hospital ships, tugs, lighters and pontoons … this heterogeneous mass of shipping would have conveyed to the uninitiated eye an impression of disorderly profusion, but was in fact one composite whole, whose every unit was an organised integral part, ready to move at a given moment to its assigned station with full knowledge of the part it had to play in the forthcoming struggle.[169]

When they arrived at Tenedos, 2,000 troops from the transports were transferred to *River Clyde*. Rosy wrote to Victoria on 23 April:

> Tonight I feel a great load off my shoulders, the hard of thinking work is over and finished and tomorrow morning I shall be fit as a lark … In the meantime my work is extraordinarily varied. I am still Governor of Mudros, where I left a locum tenens, *pro tem.*, landing or hoping to land the Army, organising supplies for the troops and besides this commanding a squadron from this ship– truly a multifarious business. It is wonderful experience but I have good fellows all around me and they all do well. We want just a little bit of luck and we shall make history.[170]

---

169 Lord Wester Wemyss The Navy in the Dardanelles Campaign, 65
170 Ibid 66

14: ADVANCE AND RETREAT

For General Hamilton, 23 April had not started well. He had boarded the *Queen Elizabeth* to be given a signal advising him that the poet Rupert Brooke had died of blood poisoning following sunstroke. His friends had carried him up into the hills of Skyros, off which the French hospital ship *Duguay-Trouin,* on which he died, was at anchor.

> We buried him the same evening in an online olive grove where he had sat with us on Tuesday – one of the loveliest places on this earth, with grey-green olives around him, one weeping above his head; the ground covered with flowering sage, blueish-grey, and smelling more delicious than any flower I know. The path up to it from the sea is narrow and difficult and very stony; it runs by the bed of a dried up torrent. We had to post men with lamps every 20 yards to guide the bearers. He was carried up from the boat by his A Company petty officers, led by his platoon-sergeant Saunders; and it was with enormous difficulty that they carried the coffin up the narrow way. The journey of a mile took two hours. It was not until 11 that I saw them coming. First came one of his men carrying a great white wooden cross with his name painted on it in black; then the firing party, commanded by Patrick; and then the coffin, followed by our officers and General Paris and one or two others of the brigade … The funeral service was very simply said by the Chaplain and after the Last Post the little lamp lit procession went once again down the narrow path to the sea.[171]

Hamilton had handed over tactical authority to his two corps commanders, so that he could be free to make such strategic decisions as might be required of him.

---

171 Quoted in Collected Poems of Rupert Brooke with a Memoir cliv

Rosy, in *Euralyus,* had arrived at Tenedos on the same day; they had weighed anchor at midnight on 24 April, and by 5:15 a.m. on the morning of 25 April were approaching the landing beaches. At that precise moment the entire fleet opened fire, continuing the bombardment until the troops were approaching the beaches in their small craft. The landings at Morto Bay, on the beaches which were designated as W and X, had been of concern to Rosy, but there were few casualties and the beaches were secured by 8:30 a.m. However, on V beach it was a different matter. The beach was gently curving, which made it easy to defend, with hills above from which fire could be directed down onto the beach from concealed positions. This was the beach on which *River Clyde*, sailing through heavy fire from the gun batteries from both the European and Asian shores of the straits, was to land her troops. She grounded at 6:30 a.m., but further out than was planned, as the beach shelved more gently than expected. Nor did the lighters on which the troops were to transfer stay in their positions alongside. So Commander Unwin, Midshipman Drewery and five others went into the water and held them in place for the troops to be transferred into them. All the while that this was going on, heavy rifle and machine-gun fire from the shore was directed onto them. After standing in water up to his chest for over an hour, it became apparent to the commander that landings from *River Clyde* would have to be suspended as the fire directed on to her was so heavy that any troops trying to cross to the lighters would have died instantly. But when darkness fell, the troops remaining on *River Clyde* were landed without further loss. After all the troops were safely ashore, Unwin and his crew then converted *River Clyde* into a pier. The landings continued against heavy resistance, and by the end of the first day, although none of the objectives had been taken, 30,000 men had successfully landed on the beaches.

However, at 11:00 p.m., General Hamilton was woken by his chief of staff. A message had come in from General Birdwood, commanding the Anzac division. When Hamilton arrived in the dining saloon of *Queen Elizabeth*, where the staff were waiting, he read Birdwood's request for permission to abandon their position; the beachhead at Gaba Tepe, where the Anzac troops had landed, was under a particularly heavy attack by Turkish troops led by Mustafa Kemal, to the extent that by nightfall the Anzacs had fallen back towards the seashore and were pinned down. Rear Admiral Thursby, who was in overall command of the landings, told Hamilton that it would take several days for an evacuation to take place. In the midst of the discussion a message came in that HM Submarine *AE2* had transited the narrows of the Dardanelles and reached the Sea of Marmara. Hamilton then replied to Birdwood:

Your news is indeed serious. But there is nothing for it but to dig yourselves right in and stick it out. It would take it least two days to re-embark you as Admiral Thursby will explain to you. Meanwhile the Australian submarine has got up through the Narrows and has torpedoed a gunboat at Chanak. Hunter-Weston despite his heavy losses will be advancing tomorrow which should divert pressure from you. Make a personal appeal to your men and Godley's, to make a supreme effort to hold their ground ... PS. You have got through the difficult business now you have only to dig, dig, dig, until you are safe.[172]

The Navy continued throughout to be fully employed, bombarding batteries which were firing on the ships, virtually all of which received direct hits, some causing some damage and fatalities. The strains on the ships were exacerbated by the numbers of men who were manning the small craft, tugs and other vessels, or ashore on beach duty, reducing the size of the crews to fight their ships.

Rosy wrote:

May 1

There has been no fighting for the last two days ... We have a pretty firm footing on the Peninsula now and it does not seem likely that the enemy will be able to turn us out.

However, soon after he wrote that:

suddenly the perfect stillness pervading until that moment was broken by a sudden roar of artillery. It was an attack by the enemy! We on board could do nothing, for there were no means by which the ships could give the troops any assistance. It was not long before the rattle of musketry and shouts and hurrahs reached us across the water proclaiming that the combatants were coming to close quarters.

Four days later he wrote to Victoria:

I wish I could give you some idea of the sight that meets the eye from the deck of this ship. In front that wonderfully inhospitable shore, gradually rising to the great peak called Achi-Baba, the goal for which we are striving, the key to the situation, which it is hoped to capture tomorrow. On the beach thousands of men making roads and piers, unloading lighters of their freights of guns, ammunition, stores, etc, the low cliffs crowned by

---

172 Quoted in Alan Moorhead Gallipoli, 155

masses of horses, mules, men, tents, hospitals – all crowded because they have to be out of the range of possible shellfire. On the right the entrance to the Dardanelles with the magnificent Asiatic mountains in the distance. To the right and left, battleships and cruisers which occasionally opened fire on points indicated from aeroplanes by wireless telegraphy. Behind us, clusters of transports, ships of all descriptions, from huge liners to the ordinary collier, and the whole surface of the sea dotted with steamboats of all descriptions, towing laden lighters to the beach and empty ones back … Today I have been busy writing despatches – one of them recommending those four fine fellows [from the *River Clyde*], Commander Unwin, Midshipmen Drewery and Allison and [Able] Seaman Samson for the VC.[173] It is a great pleasure doing so, but it is difficult to find a suitable language without being gushing.

The campaign continued and it became apparent to Rosy that as reinforcements would be arriving, which would first go to the harbour at Mudros, the base would require further expansion and he would be better employed there, so after consultation with de Robeck he returned to Lemnos, regretfully hauling down his flag on *Euralyus t*o return to his cramped quarters on *Hussar.* His next letter to Victoria starts:

Mudros May 17, 1915

the comparative quiet of this place is refreshing for during the last three weeks there has scarcely been an hour of the day or night when there has not been a booming of guns or rattle of musketry. My work of landing the Army over, I have returned here to develop the base and there is much to be done. The requirements are ever increasing, but the ways of meeting them do not augment in proportion. The Admiralty still pay but slight heed to our demands, and consequently it is the oldest story of bricks without straw … The transport business is becoming a very big affair indeed, and the wretched staff are undermanned and overworked.

May 18

We are in a curious position. Like Mahomet's coffin we seem to be suspended between two uncertainties. Whilst I am certain that this place must of necessity develop and become a huge base, the Admiralty on the contrary seem to think that nothing is required here, and that we ought to be able to carry out the work of a Portsmouth dockyard with no appliances and insufficient men. Last night was a regular gala in the

---

173 See: Stephen Snelling VCs of the First World War: The Naval VCs, 40–62

matter of news ... We hear that the resignations of Fisher and Winston Churchill are expected. We hear talk of a Coalition Cabinet. Of course that should have been formed at the beginning of the war. Evidently there are doings in the wind, but I fear it may be only a case of out of the frying pan and into the fire ... I see by your letters that the reports given out in London about the landing must have been very vague. I suppose that, as usual, the authorities wanted to make matters out to be better than they really were. The truth is, that the getting onshore at all was a magnificent feat accompanied of course by tremendous losses. The Army expected that, once onshore, they would be able to push on, and therein lies the disappointment. The original fault of course was in attacking the forts before the army was ready to be put onshore.

May 20

Two nights ago the Turks delivered a great attack on the Australians, who behaved splendidly and drove them off with great slaughter. I hear nothing but good of them. I have been so busy with matters naval lately, that I have not had time to put my foot on shore to see for myself how matters are going there. So many transports, supply ships, store ships, etc, and they all require much looking after, and I'm always suffering from a shortage of everything.[174]

Information came in two days later that enemy submarines were now active in the Mediterranean. This changed the way the transport operation could be safely continued. A submarine boom was put in place at the entrance to the harbour, and the transports and supply ships which had previously been able to lie off the beaches to offload their cargoes now had to stay within Mudros harbour; everything had to be shipped into smaller vessels, of which there was still a shortage, for onward delivery to the beaches. This of course slowed the entire landing process considerably.

The submarine threat became very real on 25 May when the battleship HMS *Triumph* was sunk by a torpedo, capsizing after only 8 minutes and sinking 30 minutes later. Two days later another battleship, HMS *Majestic*, was sunk by a *second* torpedo, both fired from *U-21* under the command of Otto Hersing.[175]

On 30 May, Admiral Fisher resigned as First Sea Lord, and Admiral Sir Henry Jackson took his place. Winston Churchill had also resigned, and his place as First Lord of the Admiralty was taken by Arthur Balfour. Both men

---

174 Lord Wester Wemyss The Navy in the Dardanelles Campaign, 132

175 It was noticeable, particularly on Majestic, that in the list of those lost were large numbers of reservists, either from the Royal Naval Reserve or the Royal Fleet Reserve; these were older men who had been called up for war service.

were of a very different stamp to their predecessors. Jackson is described by Arthur Marder as, *inter alia*, 'sensible and level headed but he lacked the three aces. He had little of his predecessor's leadership capacity, fertile imagination … and a talent for using the brains and energy of juniors'. Balfour was much less active than Churchill. Marder again: 'serenity and union were restored to the Admiralty, *but at a high price*. Balfour was, let us face it, a lethargic man. His energy was desultory; he lacked sustaining power.'[176] Rosy also noted 'I cannot enthuse over AGB as First Lord.' He was otherwise wholly concentrated on his duties at Mudros, commenting on 9 June, 'I don't know the latest ideas on the business but one thing is certain and that is, that it is going to be an extremely long job.' His working conditions were alleviated on 15 June when the depot ship HMS *Europa* arrived and Rosy and his staff transferred on board her, leaving their cramped quarters on *Hussar* with much relief. The staff now had space to carry out their ever-increasing workload much more easily. Rosy was further helped by the appointment of the former captain of the *Triumph* as his chief of staff.

As the summer progressed the heat rose. Late in June, Rosy wrote:

June 25

The weather is very hot, which perhaps helps the work to go slower and gives me much trouble to make other people keep their tempers. Not that they lose them really, but heat always magnifies molehill troubles into mountainous difficulties … I can't tell you what an extraordinary job I have fallen into. I seem to have my finger into every sort of pie that ever was baked. It is a great experience … The military staff here seem quite incapable of grasping the fact that the sea and the dry land are two different elements.[177]

As the summer progressed, the incidence of disease increased dramatically. Typhus and dysentery were rife. The latter, because of the conditions in which the troops existed, spread even more rapidly because of the flies, which were of plague proportions. It affected virtually every man in the Army, including General Hamilton himself. Reinforcements were sent out from England, following Hamilton's urgent request. Three more divisions were to be sent, and on 10 July the first detachments arrived, on board the large liner *Aquitania*, which carried 6,000 troops. Her movements had been under a cloak of so much secrecy that even Rosy was not made aware of her arrival date. As a result, she

176 Arthur Marder Dreadnought to Scapa Flow Vol.2, 298–299
177 Lord Wester Wemyss The Navy in the Dardanelles Campaign, 142

arrived off the port in the early hours of the morning, to find that the gate in the anti-submarine net was closed. She had to wait, stopped in open water, a prime target for a submarine, before the gate could be opened. The arrival of these extra troops at Mudros had required further camps and hospitals to be put up on the shores of the harbour. In addition to the fresh troops, more ships arrived, including monitors. There were also, which gave Rosy particular pleasure, motor lighters designed for transporting horses and men to the beach. They had flat bottoms and a gangway which was lowered when the lighter ran onto the beach, to allow the horses or troops to disembark. They carried up to 400 men or 40 horses at a time.

The epidemic of dysentery which had spread throughout the Army was overwhelming the medical services. It had been envisaged that field hospitals would be set up the shore on the peninsula. But this did not happen, so the hospitals which had been set up on Lemnos were filled with men evacuated from the beaches. These hospitals also became overwhelmed, and the sick were then accommodated on the hospital ships, which were in turn unable to cope. The preparations for handling the sick and wounded had been wholly inadequate. The wounded were taken off the beaches to the hospital ships; when they were full to capacity, the warships accommodated as many as they could. Boats with wounded aboard were going from ship to ship seeking a space. Empty transports were used, but they had no doctors or medical equipment on board. In August Rosy himself was affected by dysentery and could not shake off its effects. In order to regain his health, and to have a meeting with the British minister to discuss many aspects of the administration of Lemnos, he went to Athens. He was back on 30 August, after two days away, and wrote to Victoria:

> Here I am back again after a little jaunt to Athens, which besides having proved of some political benefit has done me personally all the good in the world. Change of air, change of scenery, change of personnel and a few hours of comparative civilisation have all helped to make another man of me and I have returned feeling fresher and more cheerful than I have done for some little time.[178]

By September, Mudros had grown rapidly, to cope with the numbers of ships which were using the harbour. On any one day between 150 and 200 large ships and a huge fleet of small craft, tugs, trawlers and other vessels were inside its harbour. Up to 50 ships arrived or left every day.

He wrote again on 14 September:

---

178 Lord Wester Wemyss *The Navy in the Dardanelles Campaign*, 182

> I wish I could explain to you how this place is expanding. In the last three weeks there has practically arisen a new town of about 10,000 inhabitants. Every hut and every bit of provisions has had to be landed from the store ships, for which purposes three big piers and several smaller ones have been built.[179]

In the middle of October General Hamilton was replaced by General Sir Charles Monro, who came to Gallipoli after commanding an army in France. The political situation in the Balkans was causing difficulties for the Allies as the Greek government was demanding their support to defend Salonika. On 31 October, General Munro telegraphed to London, strongly recommending the immediate evacuation of the Gallipoli peninsula and setting out all his reasons for arriving at this conclusion. At the same time, Commodore Keyes, the chief of staff to Vice Admiral de Robeck, had travelled to London with a proposal to put before the Admiralty and the War Council plans for a squadron of ships to force their way through the straits towards Constantinople. Rosy was in favour of that idea, as it accorded with his own views. However, on 4 November Kitchener telegraphed to General Birdwood, saying that the naval plan was not likely to be approved and asking him to produce a scheme for evacuation. De Robeck went on leave on 25 November; Rosy was not informed until the evening before that he would be taking over overall command, although whether on a permanent or temporary basis was not made clear.

With the enthusiastic assistance of Commodore Keyes, he then set out the plans for a naval attack, which he put to General Munro who, it became clear, had little faith in the Navy's ability to effect major progress. The case for a naval attack suffered a further, and major, blow when on 26 November a violent gale blew up, which lasted for three days and caused major damage to shore facilities and wrecked many small craft and lighters. Despite the detailed plans for the naval attack presented to him, General Monro's views were unchanged. The move towards evacuation continued and despite Rosy's own views he saw the likelihood of that happening, so he started planning accordingly, with General Birdwood, for that eventuality. On 2 December Rosy was promoted to acting vice admiral. Six days later he received a personal telegram from the Admiralty

> announcing that: 'in the face of unanimous military opinion HM Government have decided to shorten the front by evacuating Anzac and Suvla'. The blow was bitter and all the more so since the heights to which our expectations [for a naval attack] had been raised, had been great. I have no illusions about 'shortening the front'… I knew full wll that evacuation

---

179 Ibid 187

of Suvla and Anzac could only herald that of Helles, must inevitably lead to retirement from the peninsular [*sic*] and an inglorious termination of the campaign.[180]

After an exchange of telegrams with London, which failed to make any change to the decision, Rosy turned all his attention to planning for the evacuation. The plan all hinged on absolute secrecy; the aim was to evacuate the entire force, nearly 120,000 men in total, without the enemy's knowledge. This was to be undertaken in the season of winter gales. If a southerly gale had blown up it would have made a rapid evacuation impossible; piers would have been wrecked, causing the embarkation to be carried out from open beaches and with heavy losses amongst the small craft. The removal of all the guns, thousands of vehicles, animals and all the huge quantities of stores started on 10 December and lasted for eight days, until all that could be removed had been. The Allied and Turkish trenches were only 300 yards away from each other and in places were only 5 yards apart. This was the first time that such an evacuation had been planned or even attempted. Rosy wrote to the First Sea Lord, Admiral Jackson, terrified 'should the slightest hitch occur. One wretched stupid private might well cause a disaster.'[181] At that time there remained some 43,000 men, divided between the two beaches, who were to be evacuated over the next two nights, with the few guns that remained, which were needed for holding the positions in the final hours.

> The nights of the 18th/19th and the 19th/20th were fixed upon as those of the final stage. The transportation of 43,000 men within the dark hours of those two nights required the employment of an amount of shipping that strained our resources to the utmost ... I asked for and obtained the services of Admiral Fremantle's squadron ... They arrived at Mudros on the 14th and their ships' companies and boats were a welcome addition to our means. A flotilla of more than 100 motor-lighters, trawlers, steamboats and pulling boats were collected at Kephalo by the 17th, from whence they would be dispatched to the different beaches for the conveyance of the troops to the vessels destined to carry them away from the peninsula. These consisted of 14 troop carriers each holding, on an average, 1200 men, two old battleships sent from Egypt for the purpose and two light cruisers.

At 9:00 p.m. on the evening of 18 December, Rosy embarked on a destroyer

---

180 Lord Wester Wemyss *The Navy in the Dardanelles Campaign*, 224

181 Wemyss to Admiral Jackson, 15 December 1915, quoted in Arthur Marder *From the Dreadnought to Scapa Flow* Vol.2, 325

and spent the night passing up and down the coast, watching and waiting for I hardly knew what; but in truth there was little to see. All was still, not a sound was audible except an occasional burst of musketry such as might have been heard on any night of our occupation of the Peninsula … except for the movement of the transports that glided noiselessly into their positions, eased down their anchors, took on their quota of men and as silently steamed off, to be succeeded in like manner by others; there was nothing to indicate by eye or ear that there was anything unusual going on. By 5:40 a.m. the night's work was over and at dawn all traces of this silent retirement had vanished.[182]

The morning of 19 December dawned as fine as the previous morning had been, but the risks were even greater as any mistake might have alerted the enemy and caused the annihilation of the remaining troops. On the second night, Rosy embarked on the cruiser HMS *Chatham*, with General Birdwood.

> There was as little evidence of any great undertaking as there had been the night before … The transports arrived with the same silence and with the same regularity; the whole operation was carried out with the precision of a peace manoeuvre.

At 4:30 a.m. a pre-arranged signal from the beach at Anzac indicated that the last man had left the beach. At Suvla the last boat left the beach at 5:40 a.m. Rosy had estimated that the evacuation could have lost 30,000 lives; only one life was lost.

After the event a German newspaper reported:

> The English had … realised the hopelessness of the struggle in the last week of November and about the middle of December had prepared their retreat in a manner so admirable as to call forth all praise. As long as war exists that evacuation … will stand in the eyes of all students of the strategy of retreat as a masterpiece which up to now has never been attained.[183]

Rosy laid the success down to 'faultless staff work, perfect discipline, clever devices for hoodwinking the enemy, mutual confidence between officers and men, hearty cooperation between the two services and finally good fortune as regards weather.'[184]

---

182 Lord Wester Wemyss The Navy in the Dardanelles Campaign, 239

183 Vossische Zeitung 21 January 1916, quoted in Lord Wester Wemyss The Navy in the Dardanelles Campaign, 242

184 Ibid 241

He returned to Mudros on 21 December. A gale had blown up on the day immediately after the evacuation had been completed; the weather had indeed played its part when required. On his arrival he received the news that de Robeck was due to return the next day to resume command and that he, Rosy, was offered the command of the East Indies station. He was also appointed Knight Commander of the Bath for his work in the Dardanelles. He sailed for England on Christmas Eve, his part in the Dardanelles campaign over.

15: THE FINAL WORD

The whole report of the operation of the campaign in the Dardanelles was reviewed afterwards by the Dardanelles Commission, which sat in 1917. Dispatches from the various commanders of both Army and Navy formed part of the final report. Among the naval dispatches was that of Rosy, describing the evacuation which was, for the final report, received by the Admiralty on 11 April 1917, although his report was written two days before he left on leave.[185]

[HMS] Lord Nelson at Mudros 22nd December 1915

Sir,

Be pleased to lay before the Lords Commissioners of the Admiralty the following report on the operations connected with the evacuation of the positions at Suvla and Anzac.

The evacuation was carried out in three stages, as follows:-

a) A Preliminary Stage.

During this stage all personnel, animals, and vehicles not necessary for a winter campaign were removed. This necessitated no special arrangements, and was completed by the date on which definite orders to evacuate Suvla and Anzac were received.

b) An Intermediate Stage.

During this stage all personnel, guns, and animals which were not absolutely necessary for the defence of the positions in the event of an enemy attack at the last moment were removed. This also was carried out without special arrangements beyond the withdrawal of increased amounts of material each night.

---

185 Churchill Archive WYMS3/1 The Final Report of the Dardanelles Commission

c) Final Stage.

Special and detailed orders were necessary for the operations of this stage, which had to be completed in 36 hours, and which included the embarkation of all personnel remaining, and of all guns and animals not previously withdrawn.

The principle decided upon for all three stages was secrecy and the attempt to take the enemy entirely by surprise. It was hoped that he would ascribe any unusual activity, if observed, to the preparation for an attack. Every effort was therefore made during the whole of the operations to maintain the beaches, offing, etc. in their usual appearance, and all embarkations were carried out during the dark hours. The increase in the number of motor lighters, boats, etc, in use at the beaches was hidden as far as possible during the daytime. The preliminary stage was completed satisfactorily by 10 December, when the definite orders to evacuate were received.

It had been computed that 10 nights would be required for the intermediate stage, on each of which 3000 personnel and a proportion of guns and animals would be embarked from each beach. This estimate was eventually reduced, special efforts being made in order to take advantage of the fine weather, the duration of which could not be relied on at this season.

The intermediate stage was completed on the night of the 17th/18th of December and, from the absence of any unusual shelling of the beaches during these nights, it was apparent that the enemy had no idea of the movement in progress.

Some forty-four thousand personnel, nearly 200 guns, numerous wagons, and 3000 animals were evacuated during this period, together with a large amount of stores and ammunition.

The final stage commenced on the night of the 18th /19th December and was completed on the night of the 19th/20th of December. The fixing of the date for this stage had been a question of some discussion. On the one hand, it was deemed most advisable that the operation should be carried on with the utmost despatch and without loss of time for fear of the weather breaking; on the other hand, the moon on the 18th was very near its full. It was considered, however, that this fact might not altogether be a disadvantage, as the benefit accruing to us would probably counteract any advantage gained by the enemy. The weather conditions, however, proved to be ideal. An absolutely smooth sea, no wind, and a cloudy sky caused grey nights which were of the utmost benefit to the work on the beaches, and were apparently not sufficiently light to enable the enemy to get an idea of what was taking place.

On each of the two nights of the final stage it was necessary to evacuate rather more than 10,000 personnel from each beach and for this special arrangements were necessary. For the successful achievement, the possible difficulties to contend with were:- Firstly, the bad weather to be expected at this season; secondly, interference by the enemy.

After some heavy winds fine weather set in with December [*sic*], and, except for a strong north-easterly wind on the 15th continued until 24 hours after the completion of the evacuation. This prolonged period of fine weather alone made possible the success which attended the operation. It enabled light piers [to be constructed], and improvements of a temporary nature to existing piers, to be carried out. A southerly wind of even moderate force at any time during this period must have wrecked piers, and have caused very considerable losses among the small craft assembled for the operations, and would have necessitated the embarkation being carried out from the open beaches. Such loss of small craft would have made anything in the nature of rapid evacuation an impossibility, and would have enormously increased the difficulties. To cope with such an eventuality a reserve of small craft up to 50%, would not have been too great; actually the reserves maintained had to be very much smaller.

Interference by the enemy would have been most serious, as the beaches were fully exposed to shellfire, and the damage inflicted to personnel, small craft, piers, etc, might have been most serious as he would have no inducement to husband his ammunition.

Under such conditions it was most improbable that anything beyond personnel could have been evacuated. Casualties would also have been heavy and removal of wounded out of the question. To meet the latter possibility, arrangements were made to leave the hospital clearing stations intact, with a proportion of medical staff in attendance, and thus ensure that our wounded would not suffer from want of attention, which the enemy, with all the good will in the world, might have been unable to supply. It was also arranged that in such circumstances an attempt would have been made to negotiate an armistice on the morning after the evacuation to collect, and if possible, bring off our wounded. Fortunately neither of these two dangers matured, but the probability of either or both doing so made this stage of the operations most anxious for all concerned.

The final concentration of the ships and craft required at Kephalo was completed on 17 December, and in order to prevent enemy aircraft observing the unusual quantity of shipping, a constant air patrol was maintained to keep these at a distance.

Reports of the presence of enemy submarines also were received during these two days: patrols were strengthened but no attacks by these craft were made.

The evacuation was carried out in accordance with orders. No delays occurred, and there were no accidents to ships or boats.

On the night of the 18th/19th of December when I embarked in HMS *Arno*, accompanied by General Sir William Birdwood, the embarkation was finished in Suvla by 3 a.m. and at Anzac by 5:30 a.m., and by daylight the beaches and anchorages at these places had resumed their normal aspect.

The second night's operations, as far as the Navy was concerned, differed in no wise from the first; precisely the same routine being adhered to. The weather conditions were similar and could not have suited our purpose better. On this night I hoisted my flag in HMS *Chatham* and was accompanied by General Sir William Birdwood and members of out two Staffs.

The last troops left the front trenches at 1:30 a.m. and I received a signal that the evacuation was complete at 4:15 a.m. at Anzac and 5:39 a.m. at Suvla.

A large mine was exploded at about 3:15 a.m. by the Australians and at Suvla all perishable stores which had not been taken off and which were heaped up in large mounds with petrol poured over them, were fired at 4 a.m., making a vast bonfire which lighted everything around for a very long distance.

In spite of all this, the enemy seemed perfectly unaware of what had taken place. As day dawned, soon after 0630, the anchorages of both places were clear of all craft, except the covering squadrons, which had been boarded up during the night. When the sun had sufficiently risen for objects to be made out, the bombardment of the beaches commenced with the object of destroying everything that remained. At Suvla this consisted only of some water tanks and four motor lighters, which, I regret to say, had been washed ashore in the gale of 28th of November and had never been recovered, owing principally to lack of time. At Anzac it had been deemed inadvisable to set light to the stores which had been found impossible to embark, so that here the bombardment was more severe and large fires were started by bursting shells.

A curious spectacle now presented itself, certain areas absolutely clear of troops being subjected to a heavy shell fire from our own and the enemy's guns.

It seems incredible that all this work had taken place without the enemy becoming aware of our object, for although the utmost care was taken to preserve the beaches and offing as near as possible normal, yet it proved quite impracticable to get up boats and troop carriers in sufficient time to carry out the night's work, and yet for them not to have been visible from some parts of the Peninsula.

The morning bombardment lasted but a very short time, for I felt that the use of much ammunition would merely be a waste; moreover, the risk of the submarines appearing on the scene of action had never been absent from my mind at any time during the whole operation. Consequently, at 7:25 a.m., I ordered the squadron to return to Kephalo, leaving two specially protected cruisers to watch the area. These subsequently reported that they had caused a good deal of damage amongst the enemy when they eventually swarmed down to take possession of the loot, the realisation of which, I trust, was a great disappointment to them.

All the arrangements were most admirably carried out, and the timetable previously laid down was adhered to exactly.

Before closing this dispatch, I would like to emphasise the fact that what made this operation so successful, apart from the kindness of the weather and of the enemy, was the hearty cooperation of both services. The evacuation forms an excellent example of the cordial manner in which the Navy and Army have worked together during these last eight months.

For the Army the evacuation was in operation of great probable danger, shared by the Naval Beach personnel; it was also, especially for the former, one of considerable sadness. Throughout the whole proceedings and nothing could have exceeded the courtesy of Generals Sir William Birdwood, Sir Julian Byng and Sir Alexander Godley, and their respective Staffs, and this attitude was typical of the whole Army. The traditions of the Navy were fully maintained, the seamanship and resource displayed reaching a very high standard. From the Commanding Officers of men-of-war, transports, and large supply ships, to the Midshipmen in charge of steamboats and pulling boats off the beaches, all did well.

I am, Sir,

Your obedient Servant,

R E WEMYSS

16: EAST INDIES AND EGYPT STATION

Rosy sailed from Mudros to Marseilles with his staff, before taking the train from there to Paris, where he was joined by Victoria before proceeding to London. He received a very warm welcome when he arrived: he had already been awarded the KCB, and Asquith had mentioned him in the House of Commons in very warm terms. From London he travelled to Sandringham so that the King could invest him with his knighthood. On his return to London, in preparation for his new appointment as Commander-in-Chief of the East Indies station, he attended many meetings to brief him on the area, including with Mark Sykes, who he was to encounter in the Red Sea, and with Aubrey Herbert, who later was to join his staff. He left London on 8 January, with Victoria and his staff, stopping in Paris for two days for meetings with the directors of the Suez Canal Company. They then travelled on to Rome, where Victoria left to return to Switzerland, and Rosy and his staff travelled on to Malta, there raising his flag again in HMS *Euralyus,* which had been his flagship at the Dardanelles. She sailed for Port Said on 20 January, where the headquarters was established.

The area covered by his command stretched east to Singapore, including all waters and coasts in between. The Suez Canal was the most strategically important part of his command because of its proximity to the Ottoman Empire, which had joined Germany on 31 October 1914 in declaring war on the Allies. An attack on the canal in February 1915 by a force of 25,000 Turkish troops, with artillery support, had been stopped at the very edge of the canal – indeed, a small number of Turkish troops had managed to cross the canal but were repulsed by Indian troops from the 62nd Punjabis, with fixed bayonets.[186]

In addition to the threat from east of the canal, a further threat came from the Western Desert, where the Moslem Senussi tribesmen, who were very pro-Turkish, had declared war on Egypt.

---

186 John Johnson-Allen T E Lawrence and the Rea Sea Patrol, 39

With Rosy's arrival, the captain of one of the cruisers, William Boyle, who had been appointed in the autumn of 1915, was now to find a marked difference in the way the East Indies station was to be commanded. On his appointment in September, the commander-in chief was Vice Admiral Sir Richard Peirce, who had been in command since before the outbreak of the war. Boyle, who had left the post of naval attaché in Rome in order to have active service at sea, visited the admiral on being appointed:

> Thirsting for action as I was, it was a shock to be told that his policy was to do everything that the Army asked him to do but not to take the initiative in any way. I was warned that as I was going down the Red Sea I was to remember this and act accordingly.[187]

Boyle's ship, HMS *Fox*, was, when he arrived in Port Said, recommissioning and awaiting the arrival of her new crew, so he had to wait some days before joining her. She was an elderly cruiser, and Boyle, not altogether delighted with his new command, commented that she was 'almost the slowest and oldest ship commanded by a Captain in the Royal Navy'.

The objective of Rosy's role as commander-in-chief were to secure Egypt, the Red Sea and the Suez Canal, to project maritime power in the Red Sea littoral in support of the Arab Revolt, and in particular to wear down the forces of the Turks, and to promote Britain's image as a friend of the Islamic peoples within and without the British Empire. To do this, he had a motley collection of ships: two old cruisers, three sloops and some armed merchantmen including three Indian Marine troopships. The overall number of ships he could muster was twelve, but six were normally in continuous employment, with the remainder – for example, three seaplane carriers which had been converted from merchant ships – being called on as required.

When Rosy arrived in Port Said on 23 January, a week before Peirce was due to relinquish his command, he noted in a letter to Victoria:

> I have been looking over matters and find there is much that does not suit my views at all. It's a nuisance because I hate having to change things immediately that I assume control. Some people seem to have gone to sleep here ... It's all very interesting and I foresee lots of hard work though I am afraid there are some people who will not appreciate the change ... As soon as ever he [Peirce] has gone I am off for a little tour of inspection at the Canal and to Alexandria and possibly Cairo. All interesting and amusing.

---

187 Admiral of the Fleet the Earl of Cork and Orrery My Naval Life, 95

January 29, British residency, Cairo

I have been having a real [*sic*] strenuous week since coming here. I found things in an awful muddle and chaos reigns complete.[188]

He did not waste time but started to untangle the chaos, which was made more difficult as he needed to sort out not only the naval problems but also those involving the Indian and Egyptian governments, which had become entangled in naval affairs. He had for his use a yacht provided by the Suez Canal Company, whose staff had proved to be very helpful, in order to go up and down the canal. He had decided that rather than stay in Port Said, he would make his headquarters in Ismailia, a pleasant town on the shores of the Bitter Lakes, and the headquarters of the Suez Canal Company. He transferred his office there from on board *Euralyus,* which travelled down the canal and anchored in Lake Timsah, a convenient place from which to be able to reach Cairo, Port Said, Suez and Alexandria. He was pleased with his decision to move to Ismailia, as he considered it

A perfect paradise compared to Port Said. Quite pretty it is with lots of trees and flowers, – a sort of tiny independent republic belonging to the Canal Company. Everybody very nice and kind. I have a motor car belonging to King George V and horses belonging to the Army.[189]

His changes and reforms were taking place and the organisation was now running more smoothly. However, he noted:

I find I have to use the greatest tact and care in interfering with all these people. However, up till now I have succeeded in keeping them all in good humour and yet have egged them on. There exists a naval mentality which thinks that anything beyond the handling of a ship or a naval gun is either a purely diplomatic or a purely military question. I, on the contrary, butt in everywhere for my faith is that everything English must have a naval side.[190]

An anomaly that was in place when Rosy assumed his command was the political division of responsibility for the Red Sea. The northern part, from latitude 21° North, was controlled by the Cairo government: south of that latitude control was by the Indian government through its officers in Aden. As

---

188 Lady Wester Wemyss Life and Letters, 259

189 Lady Wester Wemyss Life and Letters, 262

190 Ibid 267

a result, the Red Sea Patrol operated in two separate parts, each with differing regulations, particularly with regard to the interdiction of coastal shipping. The differences were not understood by the crews of the dhows who were not conscious of what was to them an arbitrary line. This political divide resulted in 'maximum expenditure for minimum result'. Rosy therefore went to Aden, in his flagship *Euralyus*, to head a conference to address this anomaly and to reorganise the patrol into a single unit with Captain Boyle as the senior naval officer.

From Aden he steamed east, to Muscat and then on to the Persian Gulf, whose strategic importance he was a very well aware of, particularly as the supplies of oil for the British Fleet came from the Anglo-Persian Oil Company refinery at Abadan, at the mouth of the Shatt-el-Arab, at the head of the Persian Gulf.

The campaign in Mesopotamia was in severe difficulties as the advance towards Baghdad had proceeded well until the end of September 1915, but had been halted in November by a superior Turkish force at Ctesiphon, only 25 miles from Baghdad, causing the British forces to retreat to Kut-al-Amara. They were surrounded by Turkish troops there and were cut off, under siege. Unsuccessful attempts to relieve Kut had been made as the siege progressed. General Charles Townshend, in command of the forces in Kut, had stated that if they were not relieved by 12 April they would have to surrender.

On Rosy's arrival in the port of Bushire, he had to transfer to a smaller vessel to go up the river to Basra. He then joined a small shallow-draught naval gunboat, HMS *Snakefly*, one of a class of specially built gunboats which had been built in England and then shipped out in parts, to be reconstructed for service on the Mesopotamian rivers. She took him up the Tigris to the headquarters of the Mesopotamian forces. Before Rosy arrived there, the possibility of revictualling Kut had been considered, to allow a further period for the Army to break through and relieve the siege. He was therefore asked if the Navy could try and break the blockade. The likelihood of success seemed very small: there was a strong current running down the Tigris, against which any ship would have to fight, reducing its speed; both banks had gun batteries which would bring down heavy fire on any passing ship; and lastly it was believed that a heavy chain had been laid across the river to prevent such an attempt. However, despite all this Rosy was persuaded to agree to the mission. The official report records the events of that evening of 24 April, on which Easter Monday fell that year.

> The Turks knew that the attempt was going to be made, and their outposts on the bank soon reported that a steamer was passing their positions.

Rifle fire was soon opened up on her, but Lieutenant Firman held on steadily at 6 knots over the bottom: owing to the strong current he could do no more. At Aanniayat the rifle fire became extraordinarily heavy; but the *Julnar* was taken past it and negotiated round all the bends as far as the Es Sinn position, only 10 miles from Kut. Here she came under artillery fire for the first time; and it increased steadily as she passed along the reach of the river between Es Sinn trenches and the Maqasis. Some moments before she reached the Maqasis bend, a shell struck the bridge. Lieutenant Firman fell dead, thinking doubtless that success was in sight, for the *Julnar* was then within about 8 miles of the town. Lieutenant Commander Cowley, though wounded by the same shell, now took charge. In a few more minutes the *Julnar* struck a cable which had been stretched across the river at Maqasis, and drifted onto the right bank of the river near the Fort. She could not be got off and Lieutenant Commander Cowley surrendered. The Turks harboured nothing but a desire for vengeance against an officer who had shown such dauntless courage. Sometime after they had carried off their prisoners, the Turks separated Lieutenant Commander Cowley from his men, and he was never heard of again; but there are strong grounds to believe that he was shot by his captors in cold blood.[191]

Both the commanding officer of the *Julnar*, Lieutenant Firman RN and Lieutenant Commander Cowley RNR (who had a detailed knowledge of the river, through his pre-war employment with Lynch Brothers who ran a fleet of river steamers on the Tigris and the Euphrates) were awarded posthumous VCs for their part in the operation, as it emerged that Cowley had indeed been shot by the Turks the next day.

Rosy remained in Mesopotamia for two more weeks. Most of the time he spent on board the small naval gunboats, in significant discomfort which he accepted cheerfully, all but the flies. He remarked: 'But the flies! They are absolutely in sheets and curtains!' By a happy chance on one of the gunboats he discovered that one of the crew was from East Wemyss, close to Wemyss Castle, and had a long conversation with him; he also noticed on the riverbank on one occasion a piper from the Seaforth Highlanders, who, he discovered came from Kirkcaldy, also close to Wemyss Castle.

The fall of Kut and the conditions that the troops were experiencing in Mesopotamia, including the complete inadequacy of any medical care, caused Rosy great distress. The conditions were the result of the lack of necessary funds coming from the Indian government, which had provided the troops for the

---

191 The Official History of the War, Naval Operations Vol.4, 90, quoted in Lady Wester Wemyss Life and Letters, 292. Also see: Stephen Snelling, VCs of the First World War, the Naval VCs, 98–110

campaign. So Rosy planned, on his arrival at Bombay, the next port on his tour, to travel to Simla to speak directly to the viceroy to make the situation in Mesopotamia clear and put the case for more support for the campaign. However, before he arrived at Bombay, he had to deal with matters in Basra and visit some of the small ports in the Persian Gulf, to visit the ruling sheikhs to show the flag and assure them of British support. In Bombay he received news of the Battle of Jutland, followed by the news of the loss of HMS *Hampshire*, which had on board Kitchener and his staff, who were all lost in the tragedy.

After his arrival he travelled, as he had intended, to Simla to speak to the viceroy about Mesopotamia. From Bombay he sailed on to Colombo, and then to Penang for a meeting with the commander-in-chief of the China station, before returning to Colombo, to stay at Admiralty House in Trincomalee, intending to spend the summer there, thus escaping the heat of the Red Sea. However, on 9 July he received a telegram from the Admiralty which gave him the news of the start of the Arab Revolt and of an impending attack by Turkish forces on the Suez Canal; the latter were successfully defeated in the Battle of Romani, with 2,000 Turkish troops taken prisoner and the Turks pushed 30 miles back from the canal. Exactly a month before he received the telegram advising him of the Arab Revolt, two of the ships of the Red Sea Patrol, HMSs *Fox* and *Hardinge*, which were anchored off Jeddah, switched on their searchlights after sunset to illuminate the town and opened fire with their main armament: 6-inch guns on *Fox* and 4.7-inch on *Hardinge*. The Turks had anticipated an attack and had prepared defences against such an event. However, even if some of the Turkish forces may have experienced searchlights and naval gunfire, the effect on most of them, and on almost the complete majority of the Arab population, on being lit up by searchlights from the sea and then being shell from heavy naval artillery offshore would have been akin to the 'shock and awe' attacks on Baghdad in the next century. The bombardment continued for four days, with two more ships of the Red Sea Patrol arriving to add to the weight of shells landing on the town, culminating in the arrival of a seaplane carrier, HMS *Ben-my-Chree*, a converted Isle of Man ferry. The attack by her aircraft caused the white flag to be raised very soon afterwards.

In September the annual ceremony of the presentation of the Holy Carpet, the pilgrimage from Cairo to Mecca, which had not taken place the previous year as the Turks were occupying Mecca, took place. Rosy travelled to Cairo to witness the celebrations surrounding its departure to Suez:

> The ceremony took place on a huge parade ground on one side of which is a sort of Pavilion with one side entirely open. In the Pavilion

was a chair for the Sultan and on each side were arranged his High Officers and various Sheiks and Holy Men, many of whom were to do the pilgrimage. On the ground were paraded a lot of Egyptian troops, extremely smart, and soon after our arrival the Sultan drove up in state. The whole turnout was really beautiful. He himself was in the very large State Barouche, drawn by four beautiful bay horses. State harness and

Portion of Holy Carpet presented to Rosy in 1917 (author's collection)

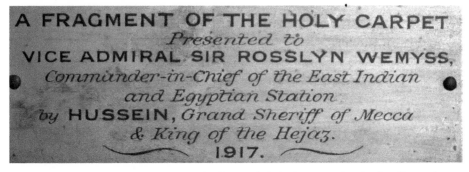

Presentation plaque attached to the frame of the holy carpet (author's collection)

The Holy Carpet leaving Cairo in 1917 (Churchill Archive)

State liveries all very much like the London ones, only of course the servants wore fezzes instead of cocked hats. The escort of Lancers was really superb, and I have never seen anything better turned out than the whole thing. On his arrival, after having warmly greeted all of us, he proceeded to his chair and then from behind the line of troops there appeared a string of camels. The leading one had on his back a very fine Howdah, all red with gold decorations and texts from the Koran. Inside of this was supposed (I say supposed because I believe it really wasn't there) to be the Carpet. This camel was followed by half a dozen others also with many trappings not less gorgeous than those of the former, and on each was a Bedouin who was playing on a reed instrument the music of which was at first quite inaudible. I naturally expected that they were producing Arab tom-tom music; imagine therefore my surprise went on the close approach, I recognise the Egyptian National Hymn! These camels, escorted by horse and foot police all turned out spick and span, proceeded solemnly to perambulate the parade ground three times, at the end of which they stopped at the steps of the Pavilion. The Sultan then came down to them, and the tassel at the end of the halter of the Carpet Camel was handed to him and he proceeded to kiss it and press it to his forehead and eyes; one or two other high dignitaries did the same and the ceremony was over.[192]

---

192 Lady Wester Wemyss Life and Letters, 328; contemporary film of the ceremony can be seen on IWM held films of the Mahmal, which can be found by online search.

The Holy Carpet was then taken to Suez, where it was to be taken on board HMS *Hardinge*, for the passage to Jeddah. The Egyptian troops, commanded by a brigadier, also accompanied by a white camel, formed its escort. Rosy followed, on board *Euralyus* two days later, arriving in Jeddah on 26 September, only a few hours after *Hardinge*.

On his return to Ismailia he had received many letters, a considerable number from friends and colleagues who had been on board ships involved in the Battle of Jutland, writing of their experiences in that major conflict. He also received a letter from Captain Rupert Gwatkin-Williams, who had written to him from the hospital in Alexandria, of the recovery of him and his crew following their privations in the Western Desert following the sinking of their ship.

At the outbreak of war, Captain Gwatkin-Williams had been recalled from retirement and given the command of HMS *Tara*, a former Isle of Man ferry which had been conscripted for naval service. She had been armed with three small elderly guns; her Merchant Service crew had been retained, signing T124 articles to serve under Naval terms of engagement, including the Naval Discipline Act. As a ferry, she had a good top speed, but this was reduced by the need to carry more coal than in peacetime, to extend her operating range: in addition to her normal coal bunkers, her holds were filled with 500 tons of coal. The Navy provided a signalman and three naval gunners. After initially spending a year patrolling in the Irish Sea, she was ordered to proceed to Alexandria. When she arrived in October 1915, she became part of the North Egyptian Coast Patrol. On 5 November of that year, only some two

The Egyptian Brigadier boarding HMS Euralyus *at Jeddah (Churchill Archive)*

weeks after her arrival, she was on an uneventful passage to Sollum, a small port which held a garrison of Egyptian troops under the command of a British officer, Colonel Snow. But her peaceful progress ceased at 10:10 a.m., when she was torpedoed. Captain Gwatkin-Williams had ordered all the lifeboats to be launched as soon as the torpedo track was seen. This enabled the majority of the crew to take to the boats; as the *Tara* sank in under ten minutes this saved a great many lives. Twelve of the crew were lost, but there were 92 survivors, most of whom were in the three lifeboats, which then picked up those who were in the water. The U-boat surfaced and took the lifeboats in tow – not as hoped to Sollum, but to Port Bardia which, unbeknown to the British, was being used as a base by German U-boats. The crew's march into the desert started two days after their arrival. In the haste of abandoning ship, many of the crew were barefoot. Fortunately, the first leg of their journey was short, although the conditions underfoot caused great pain to the barefoot walkers, stopping after a day's march at a camp, where they remained for a week. Whilst there, they were provided with Arab clothing and felt slippers. From there the march continued in earnest, until they arrived on 24 November at their final destination. Throughout their march they had been guarded by Senussi tribesmen under the command of a Turkish officer. Their destination was an oasis, which had a supply of water. It was called Bir Hakkim Abbyat, or 'White Doctor', after the colour of the mound which concealed the well. They were to stay there in captivity for four months in conditions of extreme privation, living off rice, occasional small amounts of goat meat and the local snails which were picked off the ground. The rations provided by their captors, issued weekly for 92 men, comprised three sacks of rice and one of barley flour, with an ounce of goat meat per head on alternate days. It was a particularly dry winter; such rain as did fall, less than 2 inches, fell before 7 January 1916, after which there was no more. After a further month, the rice ration had reduced and the prisoners were falling ill from malnutrition; 12 March 'was our last Sunday; we all felt the end was very near. The spectre of death stared us in the face.'[193]

On the following Friday, 17 March, their ordeal came to an end, when British armoured cars under the command of the Duke of Westminster found their encampment after an extensive search. Amongst the 43 vehicles was a Red Cross ambulance which had supplies of food on which the prisoners gorged themselves. As the armoured cars arrived, the guards ran off but were pursued and shot. The surviving crew (there had been some deaths whilst they were in captivity) of the *Tara* were taken back to Sollum, and thence by sea to Alexandria, arriving two days later. In his letter to Rosy, Captain Gwatkin-Williams wrote

---

193 R.S Gwatkin-Williams Prisoners of the Red Desert, 247

I am making a map of our wanderings. The latter was rather difficult as I had neither map, compass nor watch and all my estimated distances and directions were simply from observing the sun and stars and judging from them and my recollection of the coastline the amount we had really made good.[194]

After *Euralyus* had arrived in Jedda, on the following morning Rosy went ashore for an official welcome from the leading men of the town. In addition Sherif Hussein, the self-styled 'King of the Arabs', in a telephone conversation from his residence in Mecca, invited him to a banquet (which, Rosy confidentially reported, 'I was fortunately unable to accept') and sent by special messenger a basket of fruit from his garden in Mecca. In return,

I took the occasion to mark with all the pump and ceremony which was at my disposal the landing of the Holy Carpet at Jeddah. This was a question which I had much debated with myself as it had been hinted to me that the Muslim population would not be particularly pleased that so much circumstance was being given to it by Christians; but I now know that the contrary is the case and that the inhabitants of Jeddah and all the Pilgrims who are assembled there are much gratified at the honours paid to it.

The Escort of the Holy Carpet consisted of picked Egyptian troops and was commanded by an Egyptian Brigadier-General. We exchanged visits of courtesy and when he arrived on board, his Pilgrim's costume consisting only of a somewhat scanty bath sheet loosely wrapped around his person and kept together by a 'Sam-Browne' belt, I noticed that the guard of honour drawn up to receive him had some difficulty in keeping their countenances. On my returning his visit the situation was reversed. Myself in uniform I was confronted by a guard and band habited in Pilgrim attire. And it was I who now had the difficulty in keeping my countenance by the bandmaster who was struggling to prevent his unaccustomed draperies from interfering with his duties of conducting.[195]

Signed photograph of Emir Husein (Churchill Archive)

194 Churchill Archive WYMS 4/4
195 Ibid WYMS 4/1

Following his visit to Jeddah, he went to Rabegh, a port further up the Red Sea coast, on board HMS *Dufferin,* one of the former Royal Indian Marine ships, to meet Sherif Ali, Hussein's eldest son, to discuss with him the progress of the Arab Revolt, and Arab cooperation with the captains of the ships of the Red Sea Patrol. The revolt was being kept afloat by the monies provided by the British government. In addition to a very substantial sum provided at the outset of the revolt, a payment of £150,000 per month was paid initially, increasing in steps as the Red Sea ports fell to the Arabs, to culminate in £200,000 a month after Aqaba was taken in July 1917. By 1 October he was on his way back to Ismailia, writing to Victoria that he was planning to return to Jeddah the next month and from there visit Khartoum to visit the Sirdar of the Sudan, Sir Reginald Wingate. After a tour of inspection of the Mediterranean coast of Egypt in his yacht, *North Star,* he arrived back at Jeddah on board *Euralyus* at the beginning of November. On 4 October she sailed from Jeddah to Port Sudan. On board was T E Lawrence, then only a captain, who had asked Rosy if he could take passage across the Red Sea. Lawrence commented, in *Seven Pillars of Wisdom,* of Rosy:

> He had taken the greatest interest in the Arab Revolt from the beginning … He had given the Arabs guns and machine guns, and landing parties and technical help and unlimited transport, and naval cooperation, always making a pleasure of our requests and fulfilling them in overflowing measure. Had it not been for his goodwill and the admirable way in which Captain Boyle gave effect to it, the jealousy of Sir Archibald Murray would have wrecked the rebellion at its start. As it was Sir Rosslyn Wemyss acted godfather till the Arabs were on their feet.[196]

On 6 November, Rosy wrote to Victoria from the Palace at Khartoum, Sir Reginald's official residence:

> The Sirdar is more than kind – A special train with his own private saloon, with every comfort and luxury was placed at my disposal and I travelled here in great comfort. The heat is not very great and if it were the various electric fans, bathrooms etc with which the train is fitted would have made it quite supportable.

He goes on to describe his arrival in Khartoum:

> I was received with tremendous pomp – a guard of 100 men, a band, many officers and the Sirdar and his staff – the streets were lined with troops and

---

196 T E Lawrence Seven Pillars of Wisdom, 98

police and we were escorted from the station to the Palace by a splendid escort of Lancers mounted on white horses.

After his meeting in Khartoum he returned to Port Sudan by train and immediately went back to Jeddah for meetings with officers there, to advise them of changes in policy resulting from his meeting with Wingate. His letter continued:

> [I] am now on my way back to Egypt. I have received a most interesting souvenir from the Sherif or rather King of the Arabs as he now styles himself, in the shape of a piece of last year's Holy Carpet – about 1 yard square. It really is a curiosity – and I don't suppose any other Christians beside the Sirdar and myself have such a thing – on the arrival of the new carpet every year the old one becomes the property of the Sherif, who usually sells pieces of it to devout and rich pilgrims for fabulous sums and these pieces are treasured by their owners as the most sacred of sacred relics. He also presented me with an Arab headdress.[197]

Following his meeting with Wingate, the latter wrote to him at the end of November:

> I am very grateful for all you are doing to help matters in the Hejaz. There, as elsewhere in the world, the splendid work of the Navy and their readiness to cooperate for the general good is one of the few wholly satisfactory features. What we should have done without your assistance and practical advice I really don't know.[198]

Also at the end of November, news reached him of the resignation of the First Sea Lord, Admiral Sir Henry Jackson, who was replaced by Sir John Jellicoe, who had been the Commander-in-Chief of the Grand Fleet at the Battle of Jutland. The resignation of Jackson in the reports that had reached Rosy suggested to him that this was an anti-Admiralty intrigue by the Harmsworth Press.

He was sorry to see Jackson leave, but

> If it is beneficial to accept a change at all, I'm glad to think that one can accept Jellicoe's appointment with satisfaction and faith. I have no doubt that Jackson himself, being perfectly free of any personal ambition will not be sorry to give up.[199]

---

197 Churchill Archive WYMS7/11/3

198 Churchill Archives WYMS 4/3

199 Lady Wester Wemyss Life and Letters, 341

Jackson was indeed not sorry: Rosy received a letter from him in which he said that he was perfectly delighted to get away from the Admiralty. He had become 'heartily sick' of the politics, and had offered to resign two months before.

On Christmas Day 1916 Rosy wrote to Victoria:

> I can't tell you what a depressing effect Christmas has on me when I am away from the bosom of my family. The feeling of 'one ought to be jolly; let us attempt to be' which pervades all men at this time, quite irrespective of their surroundings, touches the wrong nerve, and so far from feeling sympathetic makes me feel irritated. ... I have just had the General round to see me to wish me a Merry Christmas! The farce of it all! How can any thinking responsible being have a Merry Christmas! As for the New Year I can only pray for a happier Year for all of us. The greatest blessing it can bring is Peace. Is it too optimistic to hope that it will do so? I do not think it. I believe 1917 will see the end of this horror and surely any other must be but small in comparison. If it was not the hope, life would indeed be a blank.[200]

His hopes of peace were not realised but 1917 did hold great changes for Rosy.

---

200 Lady Wester Wemyss Life and Letters, 341

17: ISMAILIA TO WHITEHALL

Early in January *Euralyus* went for a refit, so Rosy and his staff moved to a villa in Ismailia, which gave him more space to spread out: 'All my tables get covered with papers and my walls with maps.'

By the middle of the month he was once again on board *North Star*, and by 21 January she was at anchor off Hassani Island, in the north of the Red Sea, for the attack on Wejh. He wrote that he was working 'in conjunction with the Arabs, really an extra ordinary affair. I have four ships here and some seaplanes and I have embarked some 2000 Arabs'. This latter figure is doubtful, as Boyle noted that *Hardinge* had carried 400 troops to Wejh; T E Lawrence in *Seven Pillars of Wisdom* stated that '550 Arabs, judged to be of indifferent quality were to be put on *Hardinge*'. It may be that Rosy had conflated the Arab force that was approaching by land from the south, accompanied by Lawrence, with the troops on *Hardinge*. Rosy noted that the 'main army' were late arriving. The 'indifferent quality' of the troops which were transported on *Hardinge* became apparent. These troops were supported by a naval brigade which was to be used

Emir Feisal (on right), in desert (Churchill Archive)

as a stiffening force and to allow the Arabs to have the credit of actually taking the town. This did not work however, as only about 200 followed Major Vickery and Captain Bray, two British officers leading them and of those over 100 broke off and looted the first houses they got to: they found the houses packed with fair booty and made a sweep of it. The remainder of the Arab force sat on the beach and refused to budge. The following morning at dawn the landing party advanced and occupied Wejh, but the bulk of the enemy force had got away during the night and only slight resistance was offered. Some eighty prisoners were taken with the town. The Arab army came up the next day, having been delayed by water difficulties, which a ship had to be sent down the coast to rectify.[201]

Lawrence commented: 'The capture of Wejh, which had been a foregone conclusion when once the Navy should itself be so willing to help, gave us what we wanted.'

The situation in Egypt at the start of 1917 was very different to that when Rosy took command of the East Indies station. Then, the objective was warding off a Turkish attack on the canal; 12 months in Egypt was a base of operations against the Ottoman Empire. Rosy's part in this had been great; as a result of the naval activities in the Red Sea the prestige of the Navy was very high. By the end of April he was able to write:

> April 29
>
> The political situation with regard to Arabia, Hejaz, Mesopotamia and Palestine is rapidly developing, And I think on the whole favourably for us, though in the final settlement I am inclined to think there will be clauses not entirely agreeable. But the situation is so complicated and there are so many people mixed up with it that compromises must be used.[202]

His involvement in the political situation deepened when he sailed on HMS *Northbrook*, also one of the Royal Indian Marine ships, calling at Wejh to collect Sherif Feisal, son of Emir Hussein, to take him to Jeddah. On board he also had Mark Sykes, a diplomat with a special interest in Arabian affairs, and a French diplomat, Monsieur Georges-Picot. Of the latter, Rosy commented

> I have on board with me Mark Sykes and a Monsieur Picot, a French diplomat, who I think is one of the nicest men I have met for a very long time. He is a real gentleman, very pro-English and very open hearted,

201 'Naval Operations in the Red Sea 1916–17' Naval Review Vol.13, No.4 1925, 659
202 Lady Wester Wemyss Life and Letters, 352

loyal to the Entente Cordiale. He and Mark Sykes are working together politically – a combination from which I should hope the very best results should be looked for. They wanted to visit Jeddah so as I was also directing my steps in that direction I offered to take them with me, an offer which, of course, they gladly availed themselves.[203]

His opinion of Picot was not shared with other British officials, who found that he had 'a fluting voice' and a condescending manner. Major Edward Cadogan had come into regular contact with him and commented that

> He was a tiresome individual who, as so many of his race, was very anxious that the French should have as much kudos and incidentally as much territory in the Middle East as he could claim.[204]

On arrival at Jeddah, Rosy had a meeting with Emir Hussein, who he described as being a 'nice old man, with a twinkle in his eye' (this opinion was not shared by T E Lawrence, who had many dealings with him). During their time on board, it is more than likely that Sykes and Picot discussed the division of Arabia into French and British spheres of interest, which would become the Sykes–Picot Line and affect Middle Eastern policy into this century. From Jedda, Rosy went on to Aden for further meetings, in which both Sykes and Picot were involved; this assisted with the political side of the discussions. From Aden, which he found hot and damp, he went to Djibouti, in the then French Somaliland, to make the acquaintance of the governor. The weather there, although hotter than Aden, was not so humid and consequently more bearable.

By the start of July, the Red Sea Patrol had succeeded in taking all the ports of the Hejaz coast from Qunfunda in the south to Tiran at the mouth of the Gulf of Aqaba. At Qunfunda, Boyle, on *Fox*, had joined two other ships of the patrol. Boyle invited the Turkish commander, under a flag of truce, to dinner on board *Fox*.

> I gave them a good dinner and plenty of liquid, including champagne which was much appreciated by the Turk ... After dinner the time seemed opportune to suggest to the Turk that he should surrender. This I was anxious to do as I had not a large enough landing force to turn him out and capture the garrison. He refused, but so half-heartedly I gave him until 9 a.m. to think it over.[205]

---

203 Churchill Archives WYMS7/11/3

204 Edward Cadogan Under Fire in the Dardanelles, 142

205 Admiral of the Fleet the Earl of Cork and Orrery My Naval Life, 98

No reply was received by 9:00 a.m., so at 10:00 a.m. the three ships opened fire. After 15 minutes a white flag was raised over the town. Ten officers and 195 men were taken to Egypt as prisoners of war, and at the request of the local population, two officers and 30 sailors were landed to protect them until the arrival of Arab irregular forces. The one remaining port under Turkish control was Aqaba. It had been regularly bombarded by ships of the Red Sea Patrol and was severely damaged. What was left standing was, however, still in Turkish hands. On 6 July Lawrence and a force of Arabs largely from the Howeitat tribe, led by their sheikh, the renowned Auda abu Tayi, took Aqaba after crossing the desert and taking the Turks by surprise from the rear. When they arrived there was little food in the town either for the Arabs or for their 650 Turkish prisoners. Lawrence therefore set out from Aqaba by camel to Egypt, with a small party of Arabs, to ask for help. Riding almost non-stop across the desert they arrived at the banks of the Suez Canal after 49 hours. After crossing the canal and managing to find an intelligence officer who provided him with railway tickets and passes to travel to Cairo Lawrence arrived at Ismailia station, where passengers from Suez changed for Cairo. Lawrence described what happened next:

> When the other train arrived, I saw in it an opulent saloon. From it descended Admiral Wemyss and Burmester and Neville with a very large and a superior general. A terrible tension grew up along the platform as the party marched up and down in weighty discourse. ... I caught Burmester's eye. He wondered who I was for I was burned crimson and very worn with travel: later I knew that my weight was less than seven stone just now. However, he answered, and I explained myself and the history of Aqaba. It excited him. I said I wanted the Admiral to send a store ship there at once. Burmester said the *Dufferin* came in that day, and he would promise she should load all the food in Suez, go straight to Aqaba and bring back the prisoners immediately. This was splendid. He wouldn't do it himself, since he did not wish to interrupt the Admiral and Allenby.[206]

Whilst Rosy's efforts were concentrated in the Red Sea and the East Indies, in the Mediterranean there were different problems. On 31 January 1917 Germany had declared unrestricted submarine warfare on merchant ships, attacking them with torpedoes on sight. This campaign was having significant effects, the number of sinkings rising rapidly. A routeing system was created, but it did not achieve the desired result, as the U-boats located the traffic routes by the very presence of the patrol vessels in the area. The situation in the Mediterranean was different; the major traffic route was from the Straits of Gibraltar to Port Said, the entrance to

---

206 T E Lawrence Seven Pillars of Wisdom, 346

the Suez Canal. But the Allied navies did not operate in a coordinated way, and the number of craft available for anti-submarine patrols was inadequate.

The situation in the Atlantic changed with the introduction of a convoy system at the end of April. At the same time, an Allied conference at Corfu had convened to consider the same problem – to reduce the losses from submarine attack. It came up with four recommendations. The first three were concerned directly with aspects of merchant ship protection. The fourth finally recognised the need for the Allies (Britain, France and Italy) to coordinate their efforts by the establishment of 'a central authority, based at Malta, with responsibility for all arrangements affecting routes, escorts and patrols in the Mediterranean.'[207] The establishment of such a central authority caused problems: both France and Britain wanted to be in overall command. The compromise that was reached was that there would be a French commander-in-chief with overall command and a British commander-in chief of British naval Forces in the Mediterranean, with the rank of vice admiral, who would be based ashore in Malta. The choice for this post was Rosy, and it was announced on 20 June. To be Commander-in Chief in the Mediterranean had been Rosy's ambition throughout his naval career. However, due to events unfolding at the Admiralty he was never to achieve this aim. The post instead was given to Vice Admiral Somerset Gough-Calthorpe. When Rosy heard of the appointment at Malta, he wrote to Victoria:

June 12 Ismailia

Surprising developments are occurring to me personally. They want me to go as C-in C Mediterranean, an office they mean to re-institute. I shall be very sorry from a professional point of view to leave here, where the work has been so interesting, and of course it is a much more difficult business I'm going to but it's a great compliment to me for it is an enormous affair I'm going to take up and will require an enormous amount of organisation.[208]

Rosy's departure from the East Indies station gave rise to much comment. One observation, from after the war, arose from a meeting between Sheriff Faisal and General Botha of South Africa during the Versailles peace conference, when they met at lunch in the Hotel Majestic. Conversation had turned to discussing guerrilla warfare. Botha expressed his surprise that the Arabs had succeeded where the Boers had failed. Faisal replied 'Ah, that was because you had not Admiral Wemyss and his ships to help you.'[209]

---

207 Arthur Marder From the Dreadnought to Scapa Flow Vol. 4, 183

208 Lady Wester Wemyss Life and Letters, 357

209 Ibid 358

*Rosy (front row, right-hand end) at a meeting at a meeting of
the Allied Naval Council 1917 (Churchill Archive)*

Lawrence's comments were more effusive:

> Admiral Wemyss was in glorious contrast to the soldiers – no jealousy, no
> stupidity, no laziness; he was as keen to help as any two-year old. His support
> in the mixed councils and conferences was hearteningly useful. That was
> the main benefit he did us. In practical affairs he did all the Navy can do
> on the land. In the first days of the Revolt he came to Jeddah to lend his
> personal support to King Husein [*sic*] and to confirm what Boyle had done.
> The two years of steady help we received from the SNO Red Sea [Boyle],
> was of course the Admiral's work … The Red Sea patrol ships were the fairy
> godmothers of the Revolt. They carried our food, our arms, ammunition, our
> stores, our animals. They built our piers, armed our defences, served as our
> coast artillery, lent us sea planes, provided all our wireless communication,
> landed landing parties, mended and made everything. I couldn't spend the
> time writing out a tenth of their services. That's what I meant by saying, at
> the beginning, that the Admiral was hearteningly useful. His support, in the
> high place, made all the naval ships our active helpers.[210]

Rosy left Ismailia for the last time on the Suez Canal Company's yacht *Aigrette*,
travelling up the canal to Port Said on 22 July to board HMS *Weymouth* for passage
to Marseilles. As he left, the crew of *Euralyus* manned the side to cheer him away.

Whilst still expecting to be appointed to the Mediterranean post, he had
written to Victoria on 4 July that:

---

210 David Garnet (ed.) The Letters of T E Lawrence, 239

Egypt remains under my command and they are sending out a Rear-Admiral to be here, of course under me C-in-C. For some reasons I am sorry to give up this station, but I cannot help being pleased at the new job [as] it is the biggest thing there is after C-in-C Grand Fleet and it will mean an immense amount of work, since I since I shall have to organise the whole thing and I shall have to keep sweet with the French, not that the difficulties will, I think, prove very great. And then there is the possibility of our being together again – which is glorious. I should get you over from Taranto to Malta in a fast man-of-war so that there would be no danger.[211]

He travelled from Egypt to Paris, arriving on 26 July; Victoria and his daughter, Alice, were there, awaiting his arrival. It was a joyful reunion, as he had not seen Alice since the outbreak of war.

Not knowing of the changes that lay ahead, they contemplated life together again on Malta; as Rosy would be based ashore, Victoria and Alice could both join him. But it was to be a very short reunion, as the very next day he had to travel to London for meetings at the Admiralty. A week later he returned to Paris with the news that his appointment had been changed and that he had accepted the post of Second Sea Lord. Victoria was desperately unhappy at this change. In *Life and Letters* she wrote, in the third person:

> She was in despair; it was not only with it the abandonment of long cherished hopes on the very eve of fulfilment, the relinquishment of an appointment more important, more advantageous and more congenial in every way for one in all respects inferior, but above all she dreaded the Admiralty, which during the war had proved the grave of so many reputations, and the spirit of intrigue which ever since Fisher's reign had clung to its walls and with which she knew full well he was so unfitted to deal. She therefore besought him to refuse – but in vain! He was adamant. He realised that the sacrifice it entailed, he bitterly regretted his hopes being dashed to the ground but if it was thought he could serve his country better as Second Sea Lord he was ready to do so.[212]

Rosy took up his appointment on 6 September: Victoria noted that she had a heavy heart, and it was with dark foreboding that she saw him take up the appointment. Of his arrival at the Admiralty he wrote:

> When I went to the Admiralty in September 1917 as Deputy First Sea Lord the board had already been increased by the members who were designated

---

211 Churchill Archive WYMS 7/11/3

212 Lady Wester Wemyss Life and Letters, 362

Deputy and Assistant Chiefs of the Naval Staff respectively … The First Lord's original idea had been that I should be Second Sea Lord, but that the traditional duties of that office should be somewhat modified, so as to allow me to take up Staff Duties. The reason for this was that until now, should the First Sea Lord for any reason be absent from the Admiralty the whole of the burden and responsibility of the war devolved automatically on the Second Sea Lord, whose duties in connection with the personnel did not allow him sufficient time to study Staff matters. Consequently, he (the Second Sea Lord) might find himself called upon at any moment to give decisions on matters with which he could not possibly be familiar. On considering the situation, I advised the First Lord that it would be better not to interfere with the duties of the Second Sea Lord which was so well understood on all sides and which required the full attention of one man, but appoint me as additional, with my duties entirely confined to Staff work and that an officer should be appointed as Second Sea Lord who would be junior to me. By this means the conduct of the war would, in the absence of the First Sea Lord, automatically fall into my hands. This agreement was agreed to and carried out. It did not however work satisfactorily because Sir John Jellicoe could never be brought to see its utility – my presence, I'm afraid, in no way helped to lessen the burden on his shoulders simply because he refused to delegate to me any responsibility. Sometime in December I had a conversation with him on the subject and told him that I feared I was not being as much assistance to him as I had hoped to be. I pointed out to him that he was giving me no responsibilities and that as matters stood I was merely giving an extra opinion on dockets which could be dispensed with and I asked him directly whether he trusted me or not.[213]

There was adverse opinion in the Navy over Jellicoe's concerns over 'inconsequent little matters', and that the Board of Admiralty had too much to do. The junior sea lords, running their own departments, could not engage in the conduct of the war. A proposal by Captain Richmond, the leader of a group of junior officers, and who had the support of senior officers including Beatty, Tyrwhitt and Keyes, considered that the present board should be reconstituted – including the appointment of Rosy to the board. Beatty was pleased with Rosy's appointment as Deputy First Sea Lord:

He seems to have a fairly good grasp of the various situations and has good sound common sense to assist him in making his decisions – we are agreed on all the most important questions and I consequently feel more hopeful for the future.[214]

213 Churchill Archives WYMS 11/1
214 Beatty to Lady Beatty, 10 October, quoted in Arthur Marder From the Dreadnought to Scapa Flow Vol.4, 223

Jellicoe's supporters were doubtful about Rosy's appointment; they believed it was part of a plot to oust Jellicoe – who himself regarded the new appointment as 'the kind of fifth wheel of the coach'. Their suspicions had some foundation. Both Lloyd George and Sir Eric Geddes, the first lord, were unhappy with Jellicoe for various reasons. The press was also agitating, and the stage was being set for his removal. On 26 October a meeting was held in the Cabinet Room, including the prime minister and the first lord, to discuss the question of replacing Jellicoe. The problems in the Dover Strait proved to be the last straw; both Rosy and Keyes found the situation there, while Admiral Bacon was in command, profoundly unsatisfactory. At a further meeting on 20 December, Rosy made a critical intervention. He made the point very forcibly that the existing measures in the Dover Strait allowed enemy submarines to pass through the strait successfully and unchallenged. Bacon challenged this contention, describing it as 'puerile'. Rosy commented further:

> Towards the end of December, I brought the subject very insistently before both the First Lord and the First Sea Lord and my contention was that Bacon was not being successful in his anti-submarine measures, that we should leave no stone unturned to try and stop the passage of these craft and that we had better try somebody else and go on changing until we found somebody who could. Jellicoe maintained that Bacon was the best man we had for the job and should remain. I, on the other hand, maintained that he was not. The interview at which all this happened took place in the First Lords Room and I came away feeling that matters could not go on in this manner. The First Lord was in the disagreeable position of finding his two principal technical advisers in direct opposition to each other on a matter which was essentially the First Sea Lord's responsibility whilst he, I knew, agreed with me, the junior.[215]

The decision Geddes made was that Jellicoe must go if Bacon did. Therefore, the immediate cause of the dismissal of Jellicoe was the impending sacking of Bacon. Geddes, in a meeting with Lloyd George on 21 December, explained that as a civilian he could not override the sea lords in technical matters and that therefore he could not make any progress with Jellicoe.

> Wemyss, on the other hand, was a man who would give opportunities to the younger men and was on the best of terms with Beatty. During the time he had been at the Admiralty as Deputy First Sea Lord, Wemyss had encouraged the active brains in the Planning division and indeed throughout the Admiralty.[216]

---

215 Churchill Archives WYMS 11/1

216 Lloyd George War Memoirs Vol.3, ii 80, quoted in Arthur Marder From the Dreadnought to Scapa Flow Vol. 4, 340

Geddes therefore wrote to Jellicoe on 24 December, announcing his decision. 'After very careful consideration I have come to the conclusion that a change is desirable in the post of First Sea Lord. I have not, I assure you, arrived at this view hastily or without great personal regret and reluctance.'[217]

Rosy was appointed first sea lord on 27 December, the same day that the news reached the newspapers. With the first lord, he made a rapid visit to Edinburgh to discuss the situation with Beatty. He, as Commander-in-Chief of the Grand Fleet, had not been on good terms with Jellicoe since the Battle of Jutland, so the result of Jellicoe's departure was that relations between the Admiralty and the Grand Fleet became close, and better than hitherto.

Rosy was now installed as First Sea Lord, an appointment he had neither expected nor sought. He had hoped for a more active appointment. Throughout his career he had been a seagoing officer and had a dislike of office work. He wrote to Vice Admiral Gough-Calthorpe, who now occupied the post in Malta that Rosy had so much desired:

> People write and congratulate me but you – more than most people – will easily understand that it is hardly a question of congratulations but rather one of condolences. However, in these damnable times of war one can only do what one is told and not one likes. If the Service is content with my appointment and I'm content to do my best in it. The results we can only wait for.[218]

He was to bring a fresh perspective to his new role; he had two valuable assets, both of the negative type: he had never served in the Admiralty, nor had he specialised in any technical branch of the Service, openly commenting that technicalities bored him. However what he did put into place was the most important of modern requirements, that of organised cooperation – 'the welding together into a harmonious whole of the humblest as well as of the greatest effort, i.e. what is commonly called teamwork'.[219]

---

217 Quoted in Arthur Marder, Ibid 340

218 Churchill Archive WYMS 11/1

219 Lord Wester Wemyss The Navy in the Dardanelles, 277

18: THE END OF THE WAR

As in Mudros and in Egypt, Rosy's method of co-operative leadership started to make improvements. His personality and manner contributed to this. Arthur Marder commented:

> Rosy Wemyss ... possessed many valuable assets for the post of First Sea Lord – apart from a 'fighting face with a monocle set in it'. He was, to begin with, one of the most popular senior officers in the Navy. This he owed to his buoyancy, charming, invaluable courtesy, incomparable tact and talents for storytelling and mixing. The same attributes enabled him to get the best out of subordinates. He was also an officer of good judgement and common sense and one who in times of crisis never got rattled or even worried. For all his jolly casual manner, he had clear ideas as well as a will of his own. His great moral courage was well known: he would take risks and never hesitate to assume full responsibility for everything that was done.[220]

This opinion solidly repudiates Beatty, who, expressing the Navy's view, feared that Rosy lacked the experience and that he (Beatty) felt that matters could be leading to an uncertain future.

Rosy set to put his ideas in place from the outset. His first priority was to put the staff into a working pattern and to delegate work and authority, to build up confidence. He appointed Admiral Fremantle to the conduct of the campaign in the North Sea, to work closely with Beatty; Admiral Duff continued to focus on the anti-submarine campaign, and Admiral Hope managed the Navy's overseas operations. He instituted a pattern of formal staff meetings, held every morning

---

220 Arthur Marder From the Dreadnought to Scapa Flow Vol.5, 4

at 9:30 a.m., to discuss the general situation and to plan operations in outline. He noted:

> the results were eminently satisfactory and I can recall there was no instance when there was any friction … Confidence and cheerfulness now took the place of uncertainty and gloom at the Admiralty and I had not been seated many weeks in the First Sea Lord's chair before I had the pleasure of knowing that the machine was running more smoothly and efficiently than before.

He also set about changing the mindset that prevailed in the Admiralty, that of a defensive spirit, to one of an offensive and attacking nature. One of the areas in which this was the case was that of the U-boat menace, which up to his arrival had been dealt with in a purely defensive way. To him it seemed imperative for the Navy to hunt U-boats and sink them, rather than the U-boats doing the hunting and sinking.

Rosy again:

> Admiral Duff and Captain Fisher were full of the offensive spirit, but their hands had been tied by the moral atmosphere of defence which had imperceptibly crept into the Admiralty. Hunting squadrons were organised, deep minefields and patrols instituted, and if some of the earlier operations did not meet with the success which was expected of them, they raised the spirit of the men who organised and planned them and of those admirable junior officers who carried out and egged them onto further exertions.[221]

At the beginning of the year Beatty had announced that the German battlecruiser fleet had increased in size and power and now was a formidable force, and that as large numbers of [escort] ships were necessarily employed in countering the anti-submarine menace, he did not believe it was advisable to provoke a fleet action, which opinion was shared in the Admiralty. The offensive spirit in the anti-submarine campaign was focused on Dover. Keyes had replaced Bacon there and was revitalising the organisation. Rosy's idea was that:

> If only we could make the Straits impassable for the enemy our difficulties would be well on the way of being solved. Admiral Keyes with Commodore A. Boyle had built up an admirable staff organisation, where each man had his work to do and did it admirably. Mines were poured into Dover and

---

221 Churchill Archive WYMS 11/1

were laid with the idea of hermetically sealing the Straits. I must confess I never felt sure of our ability to do this. But I was determined to try and in the end we *did* succeed, for we had ample proof that the enemy got shyer and shyer of attempting to force the passage and eventually gave it up altogether.[222]

The submarine menace, if solved in the Dover Straits, was certainly not in any way contained. The sinking of merchant ships continued and losses continued to mount. Rosy was outwardly not rattled by this but internally he was deeply concerned. The balance between merchant ship losses and the sinking of submarines was one which was finely balanced. He wrote to David Beatty 'At this stage of the war one feels inclined like a drowning man to clutch at any and every proposal that holds out the slightest chance of being successful.'[223]

There were not only problems in the Dover Straits. Problems had arisen in the Mediterranean. The cruisers *Goeben* and *Breslau,* which had been given by Germany to Turkey to encourage the latter to enter the war on the Axis side, had sailed southwards through the Dardanelles on 20 January. Their sortie out into the Mediterranean was not an entire success: *Goeben* struck a mine, causing only little damage, and was able to proceed. *Breslau* had succeeded in opening fire on two monitors, sinking them both but then, shortly afterwards, also struck a mine, which had more serious consequences as she was disabled by it. Coming to her assistance and manoeuvring to take her in tow, the *Goeben* struck a second mine. The damage to her was more serious than the effect of the first mine, but she was still manoeuvrable so she cast off the tow and started to return to port. However, she was firstly attacked by British aircraft and then, having safely passed through the minefield, went aground on a sandbank, where she remained for the next six days.

At Mudros, the submarine *E12,* which was in port for repairs, was still sufficiently seaworthy to proceed to attack the *Goeben.* However, Rear Admiral Hayes-Sadler, the flag officer commanding in the Aegean, was not convinced that she was sufficiently operational and refused permission for her to sail. Other submarines returned from patrol and were able to attack the *Goeben,* but Hayes-Sadler refused to take any responsibility to launch an attack and the *Goeben* was eventually freed from the sandbank and returned to port virtually unscathed.

The affair disgusted Rosy:

The *Goeben* getting away is perfectly damnable and has considerably upset me, since we at the Admiralty were under the happy delusion that there

222 Ibid
223 Ibid

Rosy, when First Sea Lord (IWM),

was sufficient brains and sufficient means out there to prevent it: of the latter there were; of the former apparently not.[224]

As a direct result, the 'dithering and indecisive' Hayes-Sadler was removed from his post for his mismanagement of the matter.

A further problem arose because of the ongoing unsatisfactory command problem in the Mediterranean; in the previous year this had resulted in Rosy's aborted posting to Commander-in-Chief Malta (which post went to Gough-Calthorpe) under a French admiral. In order to try and resolve this problem, an Allied Naval Council was created at the end of November 1917, comprised of the ministers of Marine and chiefs of the Naval Staff of the Allied nations of Britain, France and Italy. Its first meeting was held in January 1918, in London, and Rosy, as First Sea Lord, attended. His knowledge of working with the French in the Mediterranean, and his fluency in French made him a very acceptable member of the council to both the French and Italians. Yet despite this, neither of those nations proved to be of any real use in the Mediterranean. Nor was the Admiralty much support, as the Mediterranean was regarded as a backwater and concentration was firmly fixed on home waters.

Rosy was determined that the Admiralty would behave differently from the way it had in the Dardanelles campaign, in which it had not provided any

224 Churchill Archive WYMS 11/1

assistance or direction. Consequently, he embarked on a series of meetings: initially with Keyes in London and in Dover, but as the first lord was away in February Rosy was in London for the whole month. He resumed his travels in March, going first to Dover, and then to Wemyss, to confer with Beatty on board his flagship *Queen Elizabeth,* moored in the Firth of Forth, and to visit experimental anti-submarine establishments. His next visit was to Ireland, where he went to went to visit the American warships which had arrived in port there, following America's entry into the war.

On 21 March the Germans launched the Ludendorff Offensive, a series of attacks on the Western Front. After only a short time the War Office had significant concerns; the Germans had made significant advances, retaking ground they had lost in 1916 and 1917. In order for the Army to be reinforced, as American troops would not arrive for a further four months it was proposed that the Royal Marines should be transferred from ships of the Grand Fleet. Rosy, writing to Beatty, wholly disagreed with this idea:

> I had a regular stand-up fight against the politicians and the Army at the War Cabinet yesterday – They actually suggested – and almost demanded – that the ships of the Grand Fleet should be reduced in the number of Marines, in order to strengthen some of the battalions abroad. I flatly refused to countenance any such suggestion and I think they were rather surprised and even hurt at the *non possumus* attitude which I took up. The soldiers actually put on a sort of aggrieved air as though we were not playing the game! To deprive a ship of any percentage, however small, of her highly trained men – which is what all the Marines are – decreases her efficiency to a very high degree, to a degree which I, responsible as I am for the efficiency of the fleet, cannot any under any circumstances be justified in doing. [I hope] we shall have no more attacks from the soldiers; though with the politicians and their ignorance of affairs naval and their short-sightedness as to the events of the future one never can tell what they may do … It is a subject on which I will hear nothing more and should they – which of course they cannot – insist on it, they will have to do without me.[225]

In February Keyes reconstituted the plan for the raid on Zeebrugge and Ostend which Bacon had proposed at the end of the previous year. Keyes presented his own detailed plans to the Admiralty and after close questioning received approval to proceed. His objectives were to block the canals to Bruges from Zeebrugge and Ostend by sinking blockships in both harbours. The effect of blocking the

---

225 Churchill Archive WYMS 11/1

canals would be to deny the U-boats the use of both ports and bottle up the large numbers of submarines based there. This was to be accomplished at Zeebrugge by several means. Firstly HMS *Vindictive*, an elderly cruiser, would go along the mighty stone mole which protected the harbour and land a party of some 200 sailors and 700 marines to attack and immobilise the defensive gun batteries and a fortified section of the mole. Then three old cruisers, HMSs *Thetis*, *Intrepid* and *Iphigenia*, which had been loaded with cement, were to act as blockships if possible, to block the entrance to the locks and the mouth of the canal. Lastly, two old submarines, each loaded with five tons of explosive, were to be driven under the viaduct linking the mole to the shore, to blow a hole in it. The German defences were thought to be almost impregnable, and the attack would call not only for a high degree of professional skill 'but also for courage, faith and self-confidence of the highest order'.[226]

In addition to all that, the right weather conditions, the phase of the moon and height of the tide all had to be in congruence for the attack to have any chance of success. The first moment when all those factors agreed was on 22 April. The Zeebrugge attack succeeded, but with heavy casualties. *Vindictive*, entering the harbour under heavy and accurate fire from the gun batteries and suffering severe damage, came alongside the mole further than planned, causing the troops landing on the mole to be subjected to heavy machine-gun fire which restricted their ability to advance and complete their objectives. Of the three blockships, also under heavy fire, *Thetis* ran aground before arriving at the entrance to the canal, but the other two did succeed in entering the canal and settled in place, blocking it. The two submarines that were to blow up the viaduct also had mixed fortunes as one parted its tow on the crossing and failed to arrive; the second, however, succeeded in wedging itself under the viaduct where the crew abandoned very rapidly to a small boat, before the high explosives blew a 100-foot gap in the viaduct. They were successfully recovered by a naval launch. *Vindictive* was towed off the mole and returned under tow to Britain. Two destroyers and a motor launch were lost in the attack. Of the landing party, 170 were killed and 400 wounded.

The attack on Ostend was, however, a complete failure; the blockships ran aground before entering the harbour as, unbeknown to the attacking force, the Germans had moved a crucial navigation buoy a mile to the east, resulting in the blockships failing to find the entrance.

Eight Victoria Crosses were awarded for the Zeebrugge raid,[227] and the operation was considered to be of sufficient success for Keyes to be made a Knight

---

226 Quoted in Arthur Marder From the Dreadnought to Scapa Flow Vol.5, 53

227 Stephen Spelling VCs of the First World War: The Naval VCs, 230–277

Commander of the Bath. Rosy had demanded a high level of secrecy to surround the operation, to the extent that the prime minister was not to be informed until the attack was under way and the attacking ships were nearing the Belgian coast. Keyes noted 'the Zeebrugge operation must for all times live as an example not only of gallantry but of a perfectly planned and carried out operation. It is the only example of a successful blocking operation.'[228]

Subsequent aerial reconnaissance on 17 May indicated that no submarines had passed down the canal from Bruges to Zeebrugge and that there were still submarines and destroyers stuck in Bruges. A week later Rosy gave further information to the War Cabinet, again from aerial reconnaissance indicating that there were 24 destroyers and 12 submarines locked up in the Bruges docks. But subsequent information from the German records showed that this information was not correct and that Zeebrugge had suffered only minor restrictions in service.

In Germany, information had been received from U-boats about the Scandinavian convoys, which had become larger and were escorted by large naval ships including American battleships. This information, although not accurate insofar as the frequency of the convoys was concerned, decided Admiral Scheer to mount a major attack by the High Seas Fleet on a convoy, with the twin aims of attacking Allied battleships and sinking numbers of merchant ships. The attack was planned for 24 April (which, coincidentally, was the day after the Zeebrugge raid). It was to take place off the west coast of Norway. A force of battlecruisers, light cruisers and destroyers would attack the convoy, whilst the remainder of the High Seas Fleet would wait 60 miles away, ready to support the attack. The fleet managed to pass out through the Heligoland Bight without being reported. This, despite the presence of British submarines patrolling in the area and being sighted by one submarine – which presumed that the battlecruisers and battleships it had seen were British and consequently did not report them. Although the High Seas Fleet was now out in the open sea no convoys were found for it to attack, so it returned to port. There had been clues that the fleet was on the move. Room 40, the intelligence department of the Admiralty, had picked up 'especial and unusually comprehensive messages sent from Wilhelmshaven to the minesweepers in the Heligoland Bight'[229] and had also become aware of an airship patrol which had been ordered to reconnoitre. These were good indications that a German naval offensive was likely. In the Admiralty War Room, Rosy took personal command in a highly charged atmosphere, although he remained 'completely calm and master of the situation.'

228 Churchill Archive WYMS 11/1
229 Quoted in Arthur Marder From the Dreadnought to Scapa Flow, Vol.5, 152

The Grand Fleet was ordered to proceed to sea, and in the early afternoon the entire fleet steamed out of the Firth of Forth at full speed – a total of over 160 ships, including 31 battleships. It was to be the last time that the entire Grand Fleet was mobilised before the end of the war. But they found nothing, as by the time they arrived in the area where it was thought that the High Seas Fleet would be, it had returned to base. The Admiralty signalled to Beatty in the afternoon of 25 April that he could return to port.

The German offensive on land had continued to progress relentlessly. At a meeting of the Supreme War Council in Abbeville, the situation was considered so grave that Rosy gave his opinion that:

> In the event of the loss of Calais and Boulogne it was certain for us that the war was lost at sea, because the whole of our strategy at sea depended on the Channel patrols. They were the key of our transport and of our anti-submarine warfare. But for the Channel patrols the enemy would be able to attack our transports in the Channel, and the trade of London could not be maintained as at present. If we lost the Channel ports the naval war would have to be fought under very bad conditions.[230]

The chief of the French naval staff agreed with this assessment. Fortunately, the German advance was held at Amiens and the eventuality did not arise.

By March the anti-submarine campaign had started to have a degree of success, as the number of merchant ships entering service for the first time exceeded those sunk. In May the success rate increased when the numbers of U-boats sunk exceeded the number that could be built to replace them. The convoy system had come into effect and was proving successful, as over 1 million American troops had safely arrived and were contributing to the fight back against the German offensive, which was in danger of making further advances. By the end of the month the U-boat campaign was lost. On 3 June Rosy was awarded the GCB to acknowledge his services towards the success of the campaign.

By the beginning of July, Rosy, for all his determination, drive and energy, was in need of a few days of leave. Ensuring that all eventualities would be adequately covered in his absence, he, Victoria and Alice departed for Wemyss. There he was able to relax and meet old friends and neighbours. The Firth of Forth, which lapped the beach in front of the castle, was busy, as the Grand Fleet was based at Rosyth, and from the castle he could see the passing shipping, including the convoys assembling off the small town of Methil, which had been built by one of his ancestors. Towards the end of his stay in Scotland he travelled to Inverness to visit the British and American bases there, and also visited other

---

230 Churchill Archive WYMS 11/1

naval installations on the east coast. He and his family returned to London on 23 July, and Rosy returned to work refreshed after that necessary break.

The deteriorating state of Russia following the revolution was causing concern. This intensified when, at the beginning of September, the British naval attaché, Captain Cromie, was murdered by Bolsheviks as he was defending the Embassy in Petrograd [St Petersburg] against their attack This was a huge insult to the Navy, compounded by the Bolsheviks' act of stripping his body and holding it up at the windows of the embassy to the delight of the mob below. His body was later recovered for burial due to the efforts of the Danish minister in Petrograd. The attitude of the British politicians who did not wish to avenge his death, or even apparently resented it, caused Rosy to be extremely angry as they 'seemed to be so incapable of upholding their country's honour. Their whole attitude indeed, was to him a constant source of wonder and amazement.'[231]

Rosy did not trust politicians, nor was he alone in the Navy in holding his views. Rosy's comments included: 'Damn all these politicians to hell. It is time we had a naval officer as dictator', 'I am under the impression that I have got on fairly good terms with the Prime Minister but with these slippery gentleman never can tell what their real opinions really are', and lastly, 'I hate Lloyd George but I think the remainder of the Cabinet are far worse than him.'[232]

As the summer progressed, the Allies gained ground in all the theatres of war. In Bulgaria a huge bombardment, with 500 guns firing along 80 miles of the front, opened on 14 September and continued throughout the day. This was followed by two weeks of heavy fighting, until on 26 September an armistice was announced.

The Red Sea campaign had moved northwards, away from the coast, following the taking of Aqaba by Lawrence and Auda Abu Tayi the previous year. By August General Allenby's army, consisting of British, Australian, Indian and Gurkha troops, and further supported by Emir Faisal's Arab irregulars, was making rapid progress through Palestine. On 25 September Amman had been taken: the ultimate target, Damascus, was entered by Feisal's Arab army, with Australian units waiting outside, on 30 September.

Three weeks later a tug flying a white flag steamed into Mudros harbour. On board was, to great surprise, General Sir Charles Townshend, who after the fall of Kut had been in captivity (in some comfort, in contrast to the dreadful privations is suffered by his troops) on a small island off the Turkish coast. He had been sent by the Turks, together with the aide-de-camp to the Turkish Minister of Marine, to arrange for the opening of peace talks. An armistice was signed

---

231 Lady Wester Wemyss *Life and Letters*, 381

232 Quoted in Arthur Marder *From the Dreadnought to Scapa Flow* Vol.5, 341

with Turkey on 30 October by Vice Admiral Sir Somerset Gough-Calthorpe, the Commander-in-Chief of the Mediterranean Fleet, and representatives of the Turkish government, on board HMS *Agamemnon*. The minefields in the Dardanelles were cleared so that on 12 November a naval squadron was able to sail up to Constantinople under Gough-Calthorpe's command – the French demand for command of the force having been denied – and anchored off the city.

In France, the Battle of Amiens had been won by the Allies, and by late September the German army began to evacuate Flanders and naval units started to be withdrawn, sailing close along the Dutch coast, protected by German shore batteries from attack by the Harwich force. All naval units had left by 5 October. Monitor bombardments of German positions ashore were undertaken over the next two weeks; by 19 October the Germans had left the Belgian coast. A last desperate operation was planned for the High Seas Fleet, which was assembled ready for action by 29 October. However, it became clear that its crews were refusing to take part; mutinies were breaking out, particularly on the capital ships.

But the ships of the Grand Fleet also had problems, as its crews were affected by the Spanish flu epidemic, which had spread from the trenches. Many ships were unable to sail due to the large numbers of men laid low by the disease.

Even so, the writing was on the wall, clearly visible to all combatants. So in the Admiralty and in the government, meetings rapidly followed each other in attempts to draw up peace terms, and Rosy was kept busy trying to placate Beatty on the one hand and Lloyd George on the other. However, eventually, on 16 October Rosy and the Board of Admiralty drew up the naval terms for the armistice. The overall terms of the armistice were finally agreed and drafted on 26 October. Rosy wrote to Beatty:

> It has been most difficult to get any satisfactory conclusion from the War Cabinet. They are always inclined not to come to any strong decisions and leave matters in a nebulous state; however, under the circumstances we are as favourably placed as we can be. The whole Board are unanimous on pressing the business. I have had many days at the War Cabinet and they are really very impressed with the fact that so far as the Naval terms are concerned it is impossible not to embody terms of peace. I'm going off to Paris tomorrow. We have an Allied Naval Council on Monday, the results of which I have not the slightest doubt of and feel perfectly certain that I can carry them all with me, and I therefore look forward to a unanimous resolution to put before the Supreme War Council at Versailles on Tuesday. The crux will, of course, come there, but the Board of Admiralty have very

satisfactorily strengthened my position. The First Lord accompanies me, and he will be at Versailles and will back me up at the final business.[233]

The next day he travelled with the first lord to Paris, where he spent days in meetings with various of the Allies, together with the first lord and the prime minister. There followed a week of negotiations and meetings, including the Allied Naval Council and the Supreme War Council. Despite this, when Rosy left to return to London on 2 November there was still no agreement as to the final terms of the armistice. Towards the end of the negotiations the Supreme War Council had however decided that the naval terms of the armistice would be the surrender of 160 submarines and the internment of surface ships. After the final terms were eventually agreed, it was also decided that Marshal Foch should represent the Allied Armies and Rosy the Allied Navies, and that these two should meet the German representatives for the peace terms to be presented. Rosy had a final interview with Lloyd George, the prime minister, and then left for Paris on the evening of 6 November to start the process of agreeing the terms of the armistice.

---

233 Churchill Archives WYMS 11/1

19: ARMISTICE

From Rosy's arrival in France on 7 November until his return to London on 11 November, he kept a detailed daily journal, which is now in the Wemyss Archive at the Churchill Archives Centre.[234]

Armistice

Thursday, November 7, 1918

Arrived in Paris at 7 a.m. and was met at the station by Brigadier General Grant of General Du Cane's staff. He is to accompany me to French GHQ when the time arrives, probably today. Meeting with Ad'l Du Bon and Ad'l Benson at Ministry of Marine, latter as tiresome as ever. Saw Townshend at luncheon, inclined to be talkative. In afternoon motored out to Senlis with Grant and called on Marshal Foch, then tea with Du Cane and joined the Marshal's train. 5 p.m. – Hope, Marriott and Bagot accompany me. We immediately steamed away and the train was taken into a siding in the forests of Compiegne. The train containing the German delegates is expected during the night and will stand in a siding close to ours.

The Frenchmen are all naturally very elated but dignified and calm, the Marshal quiet and confident. He told me he proposed to do as little talking as possible, to let the Germans do it all and then hand them the terms of Armistice. If they agree the principles he may discuss details.

Friday 8th

The train containing the Germans arrived at 7 a.m. I saw the Marshal early and found him rather nervous but dignified. A message was sent over to them to say that we would receive them at 9 a.m. The plenipotentiaries are

234 An expurgated version is to be found in Lady Wester Wemyss' Life and Letters.

Erzberger, Count v. Obendorff [*sic*], General von Winterfeld [*sic*], Capt. von Selow. The Mission walked over at 9 a.m. and were shown into the Saloon by General Weygand. The Marshal and I were next door and came in when they were all present. Erzberger presented his people and the Marshal ours. The Marshal then formally asked them what they had come for and had they their credentials. These they handed to the Marshall [*sic*] and he and I left the Saloon to examine them. They were quite in order, were signed by [Prince] Max of Baden but gave no power to sign any Armistice.

On our return to the saloon we all sat down, each mission on one side of the table facing each other and General Weygand read out the terms of the Armistice in French and they were translated by interpreters, British and French. General Winterfeld reading from a scrap of paper then asked on behalf of the German High Command that hostilities might cease immediately. He said that such an action might save many lives. Foch replied that a cessation of hostilities would only take place after the armistice had been signed. The Germans then formally asked for a copy of the terms which were given them and a short discussion took place as to the manner of transmitting them to Berlin. They have come without cyphers. The meeting then was closed and the answer has to be given by 11 a.m. Monday. All the Germans are very much distressed and naturally so, Erzberger showing most nervousness. But Winterfeld and von Selow looked the most distressed. The General in his little speech asking for cessation of hostilities used the word *Deroute* [rout] in connection with the German Armies. The naval and military terms did not seem to affect them as much as the civil and financial ones. My impression is that they must and will sign. [Colonel Comte de] Bourbon-Busset who was in charge of them said he thought they were there all very down. An extra 24 hours was asked for but this was refused. The time has been calculated and is sufficient.

The Frenchmen are naturally very elated but they are all dignified and behaving like gentlemen.

Erzerber [*sic*] – a common looking man typical German bourgeois.

Winterfeld – a horrid looking man with a cruel face.

Von Selow – fat and pasty, had nothing to say.

Von Obendorff – Looks like a gentleman and speaks good English and French.

The train is very comfortable. I have quite a good cabin, the size of two wagon-lits thrown into one. We have a whole wagon to ourselves. There is an office for Staff, dining room and the Marshal's own bedroom and sitting room. Baths are apparently not thought of.

It is a curious scene in the middle of the forest and yet there's nothing sad – at any rate for us. The two trains 200 yards off each other. Stray sentries in bluegrey can be seen amongst the trees. Nothing else in sight. We are in telegraphic communication with Paris and the world. Apparently the German Army is getting demoralised. Meanwhile papers have arrived and the whole story of the Naval mutiny is out. How will it affect the naval terms? It will be difficult for them to comply. The Marshal told me that were the Armistice not signed he would have the capitulation of the whole lot in three weeks. He also said that yesterday a whole regiment of Boche had laid down their arms and came in crying that now there was peace. Bourbon-Busset told me that the Germans were throwing away their arms and today a telegram came in to say that they are actually leaving their field kitchens behind. The mission said nothing about Bolshevism.

No further regular meeting – Hope saw von Selow who merely asked questions relative to the terms. He is afraid of the blockade and seems actually to think that we should keep it up for the purpose of starving their country during the Armistice. Such is their mentality as I suppose it is what they would have done had the cases been reversed. Von Selow also asked if we should sink any submarines during the Armistice! Really it is unbelievable. He said that Bolshevism had appeared in the Army during the months of April and May. The fact is that that is the time of their enormous losses and to speak of the decline of morale as bolshevism is ridiculous. I am told that all day Friday the state of the Parlementaires was deplorable but that they had bucked up a little during dinner.

Friday evening, I had a long conversation with Foch. In reply to my questions he told me that the hardest term in the Armistice was the time the Ninth Army had to retire. If carried out it meant that they must leave everything behind. He is determined that the German army shall be thoroughly beaten. Foch very ignorant about all matters naval. I gave him certain information which interested him and tried to explain to him what the Navy was doing and had done. I think he began to grasp the subject. He explained to me the difficulties the enemy would encounter in withdrawing from Belgium from which I began to understand why Von Selow had spoken about using German ships in Antwerp for evacuating the troops. Foch won't have this at any price. Also we must have all the German ships in the port for revictualling all countries.

Sunday 10th November

Yesterday morning we motored to Soissons. Truly a dreadful sight, not one single house is habitable. The cathedral is literally torn in two. Going through the streets gave one the impression of visiting Pompeii. We were shown some of the outlying houses which with great ingenuity and without any change in their external appearance have been made into regular fortresses. The news which reached us during Saturday was tremendous and varied. The abdication of the Emperor – at first it was thought that Max of Baden remained as Chancellor. Then a manifesto to German people and the world, saying that a socialist democratic government had been formed and that the functions of Chancellor had been taken over by Ebert. In the meantime, a republic appears to have been proclaimed in Bavaria. All seems to be confusion. It would appear that the plenipotentiaries have no longer any powers and one would think that Erzburger [*sic*] at any rate has no longer any standing. Last night I telegraphed to the Prime Minister telling him that the Mission feared that the continuance of the blockade would mean the starvation of the country and that I proposed to tell them that we should consider revictualling of the country.

Von Oberhorff [*sic*] yesterday saw Weygand and pointed out certain clauses which they think should be altered. On the Sunday afternoon I took a long walk with G. Hope – there was nothing doing. A German courier had left by motorcar at noon on Friday; in spite of all preparations being made it was found he could not get through the lines because of the German fire – the first intimation that the German fire discipline was getting bad. The courier was finally dispatched by aeroplane.

On Sunday evening I had been talking to the Marshal for a long time after dinner and was just going to bed when and ADC came and told me with the Marshal's compliments that he thought that the German envoys had received instructions and would probably want to see us tonight and would I therefore be ready. Consequently, I did not go to bed but lay down until midnight when I was told that the envoys had asked to be received immediately. They came into the main saloon and we resumed our seats as we did on Friday morning. There was but slight inclination on the part of any German to any protest. In one or two small matters such as numbers of locomotives or aeroplanes to be delivered they assured us that it was impossible to accede to the demands since we had over-estimated their strength and the Marshal showed reasonableness and to all intents and purposes the military terms of the armistice were signed. In the case of the German forces in East Africa the word 'capitulated' which appeared in the original text of the Armistice was allowed to be altered.

When it came to discussing the naval terms Von Selow showed a captiousness which was tiresome and quite unadvisable. He made the remark was it admissible that their fleet should be interned seeing that they had not been beaten. The reply to this was obvious and it gave me a certain amount of pleasure to observe that they only had to come out!

In discussing the submarine situation, he told me somewhat to my surprise that there were not nearly 160 to be had – and this gave me the chance of getting what I had always wanted viz. *all* the submarines. I may say that the question of the naval terms of Armistice had caused a good deal of discussion. I had originally asked for the surrender of eleven battleships, six battlecruisers, eight light cruisers, fifty destroyers and all the submarines. The politicians however were frightened and considered these terms as too heavy and desired to make them lighter, because they feared that there was a point beyond which the Germans would not go and that they (very rightly) considered that so far as Great Britain was concerned the present was the best psychological moment for obtaining a peace. I had many arguments with the Prime Minister on the subject and was quite aware that the French for the same reason wanted the general terms eased and that this should be done at the expense of the British Navy rather than at the expense of French army. During some of the discussions on this subject Foch had said: Do you expect my men to go on fighting for the sake of ships which do not come out?, thereby displaying an entire ignorance of the general situation and of the part that the Navy had played in the war. Lloyd George had endeavoured to whittle down their terms and had suggested every sort and kind of compromise – a reduction of the ships to be delivered etc and had eventually agreed to the internment of the ships as a compromise. This I accepted as the best to be got and with an undertaking from him that these ships should never be returned to Germany but surrendered at the peace.[235] It was the same with the question of the submarines; Lloyd George had objected to the word 'all'. By fixing a number which I felt sure would give us what they had got I had hoped to achieve my end – which I did. It was therefore a pleasure and satisfaction to me to get the opportunity of inserting the word 'all' in the terms.[236] The Armistice was eventually signed at 5:10 a.m. and it was decided that the time should be taken at 5 a.m. and that hostilities should cease at 11 a.m. The Germans then went back to their training and we

---

235 Article XXIII of the Armistice stated: 'German surface warships which shall be designated by the Allies and the United States shall be immediately disarmed and there after interned in neutral ports or in default of them in Allied ports to be designated by the Allies and the United States. They will there remain under the supervision of the Allies and of the United States, only caretakers being left on board. The following warships are designated by the Allies: Six battlecruisers, ten battleships, eight light cruisers (including two minor players), fifty destroyers of the most modern types. All other surface warships (including river craft) are to be concentrated in German naval bases to be designated by the Allies and the United States and are to be completely disarmed and classed under the supervision of the Allies and the United States.'

236 Article XXII of the Armistice stated that Germany was to: 'Surrender to the Allies and United States … all submarines (including submarine cruisers and all mine-laying submarines) now existing, with their complete armament and equipment, imports which shall be specified by the Allies and United States. Those which cannot take the sea shall be disarmed of the personnel and material and shall remain under the supervision of the Allies and the United States. These submarines which are ready for the sea shall be prepared to leave the German ports as soon as orders shall be received by wireless for their voyage to the port designated for their delivery, and the remainder at the earliest possible moment. The conditions of this article shall be carried into effect within the period of 14 days after the signing of the armistice.'

dispersed. Having to start for Paris at 7:30 a.m. I felt it was too late to go to bed and so Hope and I went for a walk in the forest and it was a queer feeling that I had that the war was at last over and that bloodshed would cease at 11 o'clock.

I drove back to Paris with the Marshal and went straight with him to the Ministry of War where we were received by Clemenceau whose joy and satisfaction he made no attempt to conceal and taking my right hand in his left and the Marshal his left hand in his right, Foch and I joining him equally all warmly congratulated one another. I went to the embassy and sent a detailed telegram to the government. On leaving the embassy the news was beginning to get about and the streets were already full of people making merry. In the afternoon the crowds in the Place de la Concorde were enormous.

I left Paris in the morning [of the 12th] and arrived at Folkestone about eight o'clock and in London just in time for the thanksgiving service at St Pauls.[237]

Victoria had come to meet him and they drove to London, 'and for the first and last time in his life he completely broke down: strain, emotional, joy, pride. He had taken over the Navy in its darkest moment when defeat seemed imminent; he had guided it to this triumphal hour.'[238]

On 21 October Admiral Beatty had submitted a lengthy note setting out his views, which he had made clear at a meeting of the War Cabinet, and wrote to Rosy on 7 November on the same subject, but just as Rosy was leaving for France. He was able to answer the letter on the morning of Sunday 10 November, when, as he had commented, there was nothing doing.

My dear David,

I received your letter of seventh November late last night and read it with a great deal of regret.

You are surely under a misapprehension as to the general state of affairs and certainly so as to my not taking you fully into my confidence. It is true that events have occurred so rapidly during these last few days that it has been impossible for me to talk to you, and letters and telegrams are, I am well aware, very inadequate under such circumstances as now obtained. I had hoped that [Captain W W] Fisher's visit to you would have to a great extent eased the difficulty. As regards Heligoland, I am and have been quite aware of your views. Unfortunately, the Prime Minister, in

---

237 Churchill Archive WYMS 11/1 Armistice
238 Lady Wester Wemyss Life and Letters, 395

spite of his original dictum that the terms of Armistice should approach as nearly as possible terms of Peace was, as I told you, anxious to cut down the naval terms. We had a great fight about the number of ships and about the difference between surrender and internment and the Prime Minister as you know, gave me an assurance that none of the ships to be interned would be given back to Germany. Heligoland however he objected to strongly, and when speaking on the subject I was obliged to tell him, in reply to a question, that I considered that if in the terms of the Armistice we got all [the] ships the holding of Heligoland was not of such vital importance *now* although eventually Germany would have to give it up … [and this] will be a matter for the peace conference. Naturally I should have liked to have obtained in full all that was asked for, but under the political and existing circumstances this was impossible. … If there is any difficulty about handing over the ships I shall reserve the right to occupy Heligoland in order that you may take such steps as you deem necessary to enforce their delivery.[239]

Rosy wrote again to David Beatty three days later in more detail, explaining the difficulties he had encountered in putting the case for the Navy to the politicians. He continued:

As for consulting you – Well, I seem to have lived for the last three weeks in trains and motorcars, and much of my business has actually been conducted in the latter between Versailles and Paris. Conditions were perpetually, even hourly changing, and it was physically impossible to keep you more *au courant* than I did. I know that you had the feeling that you were originally short-circuited … and believe that you will readily understand that nothing is further from my thoughts and intentions than ignoring the C-in-C Grand Fleet. I think I maintain that the whole of my attitude ever since I have been at Admiralty will bear me out in this. I have been having a hard and difficult time lately and I'm quite as irritated as you are with those who call themselves our masters. We both of us have the interests of the country and of the service at heart, and I believe we have worked so loyally and closely together during the last 12 months to allow of any shadow of misunderstanding coming between us. Whatever happens do not let us allow *that* to happen.[240]

One of the officers on Rosy's staff was Commander Walter Bagot, an officer from Room 40, the Royal Navy's Intelligence Division. He had been part of

239 Churchill Archive WYMS 11/1
240 The Beatty Papers Vol.II 1916–1927, 13

the team interrogating German naval prisoners of war, and he spoke excellent German.[241] He wrote an informal account of the armistice negotiations:

On Thursday, 7 November 1918 the British Mission, consisting of Admiral Wemyss (C.N.S.) Admiral Hope (D.1st.S.L.), Capt Marriott, RN (Naval Assistant to C.N.S.) and myself, arrived at the Hotel Meurice in Paris where we were the guests of the French Government. That afternoon the Mission left in cars for Senlis, where the CNS visited Marshal Foch's headquarters. Subsequently the Mission had tea at the headquarters of the British Military Liaison Officer. These headquarters are situated in a fine chateau close to Senlis, standing in large grounds containing among other things a racing stable and training track. About 5:30 p.m. the Commission again left by car and boarded Marshal Foch's train at Senlis Station. As the British Mission was living in it for three days a few details of the train may be of interest. It consists of some seven or eight coaches of which two were sleeping cars providing cabin accommodation for the British and French Officers, one coach containing an office and conference room, one coach forming Marshal Foch's Quarters, a dining-car and two or three coaches containing men's quarters, dynamo, telephone exchange etc. This train has been used constantly by Marshal Foch during the war for travelling about to various parts of the Front.

The thing that struck one was the fact that Marshal Foch appeared to run the War with the assistance of only five officers. These were the Chief of the Staff (General Weygand), two staff officers and two officers who acted as secretaries and interpreters. He was of course in constant touch by telephone and courier with his headquarters at Senlis. But this was also a comparatively modest establishment.

Marshal Foch's train arrived at some old heavy gun sidings in the middle of the Forest of Compiegne about 7 p.m. and remained there during the whole of the negotiations, except for occasional trips to Compiegne station to take in water etc. The German Mission through delay in passing the fighting front did not arrive until the early hours of Friday morning. The Germans were also accommodated in a train similar to Foch's and this was placed on another set of rails about 100 yards away, a line of duck boards leading from one to the other.

The weather which during the week had been wet and misty cleared overnight and Friday 8th November, the first day of the conference, proved to be a bright sunny day which showed to full advantage the rural setting of the whole scene. Looking out from Foch's train there was nothing to be seen but trees and the little wood fires of the sentries posted round to keep away the curious, particularly from the German train, visible through the

---

241 Derek Nudd 'The Battle of Jutland, Through a Looking Glass', in Mariner's Mirror, Vol.105.4, 427

wood a short way away. Another line of duck boards ran in the opposite direction to the main road to Compiegne. About a quarter of a mile away lies the village of Francport on the Aisne. Close by lies the Chateau de Francport, erroneously reported in the press as the place where the conference was held.

On the arrival of the train containing the German delegates, Marshal Foch had sent over a staff officer to say that he would receive them at nine o'clock. So, punctually to the time the German Mission was seen advancing in single file across the duck boards. Leading the procession was Erzberger, next came [von] Obendorff and General Winterfeld and finally Captain von Selow [sic], the naval delegate. There were also two other junior military officers acting as interpreters. Personal descriptions of the delegates will be found at the end of this report. They all walked very slowly and manifested a certain limpness about the knee joints. The officers were in uniform and wore a form of sword-bayonet, except the naval officer who wore a dirk. The civilians were in well worn dark blue suits. None of the delegates could have been described as smart.

On arrival at Foch's train they were shown into the coach containing the office, part of which was arranged as a conference room. General Weygand then announced their arrival to Marshal Foch, who immediately afterwards entered accompanied by Admiral Wemyss.

The proceedings were opened by Marshal Foch asking the German delegates what was the object of their visit, to which Erzberger replied that they had come to hear proposals for an Armistice on land, at sea, in the air and in the colonies. To this Foch replied I have no proposals to make. Count Obendorff then produced from his pocket a paper and read an extract from one of Mr Wilson's statements. Foch then stated that they could hear the terms if they wished to have an armistice and that these were the terms of the Allied and Associated Powers. The Germans then decided to hear these terms. Before proceeding with the conference Erzberger handed over his credentials. Marshal Foch, Admiral Wemyss and General Weygand then retired to examine them. The credentials having been found in order, Marshal Foch and the other officers returned to the room and requested Erzberger to introduce the members of his mission. After this had been done Marshal Foch introduced the French and British delegates.

The Germans having decided to hear the terms, General Weygand began the reading of the principal articles of the Terms of Armistice. The French interpreter translated each article into German as it was read. The proceedings were conducted in French. That is to say the French and British delegates used the French language throughout. Erzberger spoke only in German although he appeared to know enough French to be able to follow. General Winterfeld and Count [von] Obendorff however spoke French.

Captain [von] Selow played only a very small part in the proceedings, but appeared also to know French. When the reading of the terms had been completed, by which time the Germans looked rather dejected, the question of communicating the terms to the German Government arose. Marshal Foch offered to assist them in every way with wireless and other means. He stipulated however that the terms of the armistice must be sent in cypher if communicated by W/T. As the Germans had not brought a cypher with them, it was arranged that Captain Helldorf should be sent to the German headquarters at Spa with a copy of the terms. The Germans then asked to be furnished with a certified translation of the French text, but were told that no translation was available. A request was now put forward by the German delegates for an immediate cessation of hostilities so as to avoid useless bloodshed. General Winterfeld was the spokesman on this occasion and whilst he was explaining the desirability of immediately stopping all fighting, referred to the rout of the German Army (*la déroute* was the French word actually used) and the useless bloodshed entailed if this continued until the conference had finished its deliberations. This remark would appear to form a fair index to the state of mind of the German delegates at that time. Marshal Foch informed them that no cessation of hostilities could take place until the terms already read had been accepted and signed.

A plain language message was then sent at the request of General Winterfeld informing the German government that the first sitting had been held and that his request for an immediate cessation of hostilities had been refused.

This ended the first sitting and the Germans then retired with copies of the terms to their own train, the proceedings having lasted about an hour and a half.

About lunchtime Captain Helldorf departed in tears (so it was reported) for the German Headquarters at Spa. Later in the day various German delegates arrived over to discuss the details of the terms with the French and British delegates. Captain [von] Vanselow came over and was received by Admiral Hope, Captain Marriot [*sic*] and myself. He stated that he proposed to discuss the terms with us, so that, in the event of the Armistice being concluded it would save time if the details were arranged beforehand, but that it must be understood that nothing he said could be taken as implying that they intended to accept the terms. It may be of interest to record briefly some of the views he expressed. With regard to Article XX of the naval conditions which provides for the immediate cessation of all hostilities at sea and the furnishing of information as to the whereabouts of all German ships, he enquired whether we would undertake not to use such information to attack German ships. He was assured that this was out of the question as the terms of armistice provided for the cessation of all hostilities. In connection with the surrender of surface ships he stated that the *Mackensen* was at least 10 months off completion and that consequently only five Battle Cruisers could be surrendered. He also said that all work on new construction had ceased some time ago. As regards destroyers he remarked that the number 50 asked for was far too high as nothing like that could be got ready. Although the Germans had many more than this number on paper, the wear and tear of machinery and craft in general had been so great that it would be difficult to find 50 boats sufficiently seaworthy to send over at once. The next complaint concerned the continuation of the blockade provided for in Article XXVI. According to the German view the continuation of the blockade was not in accordance with the conception of the term Armistice; therefore, the blockade ought to be raised so as to allow of Germany revictualling herself with her own ships. He said that Germany was in a very bad way and that the continuation of the blockade would mean sickness and famine, more especially as the returning army would have to abandon a large part of its supplies. He also complained bitterly about the effect of the blacklist and hope that it would be abolished. As a concession on this point, the last sentence stating that the Allies contemplated the revictualling of Germany was eventually added to Article XXVI.

The meeting lasted about an hour and then Captain [von] Vanselow returned to the German train.

On Saturday morning there being no conference on, the British delegates took the opportunity to motor over to Soissons to see the damage done to this town by enemy bombardment. On arrival the French officer accompanying the party was lucky enough to find an officer who had recently conducted the French President over the town. The latter took the party around, who were thus enabled to see all the points of interest. The British delegates arrived back at the train about 12 o'clock to find that there was no prospect of any further conference that afternoon, so after lunch, the time was spent exploring the grounds of the neighbouring chateau of Francport. Late in the afternoon the Germans sent over their reply to the terms of the Armistice, or rather a reasoned paper requesting certain modifications to the terms, arising mainly from technical disabilities to carry them out. This paper contained also remarks about the naval terms by Captain [von] Vanselow and an exposition of the views he had expressed during the afternoon meeting on Friday. After dinner these remarks were considered by the British delegates.

Sunday was a busy day commencing about 9 a.m. with a conference with Captain [von] Vanselow, during which the various points raised by him in the above mentioned paper were discussed. The procedure was to go into all the details, to discuss these and the various difficulties arising but to leave them over for ultimate decision at the final conference with all the delegates. An interesting point arose at this conference. The question was whether Germany under the then existing political situation would be in a position to carry out the terms of the Armistice, more especially the surrender of the ships. Captain [von] Vanselow was of [the] opinion that although the Kaiser and the Crown Prince had renounced their claims to the throne [information which the Germans had obtained from the French Sunday newspapers sent over to their train], and that there had been some disturbances, speaking generally it would be possible for the German Government, which ever the party in power, to carry out the conditions. He could not, however, be certain that mutinous elements in individual ships might not damage or destroy their vessels. It was then suggested that we might have to occupy Heligoland to enforce the terms. Captain [von] Vanselow did not, however, think that this would be necessary.

Various points regarding the surrender of ships were then discussed and the meeting rose shortly before lunch.

On the Sunday evening a plain language W/T message addressed to the German delegates was received instructing them to sign the Armistice, but to add a declaration regarding the danger of the spread of Bolshevism in Germany if the provisioning of that country were not undertaken by the Allies.

During the night several further meetings between the French and German delegates took place and also a further meeting with Captain [von] Vanselow. The letter stated that he had just seen the revised terms and desired to thank us for having altered the conditions regarding von Lettow in East Africa from surrender to evacuation. The next matter concerned the occupation of Heligoland, if it should be necessary to ensure the surrender of the German warships. Captain [von] Vanselow said that this could not be included in the terms without first consulting the German Government, as otherwise he might be tried for high treason on his return for having surrendered German territory. As it would however have taken some time to obtain the concurrence of the German government it was decided to attach the Heligoland stipulations to the terms as an annexure stating that the German delegates would transmit this stipulation to the German Chancellor with a recommendation that it should be accepted, adding the reason for this demand on the part of the Allies.

Finally, about 2 a.m., the German delegates arrived for the final conference. From the above-mentioned telegram the outcome of the conference was a foregone conclusion and the Germans were not a little annoyed that the instruction to sign had been sent in plain language. At least, this was the impression gathered from some remarks of Vanselow's during the preceding meetings. It could equally well have been sent in cypher as two naval coders with the necessary books had arrived on Friday night making communication in cypher possible and incidentally a number of cypher messages were received by the Germans.

The final conference then commenced its deliberations at about 2 a.m. on Monday, 11 November. The procedure was for General Weygand to read out the terms, article by article. The French officer interpreter then translated such articles into German and then, when necessary, after discussion the final form of the article was decided upon. The first point conceded by Foch was the alteration of the text of Article II to its present form in which Alsace and Lorraine are not termed occupied territory.

Most of the other points on which discussion took place arose from the technical impossibility (according to the Germans) of carrying out the terms. For instance, General Winterfeld stated that it would not be possible to surrender more than 1700 aeroplanes as this was approximately the total number of machines available, 300 less than the number asked for. The evacuation of the occupied territories was illustrated by a large map showing the lines to be occupied by various dates. This was spread out on the table and formed an annex to the terms.

When the terms relating to the blockade came up for consideration, Erzberger tried to soften the hearts of the British and French delegates by telling them that owing to the food shortage large numbers of their women and children had died during the influenza epidemic. It was quite apparent that the blockade coupled with the blacklist had hit them very hard. The black-list and the various measures connected therewith they referred to as the blockade on shore; Vanselow remarked that they had only undertaken the submarine war as a counter stroke to this shore blockade.

When the reading of the terms had been completed Erzberger rose and read out a declaration in German. In this he stated that the German Government would do everything in its power to carry out the terms. The German plenipotentiaries however desired to point out that some of the terms were so harsh as to be likely to bring about the state of anarchy and famine in Germany.

The proceedings came to an end about a 5:15 and the Germans were then asked to say whether they would call the hour of signing 5 a.m. or 6 a.m. They chose 5 a.m. French time. The various documents were then signed first by Foch and Wemyss and then by the four German delegates. They had agreed to sign without waiting for the amended version arising from the final conference to be typed. So after they had returned to their own train it was some time before the various documents were completed.

Orders were then issued for a cessation of hostilities on land and at sea and in the air at 11 a.m. French time, 11 November, the duration of the Armistice being 36 days from that hour.

One would have supposed that on such an occasion there would have been some outward display of enthusiasm on the part of the French officers on the conclusion of the armistice. Such however was not the case. About 6 a.m. the commandant of the train produced a bottle of port and some biscuits. But it was not until one of the British officers proposed it, that a toast was drunk to the great event.

Before leaving the Germans requested the British delegates to meet a food expert and a transport officer to discuss the details of revictualling Germany. These however did not arrive so about 9 a.m. Captain [von] Vanselow came over. He stated that he did not know much about the subject, but was of opinion that Germany would require about 30,000 tons of edible fats a month, this being her principal need. He was informed that his remarks would be noted.

At 8:20 a.m. Marshall Foch and Admiral Wemyss left for Paris by car to lay the terms of armistice before the French government. The train containing the Germans left at 10 a.m. for the front.

Admiral Hope and myself left for Paris about 10:30 a.m., arriving at the Hotel Meurice about half past twelve. At first as we drove through the country side there was nothing to show that anything unusual had occurred. It was only as the villages near Paris were reached that one began to notice signs of excitement. However as soon as the outskirts of Paris were reached it was evident that everybody had heard the good news. Everybody was buying flags and decorating their houses with them and by lunchtime the people of Paris were marching about arming arm crying La Victoire! La Victoire!

After dinner that night at the Hotel Meurice Admiral Wemyss was presented by two Canadian officers with a large silk table centre displaying the Allied flags. As Admiral Wemyss rose to leave several French gentlemen at a table a short way off rose intending to call for a speech or to drink his health and called out 'Admiral!' The latter had however just passed through the doors of the dining room and did not hear this shout, consequently nothing more came of this intended demonstration.

The British delegates left that night by train for Boulogne, crossing to Folkestone next morning (12 November) by destroyer. Thus ended a mission to France fraught with such great consequences to the Allies and indeed to the world at large.

Personal notes on the German Delegates:

Excellence Matthias Erzberger Age 41

Son of a postman in South Germany. Schoolmaster by profession. Member of Reichstag centre party. Catholic. Employed in 1914 in propaganda section of F. O. Lost this post on fall of Bethmann Hollweg in 1917. Led the attack of the majority party on Admiralty for making false promises about a/m campaign in July 1917. Proposed and carried the resolution of 18th of July 1917 for a peace without annexations or indemnities. In October 1918 appointed Minister without portfolio in Prince Max's government in which he was the strongest personality. Described as a man of much energy and ability. In confidential relations with the Vatican and Vienna, but not a gentleman. Ludendorff's first powerful enemy. Of medium height, fat and bloated looking, double chin, scrubby moustache, wears pincenez.

Excellence Graf von Obendorff. Age 48

Well born. Dr of Law. Now holds rank of Ambassador. Has been through the ordinary diplomatic career, being appointed as Minister at Sofia during the war and remained there until capitulation of Bulgaria. Slight build, medium height. Speaks French fluently.

General Detlef von Winterfeld Age 57

First commission in 1888. Has had very little actual military experience, never having commanded more than a company. Several years Military Attaché at Brussels – Then returned to General Staff. 1909 to 1914 Military Attaché Paris. During the war he has been active in Spain on espionage work. It is stated that He is a kindly chap, very much in earnest and of average mental calibre. He has the reputation of being a piccehur [?], Having collected a great deal of information. Is a fair, though not (except in French) fluent linguist. Is polite and quite without the aggressive manner not seldom found among his colleagues. Has probably a nervous temperament, old for his age. It is stated by a French officer that Winterfeld's father was present at Versailles in 1871 at the Peace negotiations.

Captain von Vanselow Age 44

Entered Navy in 1892. Promoted to Captain in April 7, 1917. There is apparently nothing noteworthy in his career. Appears to have served on the Admiral Staff Berlin since 1913. Has been chief of the Military Political Department of the Admiral Staff Since sometime in 1917. Short, stout, and rather subdued not very prepossessing, not much force of character.[242]

In addition to telephoning the government to advise them of the date of the armistice, Rosy had also telephoned the King – both as his monarch, and as an old

---

242 The National Archive ADM 1/8546/319

and valued friend of many years. He had been summoned to Buckingham Palace on his return, so after the service at St Paul's he made his way to his appointment with the King, when he gave an account of the success of the mission. Although summoned to the palace and also having advised Lloyd George, the prime minister, of his return, he was surprised not to be summoned to see him also. He discovered why when, on attending the War Council, he had a frosty reception. The prime minister had planned, on hearing of the signing, to announce it in the House of Commons on the afternoon of 11 November, keeping the news secret until then. However the King, not aware of Lloyd George's plan, had announced the glad news to the Court, and the armistice was made public at 11:00 a.m. Consequently, the prime minister's statement in the afternoon had been completely upstaged. Lloyd George was barely able to conceal his anger at this, and it was to cause Rosy problems later on, when the prime minister had his revenge.

A further stage in the armistice proceedings took place on 15 November, when SMS *Königsberg* arrived at Rosyth with Admiral Hugo Meurer on board so that he could be told by Admiral Beatty, on board his flagship *Queen Elizabeth,* the details of the internment of the German naval ships. Meurer did not receive the news well, and in reply told Beatty of the effect of the British naval blockade on Germany: that the revolution had spread through the country, anarchy was rampant and that Germany was destroyed completely.[243]

Three further meetings were held on the next day. The details were all complete by the evening: all the submarines would surrender to Commodore Sir Reginald Tyrwhitt at Harwich, and the surface ships would proceed to the Firth of Forth to surrender to Admiral Beatty before going to Scapa Flow to be interned, pending their eventual disposal as to be agreed at the peace conference.

On 21 November the Grand Fleet sailed from Rosyth to escort the German High Seas Fleet up the Firth of Forth to its anchorage off Inverkeithing. The Grand Fleet consisted of 370 ships, manned by 90,000 men, all the ships flying their huge battle ensigns. It formed two columns, through which the High Seas Fleet passed in silence. As they made their way up the Forth, they passed Wemyss Castle, on the northern shore, but Rosy was in London, so was not there on the ramparts to witness the spectacle. The German fleet anchored off Inverkeithing just before noon.

> And so ended the dramatic and historic day. The surrender, if one may call it that, was one of the most decisive and dramatic events in the illustrious annals of seapower.[244]

---

243 Jim Ring How the Navy Won the War, 200

244 Arthur Marder From the Dreadnought to Scapa Flow Vol.5, 190

*With Admiral David
Beatty on the deck
of HMS Queen
Elizabeth (IWM)*

The High Seas Fleet then sailed from its anchorage to its eventual destination in Scapa Flow, starting only two days after its initial arrival. Its ships were escorted in groups, the first two comprised of torpedo boats. There followed over the next four days all the remaining ships, escorted by units of the Grand Fleet. In Scapa Flow, three separate areas had been allocated for different classes of ships, the first area allocated to battleships, the second to battlecruisers and a third to torpedo boats. The anchorage is surrounded by flat, treeless land over which gales can blow unimpeded; the German sailors realised that internment was not going to be pleasant, effectively imprisoned as they would be on rusting ships for an indeterminate period.

PART 3: POST BELLUM

20: FROM ARMISTICE TO EXODUS

At the predetermined meeting in France to renew the armistice, the Germans asked when the peace conference would start; they had been asking this for some time. They were not told, although Rosy knew the answer: the conference could only start when President Wilson of the USA arrived, which he did on Boxing Day, 26 December. This resulted in many Christmas holidays, the first in peacetime for five years, being cut very short, including Rosy's, who had to return to London to meet the president. Two days later the general election was held, and Lloyd George and his party were returned with a large majority.

Rosy did not like President Wilson; his dislike of politicians, expressed earlier, caused him to instinctively mistrust him. He was, on the other hand, very pleased to see another arrival; Emir Feisal landed in England and came to lunch with Rosy, accompanied by T E Lawrence, now a colonel. It was a happy few hours, as Rosy was able to reminisce about his time as Commander-in-Chief East Indies.

Rosy travelled to France for the start of the peace conference at Versailles on 24 January, accompanied by Victoria. Three days later Marshal Foch invested Rosy with the Grand Cross of the Légion d'Honneur for his efforts in connection with the armistice. Whilst in Paris, Rosy and Victoria met many French friends, in addition to other friends from the past. The location of the conference in France had not been popular with either the British or the American government, as it was feared that as France was a combatant nation, the necessarily calm atmosphere would not be forthcoming and that, furthermore, the French were considered to be too excitable and too bitter towards the Germans. However, Clémenceau had continued to insist on the conference being held in Paris. Lloyd George commented:

I never wanted to hold the Conference in his bloody capital – I thought
it would be better to hold it in a neutral place, but the old man wept and
protested so much that we gave way.[245]

Rosy returned to England for a week at the end of January, before returning
to Paris on 6 February for a sitting of the peace conference, where he and Foch,
as signatories of the armistice, were to give evidence. They were summoned to
appear at 3 p.m., but at 5:30 p.m. the meeting ended and they were told that
their presence was no longer required. On the following day, at a tempestuous
meeting of the Supreme War Council at which Marshal Foch had stormed out,
followed by General Weygand, Rosy insisted on being heard. He made clear the
necessity of opening discussions for a naval and military peace. President Wilson
was shocked to hear this: 'Does the Admiral speak of peace?'[246] Rosy's retort was
that he understood that this was the purpose of the conference.

In January, Geddes was replaced as First Lord of the Admiralty by Walter Long,
who had previously been the colonial secretary and had no naval experience, but
was an experienced and capable administrator who worked with his professional
advisers. The Navy was not unhappy with this appointment, Beatty commenting
'I think we are lucky to get Long who is straight and a gentleman'.[247] However the
Admiralty Board under the command of Long and Rosy was not harmonious,
because of the rapidly deteriorating relations between Rosy and Beatty. Rosy had
intimated to Beatty that with the war over he had no great interest in remaining
at the Admiralty and he had hoped to take up the position of Commander-in
Chief Mediterranean and Governor of Malta when the peace conference ended.
This position did not materialise and Beatty was advised of this by a letter from
the first lord:

My Dear Sir David,

I have now been able to make myself thoroughly acquainted with the
position as regards your coming here as First Sea Lord. As I told you when
I was on board your flagship I had heard no dates definitely mentioned,
but I believed it was contemplated that the changes would probably take
place in June or July. I find this was also due to the belief that a post would
fall vacant about this time which would be offered to the First Sea Lord
and be acceptable to him. It turns out, however, that this was a mistake,
and so far as I am able to judge no appointment which he could accept is
likely to be open for some time to come. In these circumstances he will of

---

245 Quoted in Margaret MacMillan Paris 1919, 27

246 Lady Wester Wemyss Life and Letters, 417

247 Churchill Archive WYMS 11/1

course remain here for the present. I'm very sorry that there should have been any misunderstanding and still more sorry for any annoyance it has caused you.[248]

This, of course, only exacerbated Beatty's anger in regard to the matter. Rosy wrote to him on 28 February, three days later:

My dear Commander-in-Chief,

The First Lord has told me of his interview with you on Wednesday last and it is with great regret that I gather that you are displeased at the general state of affairs existing between the Admiralty and yourself – the Admiralty in this case probably meaning me! I gather that you feel that you have three principal causes of complaint … 2. that you are not coming to relieve me immediately … As regards 2. you will remember the conversation that we had at Hanover Lodge. I came to talk to you on that occasion with the idea of finding out what you wish to do now that hostilities had ceased, and it was then for the first time that I realised that your desire was to come and relieve me. I then told you of what was at that time just a possibility, namely, that I might go out as Governor of Malta and Naval Commander-in-Chief; But I am afraid you must have inferred from our conversation something much more definite than I intended to convey. As I have since told you I looked upon that friendly conversation as purely speculative. The possibility of my going to Malta, has, for various reasons, fallen through. The situation, therefore, has quite altered since that day; and I am quite sure you do not desire to appear to be trying to push me out … I suppose it is more than can be humanly expected that two men, placed as you and I are, should actually see eye to eye on every subject that may arise, but that does not seem to be a reason for any personal feeling to be brought into the matter, and so far as I am concerned that me assure you that there is none.[249]

This did not assuage Beatty's anger at the situation, which continued to deteriorate. However, Rosy, as First Sea Lord, was fully engaged in the peace conference at Versailles; the interned German fleet at Scapa Flow and its subsequent disposal was a major problem. In January the Admiralty had set out its proposals that all the interned ships and the nine remaining battleships be surrendered and then sunk in deep water within three months of the signing of the peace terms. These terms were accepted by the Allied admirals and approved

248 The Beatty Papers Vol.II 1916-1927, 22
249 Churchill Archive WYMS 11/1 also The Beatty Papers Vol.II 191–27, 24

by the Supreme Council at a meeting on 6 March. However, the agreed plan was not accepted by the French or Italians who wished to incorporate some of the German ships into their own navies, to offset war losses. The Americans too were displeased; Admiral Benson, in charge of the American naval delegation, feared that Britain would take the majority of the surface ships for the Royal Navy. The dispute continued. The American position changed to accept the sinking of the ships, concerned that if not, the British would, in view of their present location, acquire the majority of them. The Admiralty had calculated that on a replacement basis for war losses, Britain should receive thirteen battleships and four battlecruisers, France four battleships, Italy three, Japan one battleship and one battlecruiser, and the USA none. Rosy, however, noted:

> There are obvious and weighty objections to such a division of the spoils, which would be directly opposed to the generally accepted principles of reduction of armaments, having anything but a good moral effect on the world and might well even give rise to disagreement among the allies as to the basis of distribution ... British and American naval opinion is in favour of sinking as being by far the most satisfactory solution; the moral effect on Germany and the whole world would be good, and all possibility of disagreement among the allies would be avoided.[250]

Rosy's comments were endorsed by Lloyd George.

The disposal of the submarines, now nearly all interned in Harwich harbour, was not disputed. The British and Americans were in agreement; the sentiment was that submarines were pests and, in the view of the American Secretary of the Navy, Joseph Daniels, could be compared to poison gas, and that not only should they be disposed of but no more should be built.

The disposal of the surface fleet continued to be a major problem. The British position was influenced by the announcement of a major American shipbuilding programme at the end of 1918. The Admiralty did not want to lose the two-power standard[251] that the Navy had maintained before the war. Joseph Daniels came to Versailles to try and ease the situation, but did not succeed. He was told by Walter Long, First Lord of the Admiralty, that 'The supremacy of the British navy was an absolute necessity not only for the existence of the British Empire, but even for the peace of the world.'[252] Benson, the American admiral, had replied to this that the American Navy was quite able to take a part in peacekeeping. The disagreement was so violent that he and Rosy came close to fisticuffs. Daniels noted that:

---

250 Quoted in Arthur Marder From the Dreadnought to Scapa Flow Vol 5, 265

251 This was the ability to engage two other navies simultaneously.

252 Quoted in Margaret MacMillan Paris 1919, 179

He never saw two men of their high standing so infuriated as Admiral Benson and Admiral Weymss [sic] in that conversation. They exchanged such bitter comments that at one time I feared they would pass the bounds and have an altercation. But happily nothing worse occurred than very violent expressions and violent words.[253]

Rosy's view was that Britain should have the right to build sufficient ships to return to the pre-war position of having the biggest navy in the world. Benson's view was diametrically opposed. Eventually a truce was declared, but this did not settle the matter of the ships at Scapa Flow. The deadlock continued, Rosy noting to the Deputy First Sea Lord:

You and I know what an embarrassment it would be to us to have any of these German ships and you and I know that we should like to see them sunk, but I do see that they are a pawn in the game.[254]

In London, the press campaign to replace Rosy by David Beatty continued, led by the Northcliffe Press. This was brought to an end by a statement by Walter Long, the First Lord of the Admiralty, following a question in the House of Commons, that there was no intention to change the First Sea Lord, and he commented on 'the attempt to create a difference of opinion in the Navy to bring about the sort of trouble we had in the Fisher–Beresford controversy'. Rosy's position in all this had been strengthened by the dignified way in which he had borne these most undeserved attacks. Long went further:

Whatever justification there may be for dissatisfaction in regard to the Peace terms, the Naval conditions are absolutely satisfactory and for this we have to thank Wemyss more than anybody else; and in addition I should like to say that I find him a most excellent First Sea Lord. I think it will be very difficult to improve upon him, very easy to have a worse one and I, at all events, am not prepared to 'put him on the beach' simply because it is thought in some quarters that Beatty ought to come to the Admiralty.[255]

Whilst it was not thought that Beatty himself had ever had any part in the instigation of the press campaign, there was an impression that Lady Beatty may have had some involvement.

---

253 Quoted in Arthur Marder From the Dreadnought to Scapa Flow, 231

254 Churchill Archive WYMS 11/1

255 Quoted in Arthur Marder From the Dreadnought to Scapa Flow Vol.5, 210

The problem of the interned ships was to come to a dramatic conclusion. On 21 June 1919, at Scapa Flow, where the German fleet lay at anchor, the squadron of Royal Naval ships stationed there – the First Battle Squadron, consisting of five battleships escorted by two light cruisers and nine destroyers – steamed out of the anchorage on exercise. Only two destroyers were left on guard duty, and one of those was away refuelling. Nearly two hours after the British squadron had sailed, on board the battleship SMS *Emden*, Admiral Reuter sent a two-flag signal to all the German ships, which was the pre-arranged signal to start scuttling their ships.[256] The signal was repeated until all the ships had received it. At the same time, a party of schoolchildren was boarding the tug *Flying Kestrel* to go on a tour of the anchored ships, little knowing that they were about to become witnesses to the scuttling. The German ships had been prepared for the event. Seacocks had been greased to ensure that they would open easily to flood the ships, and the linkages from the seacocks to the deck, once opened, were removed so that the cocks could not be shut off. After the valves were open, the crews abandoned ship to the boats which had been made ready. The sinking of the ships was a spectacular event; as the cold waters of the Flow flooded in, the hot steam pipes reacted violently and the air expelled from the ships was accompanied by whistles, screeching and explosions as steam pipes ruptured. The ships sank quickly, some rolling over, some listing. The first to sink was the SMS *Friedrich der Grosse*, rapidly followed by the five other ships of her class. At 12:00 noon a signal was received by Admiral Fremantle on the flagship of the First Battle Squadron, advising him of events in the Flow. The exercise was cancelled 30 minutes later. The squadron returned at full speed, the destroyers arriving first at about 2:00 p.m. As the battleship HMS *Revenge* entered the sound:

> The sight that met our gaze ... is absolutely indescribable, ships going down all around, *Bayern* listing heavily over, her bow rising sharply.[257]

The success of the scuttling operation had predictably produced a significant reaction at the peace conference: the Allies severely condemned the scuttling, whereas the Americans' view was that it was a 'good riddance'.

Rosy wrote to Admiral Hope, the Deputy First Sea Lord:

> I look upon the sinking of the German Fleet as a real blessing. It disposes once for all of the thorny question of the distribution of the ships and

---

256 This was to coincide with the original date for the expiry of the Armistice, which date Reuter knew. He had no direct communication with Germany, so he did not know that the date had been moved to the 23rd. (Aidan Dodson & Serena Cant Spoils of War, 34)

257 Quoted in Nicholas Jellicoe The Last Days of the High Seas Fleet: From Mutiny to Scapa Flow, 167

eases us of an enormous amount of difficulties. It appears that the German Admiral thought that the Armistice expired at noon on Saturday and consequently believed he was not breaking the terms of Armistice. There was not a moment during which they could not have done this, though I must confess I was beginning to think that they would never do it. We were all prepared to seize the ships as arranged, but they forestalled us by 48 hours. I do not know what the opinion in Paris will be; probably they will be rather sick; but as I said before, it is a happy conclusion. As you know, the terms only interned these ships, and did not make them our property. I suppose there will be an outcry at the beginning but when the facts of the case become known I think that everybody will probably think like me, Thank the Lord.[258]

A week after the scuttling, on 28 June the Treaty of Versailles was signed. Rosy had travelled there for the occasion:

I had hurried over to Paris from London on purpose to be present on this historical occasion and drove out to Versailles in a motorcar with G. Hope [Deputy First Sea Lord]. Groups of people thronged the roads and cheered the more or less distinguished personages as they drove by. Our naval uniforms were quite sufficient to ensure us a warm welcome from them all. The crowds grew in density as we approached Versailles and the spectacle as we drove up to the Palace by the Place d'Armes was truly magnificent. That enormous space was lined by troops, mostly cavalry, whose smart, new light blue uniforms together with the pennons of the lancers gave a wonderful air of animation and brightness to the scene. ... On entering the Palace all ideas of dignity or solemnity vanished. The arrangements were atrocious, and from the foot of the staircase right up to the Galerie des Glaces. It was a struggling mass of sparring men and women elbowing and pushing their way. ... Nor were matters much better within the famous Galerie des Glaces ... Any lingering hope that I might have had of the scene being worthy of the occasion was shattered directly I entered. In the middle of the Gallery were three long tables, placed as to form three sides of the square. In the centre of the middle one, facing the windows, was a seat reserved for Clemenceau, and the other signatories were grouped to the right and to the left. These tables were railed off from the remainder of the room which was filled with rows and rows of cane-bottomed chairs giving the hall, except for its size, the appearance of having been prepared for a village concert. The crowd, alas! was worthy of the arrangements. The German delegates in themselves cut but a sorry

258 Lady Wester Wemyss Life and Letters, 432

figure. Clothed in ill-fitting frock-coats, they came into the vast Hall looking more like miserable criminals than anything else.[259]

Despite the signing of the peace treaty, the Royal Navy was still on active service in the Baltic, supporting the White Russians against the Bolsheviks. On 17 July Lieutenant Augustus Agar in his coastal motorboat attacked and sunk the Bolshevik cruiser *Oleg*. Torpedoes were launched from the stern of a coastal motorboat so as soon as a torpedo landed in the water the launching boat had to alter course sharply to avoid being blown up. For this action Agar was awarded the Victoria Cross and promoted lieutenant commander.

Admiral Cowan, in command of the Baltic Fleet, realising the value that these small craft had in the Baltic, arranged for more motorboats to be towed from Sheerness in Kent for an attack on Kronstadt, the Russian naval base close to Petrograd (now Saint Petersburg). The attack, authorised by Rosy, took place on 18 August, using seven of the motorboats. Although it was highly successful, sinking two dreadnought-type battleships and a large depot ship, the losses suffered were heavy; three of the boats were sunk and two of the commanding officers were killed, as well as many of the crews. However, as a result there was no significant further Bolshevik naval action in the Baltic.

Six weeks after the Versailles treaty was signed, the War Honours list was published, on 7 August. Field Marshal Haig and Admiral Beatty were both created earls (the original idea had been that Beatty should be made a viscount, but Rosy recommended strongly that he should be treated equally with Haig, to prevent a slur on the Navy being perceived). They both also received a bounty of £100,000. Jellicoe, who had already received an earldom, received a bounty of £50,000.

Rosy, like four other admirals, was created a baronet and received £10,000. He had been told by Walter Long, First Lord of the Admiralty, that he would receive a viscountcy and a considerably larger grant, but this was countermanded by Lloyd George, who took the opportunity to get his revenge on Rosy for spoiling his moment for the announcement of the armistice. Rosy wrote to Walter Long immediately, tendering his resignation and commenting 'What measures of success I achieved I leave to the nation to judge; that I have not succeeded in pleasing the government is evident.'

Long, however, refused to accept his resignation. Rosy agreed, but only for a matter of weeks. The view of his friends was that an immediate resignation could be seen as a personal comment. He did not want to end his career in an atmosphere of ill will and controversial newspaper opinions. His formal

---

259 Lady Wester Wemyss Life and Letters, 434

resignation was therefore submitted on 20 August, to take effect at the beginning of November. He wrote again to Walter Long:

> The war has come to a successful end: Peace has been signed: the Naval Staff has been reorganised and placed on a sound footing and I therefore consider that the tasks, for the carrying out of which I was asked to the Admiralty have been satisfactorily performed.[260]

> His view of the government was reinforced when the Cabinet was advised of the success of the attack on Kronstadt. The admiral who delivered the news was received coldly, as the government had been secretly negotiating with the Bolsheviks and the sinking of their fleet was not welcomed.

At the end of October, Rosy wrote to Victoria:

> Tomorrow, Thursday, will appear the official announcement of my leaving, together with the Gazette of Admiral of the Fleet – and a pronouncement from me that I am leaving neither to take up an appointment nor for the sake of my health – so there it is. I think people are really sorry that I'm going – I have had one or two letters from strange people saying that they hope the rumour was not true.[261]

On 1 November 1919 he was promoted to Admiral of the Fleet, and was raised to the peerage three weeks later as Baron Wester Wemyss. That morning he said that he felt as if an alp had been lifted off his shoulders; he had not realised what a huge burden he had been suffering for so long. He was still only 55 years old. Two weeks after his retirement he was the guest of honour at a dinner at the House of Commons given by the First Lord of the Admiralty and attended by the Duke of York, at the request of the King. But Lloyd George, the prime minister, made his excuses and did not attend.

He and his family left for Paris on 23 November. Victoria commented:

> He left the Admiralty poorer in health, poorer in pocket and the poorer of many illusions but ever having steered a straight course in deed and in thought.

---

260 Quoted in Arthur Marder *From the Dreadnought to Scapa Flow* Vol.5, 212

261 Churchill Archive WYMS7/11/4

21: THE FINAL CHAPTER

Rosy, Victoria and Alice returned to Villa Montbrillant, the home that they had not seen since the start of the war, to find it unchanged, although the garden on which they had worked so hard was now completely overgrown.

Over the course of the winter Rosy regained his strength and health, playing golf and working in the garden, and by the end of April was back to his usual self. He travelled to London to take his seat in the House of Lords on 12 May 1920, introduced by the Earl of Wemyss and Lord Weardale. The title that he had adopted, Wester Wemyss, was an ancient one, dating to 1511 and recorded in the Charter of Wemyss. He wrote home to Victoria:

> My first letter written in the House of Lords must be written to you. I find the atmosphere very congenial for here at least is to be found dignity and freedom from a hustling world which is pleasant.[262]

He had become very concerned with the terms of the Turkish treaty following the Treaty of Versailles, and in his maiden speech forcibly expressed his criticism of the terms of the treaty, which he believed would lead to further conflict in the region. His speech was met with a vitriolic reply from Lord Curzon who had led the conference which had agreed the terms of the treaty. Rosy's letter continued:

> I think there is no doubt but that my speech was a real success. He described my language as the most forceful that had ever been heard in the House of Lords and rather intimated that it was not for me, a new peer to criticise the government.[263]

262 Lady Wester Wemyss Life and Letters, 455
263 Ibid 459

He returned to Montbrillant in the summer, to spend more time restoring the garden and entering into the life of the British community, amongst other interests becoming captain of the golf club.

He did not return to London until the following July, 1921, to attend the House of Lords, but returned to Montbrillant in time to spend the rest of the summer with his family. A major international conference was held in Cannes in June of the next year, and he was present as a spectator. His experience of conferences were such that he was happy not to be involved. However, by the following year he was chafing at retirement; he needed to exercise his mind, and at the age of 58 he felt he still had much to offer. Nothing had come his way from the government and he realised that his independent views and his habit of speaking his mind had caused him to be viewed with hostility in government circles and therefore was not likely to be considered for any official appointment. In November of that year he was invited to the unveiling of a monument commemorating the signing of the armistice; this event was held at Rethondes, the small village in northern France close to the clearing in the Forest of Compiegne, at which he had been awarded the *Médaille Militaire*, one of the highest honours awarded in France and the first ever bestowed upon a British admiral.

He, with Victoria and Alice, spent time every year at Wemyss, and he was appointed a director of the Wemyss Coal Company, which extracted coal from the Wemyss estate. They stayed not in the castle but in a simple single-storey cottage overlooking the Firth of Forth. He continued to spend time every summer in London, taking part in the business of the House of Lords, staying whilst

The cottage at Wemyss used by Rosy and his family in the 1920s (author's collection)

in London at the Naval and Military Club in Piccadilly. In 1928 an invitation to become President of the Institute of Naval Architects was made and he accepted enthusiastically. He became even busier, having accepted directorships in the Cable & Wireless company and other companies.

He also became involved in the creation of the British Oil Development Company, which had been set up to take advantage of the opportunities opening up in Iraq; his friendship with Emir Feisal, dating back to his time in command of the East Indies station and his involvement with the Arab Revolt, was key to this, as Feisal, in the post-war reorganisation of the Middle East, had become King of Iraq. He had visited England, invited by the government, and on a visit to Lord Winterton's country house had agreed to take the crown of Iraq. At the Cairo Conference of 1921, at which both T E Lawrence and Gertrude Bell had been present, Churchill, then the colonial secretary, had ratified the decision. Feisal had arrived in Basra on 23 June 1921 on board a British ship to begin his reign. It was his first visit to Iraq.[264]

After a very successful meeting of the British Oil Development Company in London on 27 November 1927, Rosy was invited to visit Baghdad and left London in May 1928, on the day that he was created a Knight Grand Cross of the Bath. He arrived in Baghdad on 18 May, very excited at arriving only one week after leaving London, as he had flown part of the way. It was a ten-hour flight and although he enjoyed it he noted that he was not anxious to repeat the process. He was met by the aide-de-camp to the King:

> The ADC who met me brought the most cordial greetings from the King and informed me that the latter had engaged a suite of apartments at the hotel because owing to alterations going on in the palace he was unable to give me both a bedroom and a sitting room ... the ADC is at my disposal when ever I want anything and a motor [car] of the King is to do what I want with all day and all the time I am here ... I awoke this morning feeling fresh and fit and at 9.30 went off ... to pay my first visit to Feisal. I was really touched by the warmth and cordiality of his greeting. He was genuinely pleased to see me ... He gave me his assurance that he would do all that lay in his power to help. After Feisal I went to see the High Commissioner, (Sir P. Dobbs) and two other officials; after a conversation of more than an hour and a half came away very well satisfied ... As soon as I can ascertain for certain and prove to be correct the assurances that I have received I shall hurry home to take up the negotiation in London.[265]

---

264 Kerry Webber 'S F Newcombe and T E Lawrence Beyond Arabia' in the Journal of the T E Lawrence Society, Vol.29, No.1, 40

265 Churchill Archive WYMS7/16

The negotiations in London however were not a success as the Turkish Oil Company[266] had re-formed itself as the Iraq Petroleum Company and had retained control of the concessions which it had been thought would be reassigned. Rosy made a second trip to Baghdad later in the year but without much success, so hastened back to Montbrillant in time for his and Victoria's silver wedding anniversary celebrations on 21 December 1928.

He was back in London in January, writing from the Naval and Military Club, noting among other matters that there had been no further news from Baghdad following his latest visit. He then travelled to Scotland for a visit to Wemyss, before returning to London, from where he wrote to Victoria:

> I have just got back from Wemyss to find awaiting me a letter asking me whether I will consider going to South America as the head of an important mission [for Cable and Wireless] ... It also intimates that [they] hope you will go ... and ends up by saying that of course they would do everything to make the trip pleasant and enjoyable. Naturally, all expenses would be paid.

He then went on to discuss the problems relating to Alice, as she could not be left alone, and continued:

> That is to say if you thought you could face such a voyage (which at that time of year should be a fine one) for the undoubted amusement and interest you would derive – to say nothing of the pleasure it would give me![267]

When the trip took place, in the summer of 1929, Alice, who by now was 25, took her mother's place with Rosy, whilst Victoria went to a spa to take a cure. Rosy and Alice sailed on a ship of the Royal Mail Steam Packet Company, as it was then known. Rosy wrote from on board on 23 August; he was enjoying being a passenger:

> A great deal of sleep, much reading and a little gentle exercise, with Bridge after dinner is our daily routine. Many of the passengers (amongst whom I am not numbered as you may imagine) amuse themselves in various deck sports ... The kitten flourishes like a rose. She tells me she never feels tired now and as she is very particular about her diet the poison seems to be fast being eliminated.[268]

---

266 The Turkish Oil Company was formed to try to take advantage of concessions granted by the Ottoman Empire to the Iraqi Oil Company in the post-war confusion. The concessions were likely to become void and the company was formed, with Rosy as its innocent figurehead, to try to take advantage of the situation.

267 Ibid

268 Ibid

On the last day of August, after a brief stop at Pernambuco, they arrived at Rio de Janeiro, with which he was much impressed:

> Sept 2
>
> What a lovely place this is! Quite unlike any other I have seen, and indescribable. The Bay is so large and so full of lesser bays that one is never quite sure what one is looking upon, the ocean or not. The great hills, many of them of sugar loaf shape, appear scattered in all directions … In the afternoon we went for a long drive in the town and the environs and it is there that I received the impressions with which I began this letter. The distances are enormous, the magnificent avenues beautifully laid out, the streets clean and well kept.[269]

He had a busy time there, attending many meetings with local dignitaries and businesspeople. From there, he and Alice then travelled on to Buenos Aires before returning home.

Back in London, he wrote to Victoria on 25 September when he read of the financial crisis in the City.

> Hurriedly I went into the City to try and learn what had happened – The City was like one of the dead – in the streets, that is to say, because the Stock Exchange was closed – and is I hear likely to remain closed for some days – luckily we are all right in our bank – liquid and solvent … As regards ourselves if you have no francs in the bank I have enough for now, so just like everyone else we shall have to go slowly and spend as little as possible for the present. In the near future we shall do all right because I shall have some French money coming in shortly.[270]

There had been, however, no more progress with the British Oil Development Company. It became apparent that Rosy had been the unwitting figurehead of an organisation run by clever financiers, using his friendship with Feisal to promote the company, which had unrealistic prospects. This was a second blow to his financial stability, following Lloyd George's revenge resulting in the huge reduction of his war bounty. He made a further trip to Baghdad, still hoping that progress might happen now that European financiers had joined the company, but returned to Cannes quietly and without success.

As 1932 came, after some peace and quiet at home in Montbrillant, he travelled to Paris and then to London where, after a dinner at the Naval Club at

269 Churchill Archive WYMS7/16

270 Ibid

which he was the guest speaker, he wrote to Victoria saying that he was as well as ever and was travelling to Wemyss for 'a peaceful time after this horrible stuffy and dull London'. On his return home in September, Victoria was shocked at his appearance, but treatment following medical advice had a good effect. He had received a letter asking whether he would accept the post of High Commissioner of Danzig, [now Gdansk] for the League of Nations. He was now well aware that his health was such that he could not accept, although the offer of the position much pleased him.

He stayed at home and recovered much of his strength. However the death of his brother Hugo, who lived in nearby Grasse, gave him great sorrow. In the spring of 1933, the Mediterranean Fleet visited Cannes and he was delighted to visit HMS *Queen Elizabeth* and HMS *Glorious*. The latter was of particular interest, since the last time he had seen her she had been a battlecruiser but in 1930 she had been converted into an aircraft carrier.

His health had recovered sufficiently in May for Victoria to be able to leave him to travel to London to deal with some financial matters. But only five days after she arrived, she received a telegram calling her home urgently. Rosy had had an attack of uraemia, the kidney disease which he had first suffered at the end of the war, and was thought unlikely to live through the night. She arrived home a week after setting out for London, to find that he had recovered slightly, but from then on his health worsened and he died peacefully on 24 May at 11:00 a.m., the hour of the armistice, with a smile on his face.

The letters of condolence flooded in, led by the King, who sent a telegram:

> In Rosy I have lost one of my best and oldest friends of 56 years standing. The Navy will join me in mourning the loss of one who will for all time occupy an honoured place in its history.[271]

The very many letters from his former colleagues and friends in the Navy included those from Roger Keyes, Bryan Godfrey-Faussett (who had sailed on HMS *Ophir* with Rosy in 1901 – see Chapters 6 and 7) and most poignantly from Dick Bevan, who had been Rosy's flag lieutenant and had become a close friend. He was now a captain and in command of the Second Cruiser Squadron; he wrote from HMS *York*:

> It is heartbreaking to find myself attempting to tell you how truly and how deeply I sympathise with you in these terrible days but I must try. Since 1911 my affection and admiration and I believe I can say my friendship with the Admiral have grown until his death has taken away someone who

---

271 Lady Wester Wemyss Life and Letters, 500

can never be replaced in my life. You know that for three years of the war I hardly spent a single day away from him and when I deserved harsh words I used to receive only encouragement and advice … It was his courage, simple directness and charming personality that we all loved and I hope you know how great a boon he has been to his service friends. I cannot ask you to read more though I might say so much.[272]

His death caused great sorrow throughout France, where he was revered as greatly as Marshal Foch for the success of the armistice.

His coffin was taken from his home on a gun carriage covered by the flag of HMS *Euralyus,* his flagship both at Gallipoli and on the East Indies station, to the railway station. From Calais he was taken by the destroyer HMS *Tempest* to Chatham, where he lay in the dockyard church until the funeral service at Westminster Abbey. The service was described in the obituary from the Institute of Naval Architects:

> The sombre and impressive tribute paid by the nation at the funeral service held on May 30 in Westminster Abbey marked the value which was rightly attached to Lord Wester Wemyss' service to his country. Naval and military officers were there in large numbers and His Majesty the King was represented by Admiral Sir Reginald Tyrwhitt, while the Admiralty, the Overseas Dominions and other Government departments sent official representatives. The embassies were represented by the French Ambassador and by the Naval attaches of all the principal powers.[273]

From there he returned to Wemyss, where, on 1 June he was laid to rest in the Chapel Gardens, the Wemyss family's walled private graveyard of the overlooking the Firth of Forth, past which the defeated German fleet had sailed in 1919. His grave is marked by a simple cross; next to him is Victoria, whilst a short distance away is Alice's grave.

Throughout his life he had lived by his motto:

> Steer a straight path in deed and thought. Let God be your pilot and wisdom your port.

---

272 Churchill Archive 8/4

273 Churchill Archive WYMS1/3

Rosy's book plate (author's collection)

BIBLIOGRAPHY

Primary Sources

Churchill Archives Centre

The Papers of Admiral of the Fleet Lord Wester Wemyss

WYMS 1/1-1/3	WYMS 8/1-8/8
WYMS 2/1-2/9	WYMS 9/1-9/21
WYMS 3/1-3/2	WYMS 10/1-10/8
WYMS 4/1-4/5	WYMS 11/1
WYMS 5/1-5/11	WYMS 12/1-12/9
WYMS 6/1-6/9	WYMS 13/1-13/6
WYMS 7/1-7/16	

The Papers of Sir Bryan Godfrey-Faussett

BGGF1/1	BGGF 1/49-50
BGGF 1/5	BGGF 3/1
BGGF 1/13	BGGF ¾

The National Archive

ADM11/124
ADM1/8546/319

Principal Secondary Sources

Wester Wemyss, Lady *The Life and Letters of Lord Wester Wemyss, GCB, Admiral of the Fleet,* Eyre & Spottiswoode, London 1935

Wester Wemyss, Lord *The Navy in the Dardanelles Campaign,* Naval and Military Press, Uckfield 2010

Other Secondary Sources

Albert Victor, Prince, and George, Prince *The Cruise of HMS Bacchante 1879–1882, compiled from the Private Journals, Letters and Notebooks,* MacMillan and Company London, 1886, Digitised by the Internet Archive 2007

Bell, Christopher M *Churchill and Sea Power,* Oxford University Press, Oxford 2013

Black, Jeremy 'The Victorian Maritime Empire in its Global Context' in *The Victorian Empire and Britain's Maritime World 1837–1901,* pp.167–187, Palgrave MacMillan, Basingstoke 2012

Brooke, R *The Collected Poems of Rupert Brooke with a Memoir* Sidgwick & Jackson, London 1924

Burns, Ian M *Ben-my-Chree* Colin Huston, Leicester 2008

Cadogan, Major Edward *Under Fire in the Dardanelles* Pen & Sword, Barnsley 2006

Coad, Jonathan *Support for the Fleet: Architectural Engineering of the Royal Navy's Bases 1700–1914* English Heritage, Swindon 2013

Cork & Orrery, Earl of, Admiral of the Fleet *My Naval Life* Hutchinson, London 1942

Dixon, Conrad *Ships of the Victorian Navy* Ashford Press, Southampton 1987

Dodson, Aidan *Before the Battlecruiser* Seaforth Publishing, Barnsley 2018

Dodson, Aidan, and Cant, Serena *Spoils of War* Seaforth Publishing 2020

Dunn, Steve R *Southern Thunder* Seaforth Publishing, Barnsley 2019

Dunn, Steve R *Battle in the Baltic* Seaforth Publishing, Barnsley 2020

Falk, Quentin *Mr Midshipman VC* Pen & Sword, Barnsley 2018

Faulkner, Marcus *The Great War at Sea: A Naval Atlas 1914–1919* Seaforth Publishing, Barnsley 2015

Friedman, Norman *Fighting the Great War at Sea: Strategy, Tactics and Technology* Seaforth Publishing, Barnsley 2019

Garnet, David *The Letters of T E Lawrence* Jonathan Cape, London 1938

Goldrick, James *After Jutland* Seaforth Publishing, Barnsley 2018

Gough, Barry *Pax Britannica, Ruling the Waves and Keeping the Peace before Armageddon,* Palgrave MacMillan, London 2014

Gough, Barry *Churchill and Fisher: Titans at the Admiralty* Seaforth Publishing, Barnsley 2017

Gregory, David *The Lion and The Eagle: Anglo-German Naval Confrontation in the Imperial Era, Volume 1* Writersworld, Woodstock 2012

Gregory, David *The Lion and the Eagle: Anglo-German Naval Confrontation in the Imperial Era, Volume 2* Writersworld, Woodstock 2014

Grehan, John and Mace, Martin *Gallipoli and the Dardanelles* Pen & Sword, Barnsley 2014

Gwatkin-Williams, R S, Captain RN *Prisoners of the Red Desert* Leonair Ltd, Driffield 2008

Heald, Henrietta (ed.) *The Chronicle of Britain and Ireland* JOL International Publishing, Farnborough 1992

Holland, Robert *Blue Water Empire: The British in the Mediterranean since 1800* Penguin Books, London 2012

Hore, Peter (ed.) *Dreadnought to Daring* Seaforth Publishing, Barnsley 2012

Hythe, Viscount *The Naval Annual 1913* David & Charles, Newton Abbot, reprinted 1970

Jameson, William *The Fleet that Jack Built* Periscope Publishing, Penzance 2004

Jellicoe, Nicholas *The Last Days of the High Seas Fleet* Seaforth Publishing, Barnsley 2019

Jellicoe, Nicholas *Jutland: The Unfinished Battle* Seaforth Publishing, Barnsley 2016

Johnson-Allen, John *T E Lawrence and the Red Sea Patrol,* Pen & Sword, Barnsley 2015

Judd, Dennis *The Life and Times of George V* Weidenfeld & Nicolson, London 1973

Lambert, Nicholas A *Sir John Fisher's Naval Revolution* University of South Carolina Press, Columbia, USA 2002

Lawrence, T E *Seven Pillars of Wisdom: A Triumph* (1922 text) Castle Hill Press, Salisbury 2003

McMillan, Margaret *Paris 1919: Six Months that Changed the World* Random House, New York 2003

Marder, Arthur J *From the Dreadnought to Scapa Flow, Volumes 1–5,* Seaforth Publishing, Barnsley 2013 and 2014

Massie, Robert K *Dreadnought: Britain, Germany and the Coming of the Great War* Jonathan Cape London 1992

Maxwell, Gordon *The Naval Front* A & C Black, London 1920

Moorehead, Alan *Gallipoli* Aurum Press, London 2015

Nash, N S *Chitral Charlie: The Rise and Fall of Major General Charles Townsend,* Pen & Sword, Barnsley 2010

Nunn, Wilfred, Vice Admiral *Tigris Gunboats,* Naval & Military Press 2007

Padfield, Peter *Rule Britannia: The Victorian and Edwardian Navy* Pimlico, London 2002

Palmer, Alan *Victory 1918* Weidenfeld & Nicolson, London 1998

Parkinson, Roger *Dreadnought: The Ship that Changed the World* I B Tauris, London 2015

Price, Harry *The Royal Tour 1901 or the Cruise of HMS Ophir 1901* Webb and Bower, Exeter 1980

Ranft, B McL (ed.) *The Beatty Papers Volume 2 1916–1927* Navy Records Society/Scolar Press, Aldershot 1993

Redford, Duncan, and Grove, Philip *The Royal Navy: A History since 1900* I B Tauris, London 2014

Ring, Jim *How the Navy Won the War* Seaforth Publishing, Barnsley 2018

Snelling, Stephen *VCs of the First World War: The Naval VCs* The History Press 2002

Sondhaus, Lawrence *The Great War at Sea* Cambridge University Press, Cambridge 2014

Thomas, David *Royal Admirals 1327–1981* Andre Deutsch, London 1982

Wells, John, Capt RN *The Royal Navy: An Illustrated Social History 1870–1982* Alan Sutton Publishing, Stroud 1994

Wilson, A N *The Victorians* Arrow Books, London 2003

Websites

www.naval-history.net

Articles

McCreery, Cindy 'Reviews Across the Deck of HMS *Ophir*: Revisiting the 1901 Imperial Royal Tour' *Royal Studies Journal*, Vol.5, No.1 (2018), 81

Romans, E 'Britannia's Sons – Junior Royal Naval Officers in the First World War' *Journal of the Institute Seamanship*, Vol.13, No.4

Webber, Kerry 'S F Newcombe and T E Lawrence Beyond Arabia' *Journal of the T E Lawrence Society*, Vol.29, No.1, 40

Naval Review (anon.) 'Naval Operations in the Red Sea 1916–17', Vol.13, No.4 1925

INDEX